101 Flower Power
GROOVY COLORING BOOK
Currated by Todd Cotton

---

*"No matter how much we grow taller, grow older,
we are still forever stumbling...forever wondering, forever young.*

This publication is part of a series of products and publications.
For more information, please visit: **http://www.101bookclub.com.**

"101 Book Club" is a subsidiary of
Top of the Nation Enterprises, Inc.

Copyright © 2018 Top of the Nation Enterprises, Inc.

ALL RIGHTS RESERVED. One or more global copyright treaties protect the information in this document. This book is not intended to provide exact details or advice. This book is for informational purposes only. Author reserves the right to make any changes necessary to maintain the integrity of the information held within. This book is not presented as legal or accounting advice. All rights reserved, including the right of reproduction in whole or in part in any form. No parts of this book may be reproduced in any form without written permission of the copyright owner.

NOTICE OF LIABILITY
In no event shall the author or the publisher be responsible or liable for any loss of profits or other commercial or personal damages, including but not limited to special incidental, consequential, or any other damages, in connection with or arising out of furnishing, performance or use of this book.

101 Flower Power

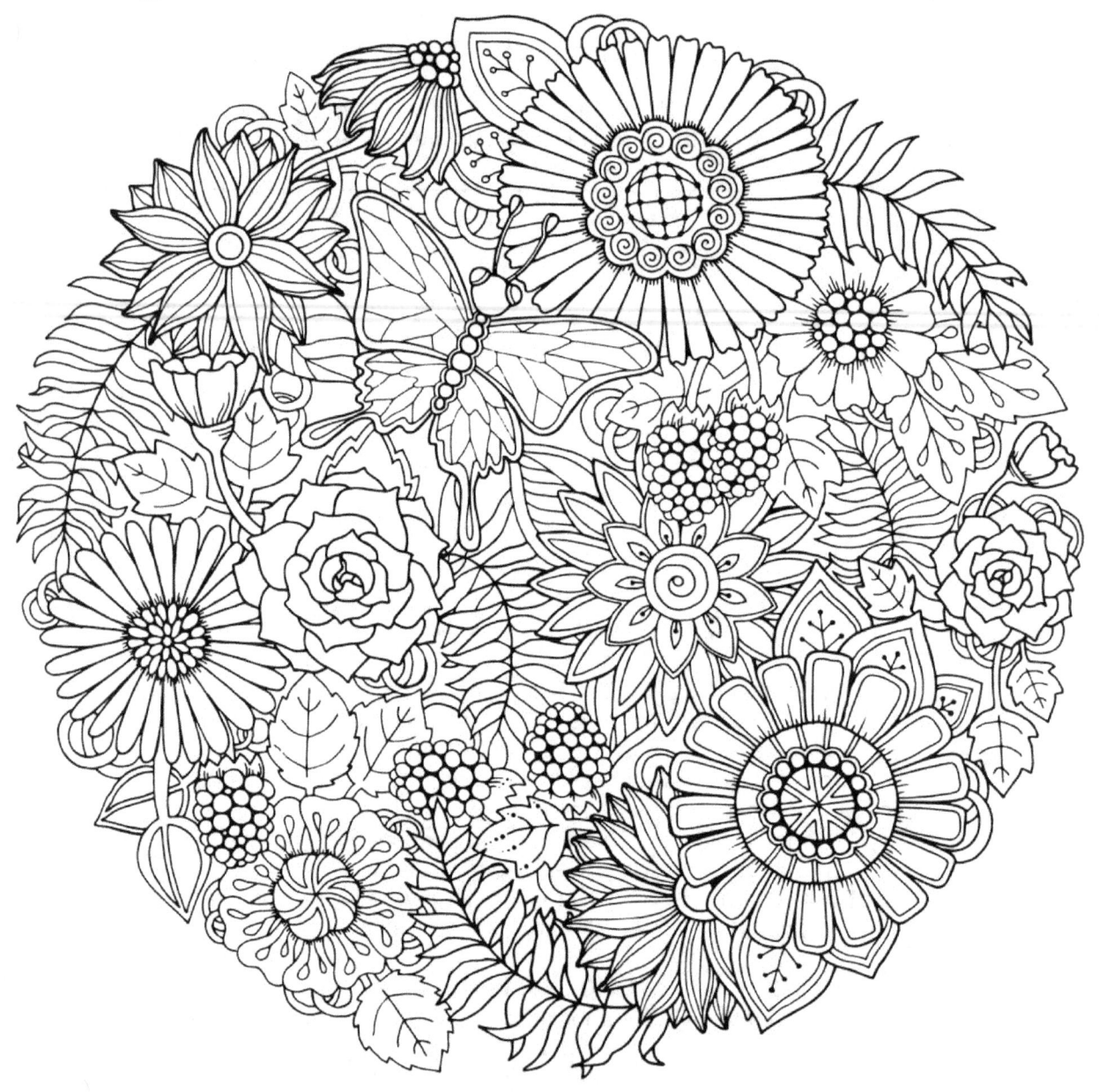

101bookclub.com

101 Flower Power

101bookclub.com

101 Flower Power

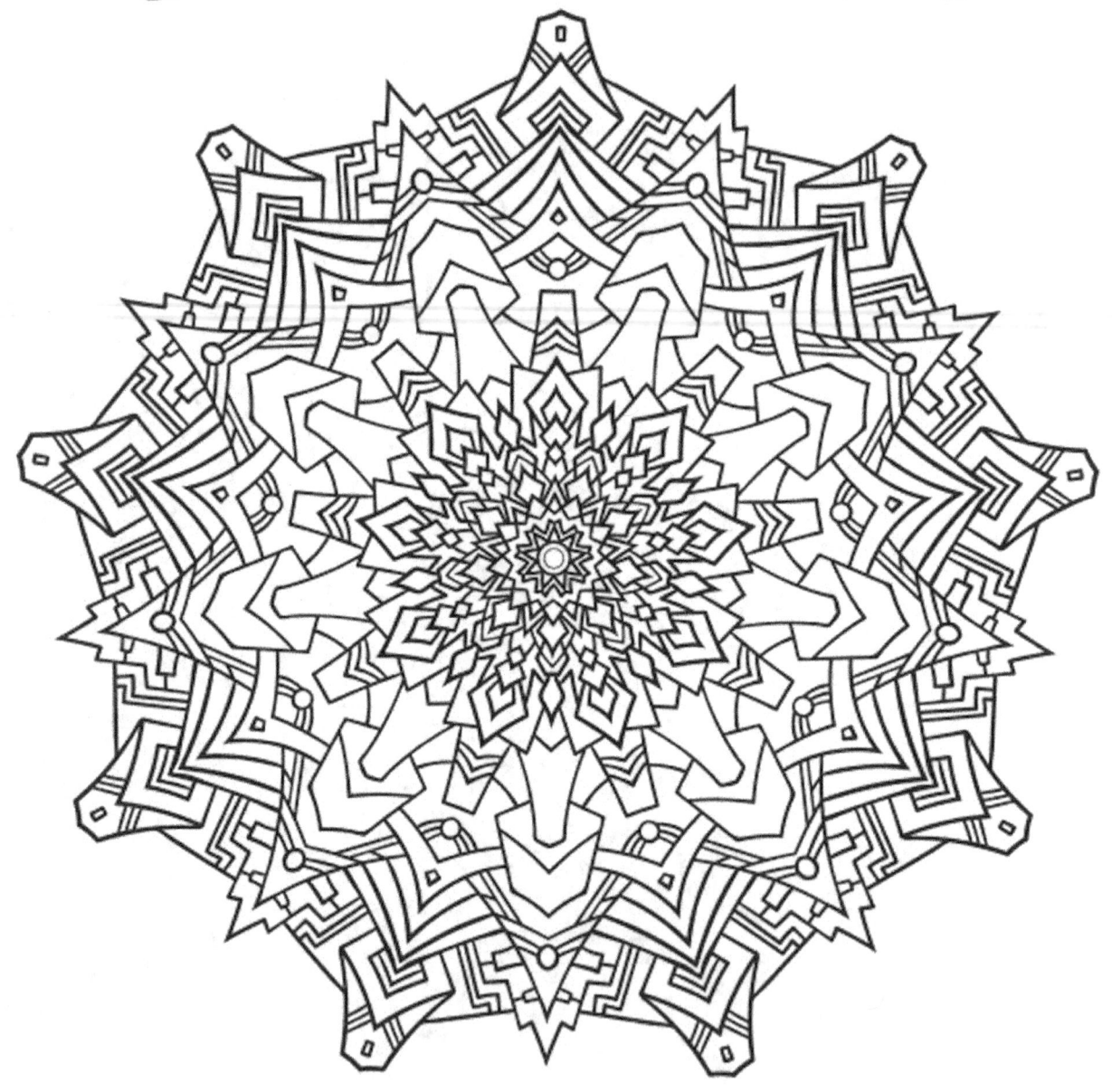

101bookclub.com

101 Flower Power

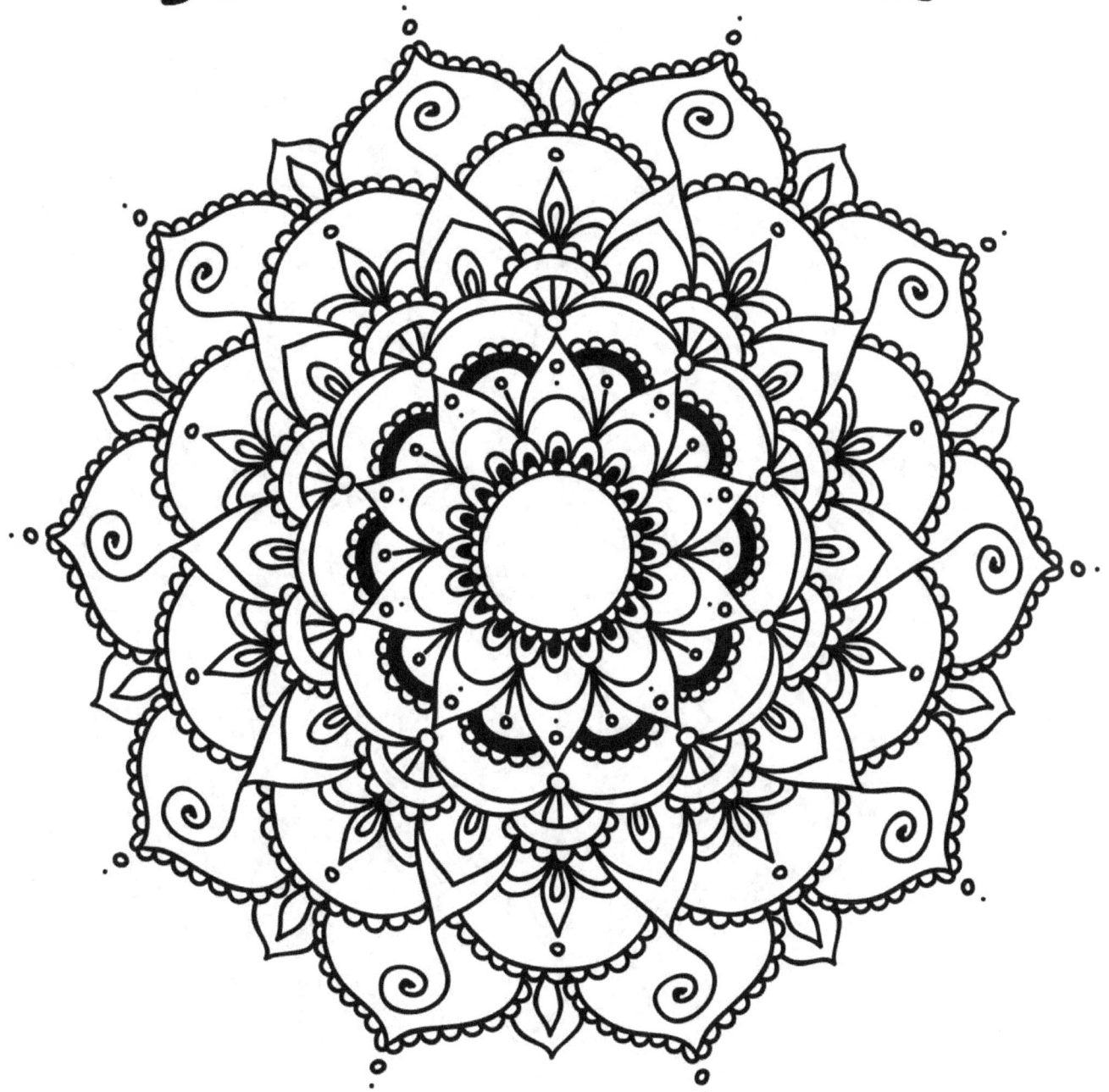

101bookclub.com

101 Flower Power

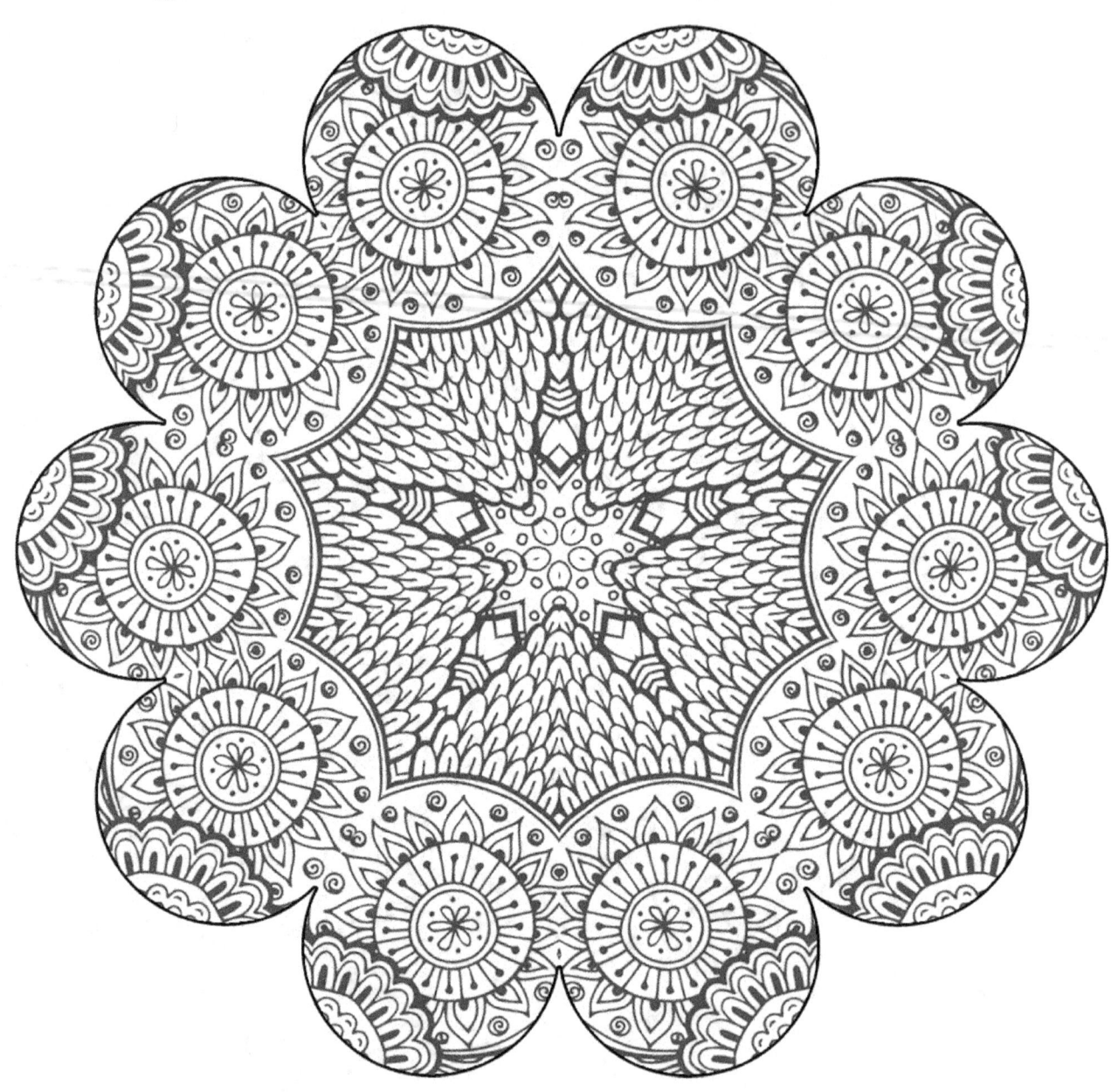

101bookclub.com

101 Flower Power

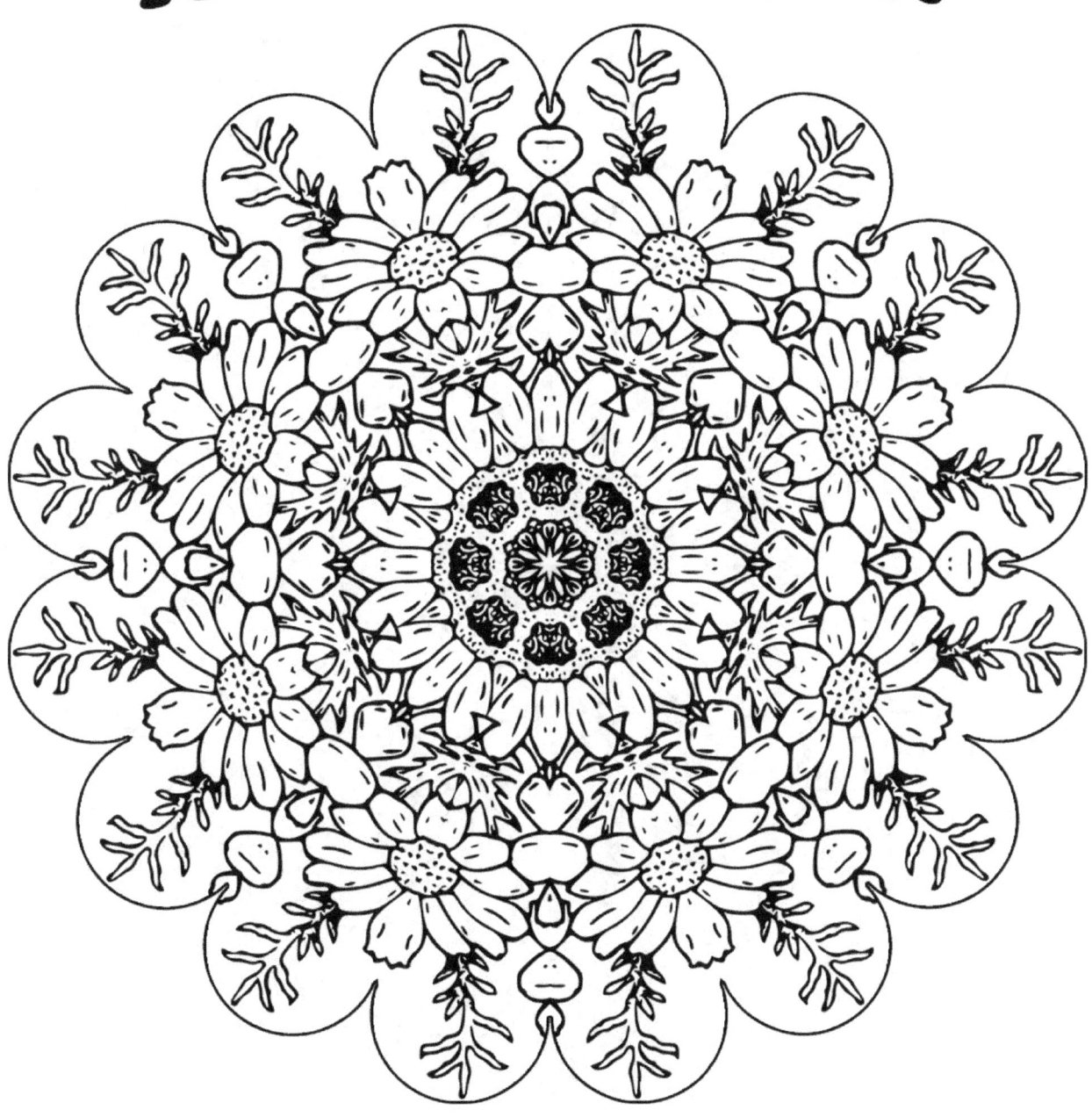

101bookclub.com

101 Flower Power

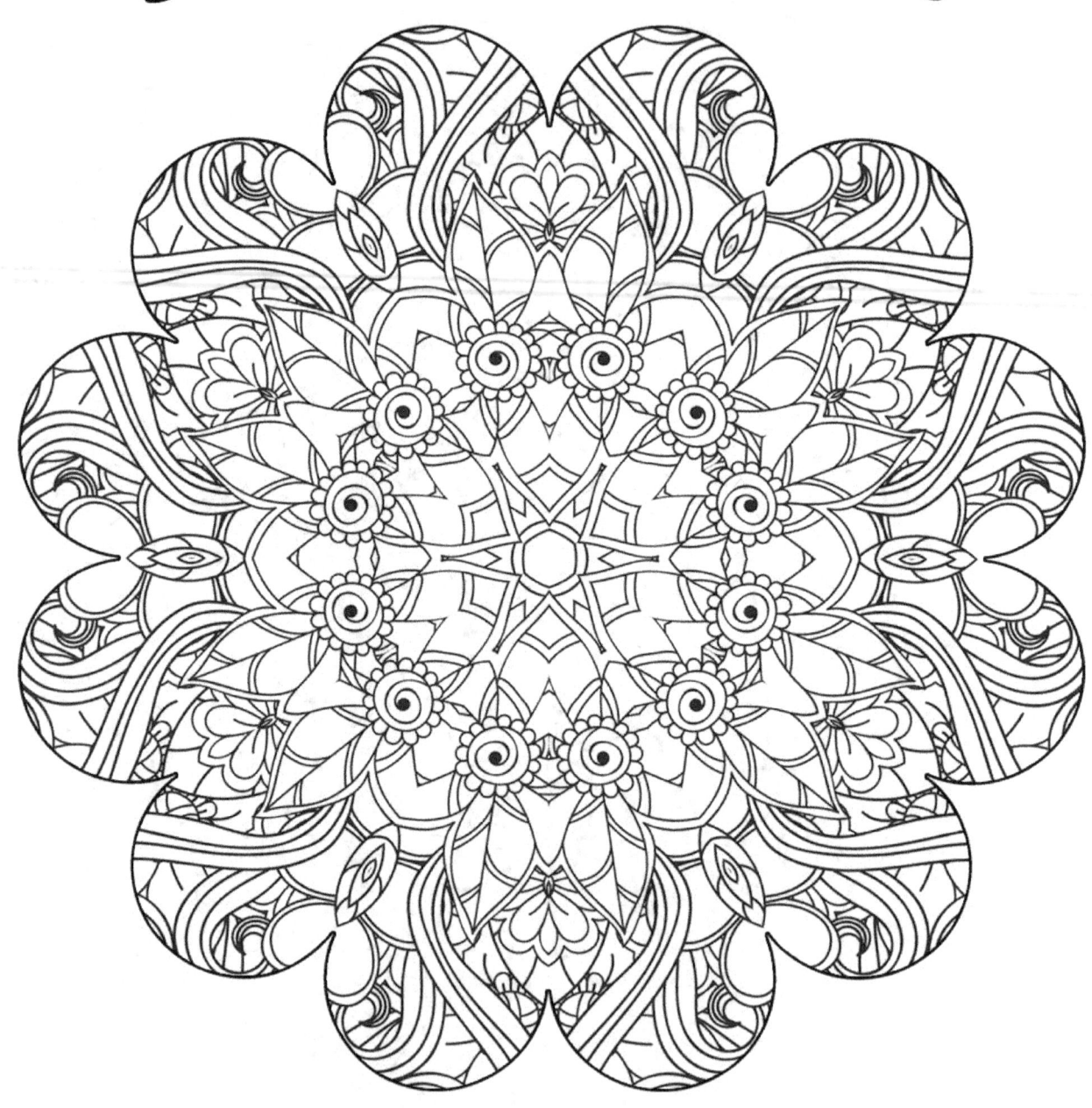

101bookclub.com

101 Flower Power

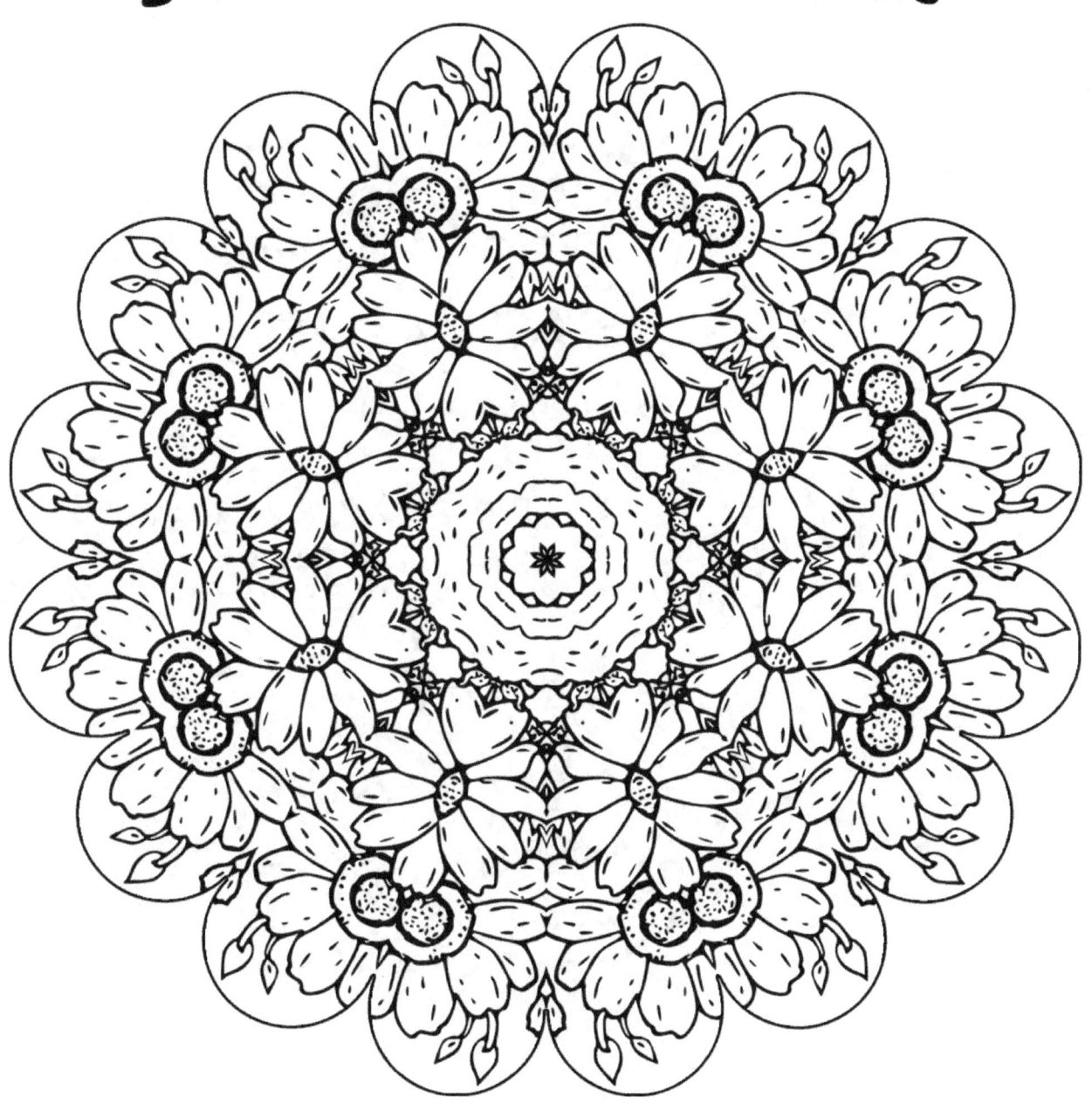

101bookclub.com

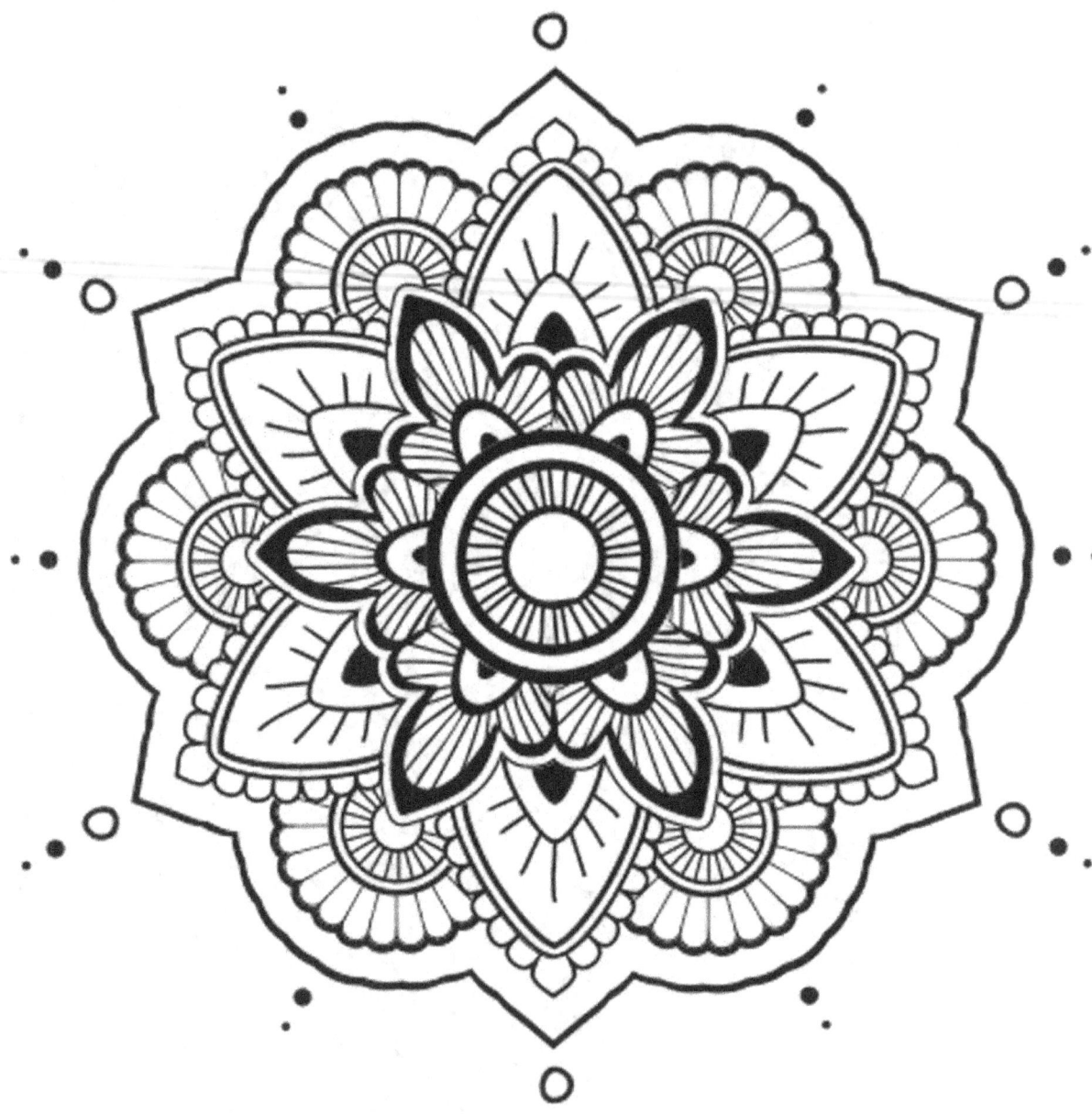

101 Flower Power

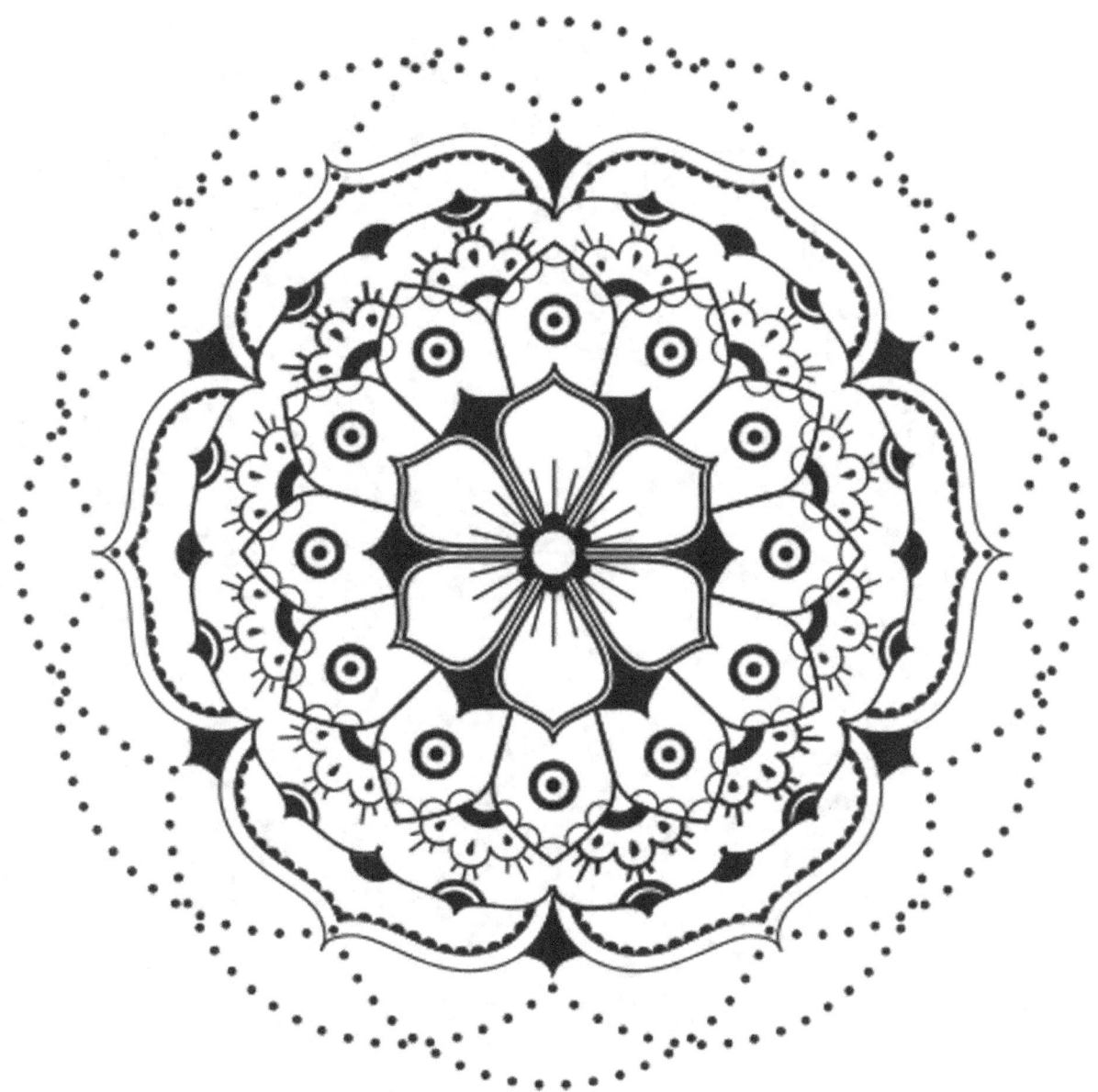

101bookclub.com

101 Flower Power

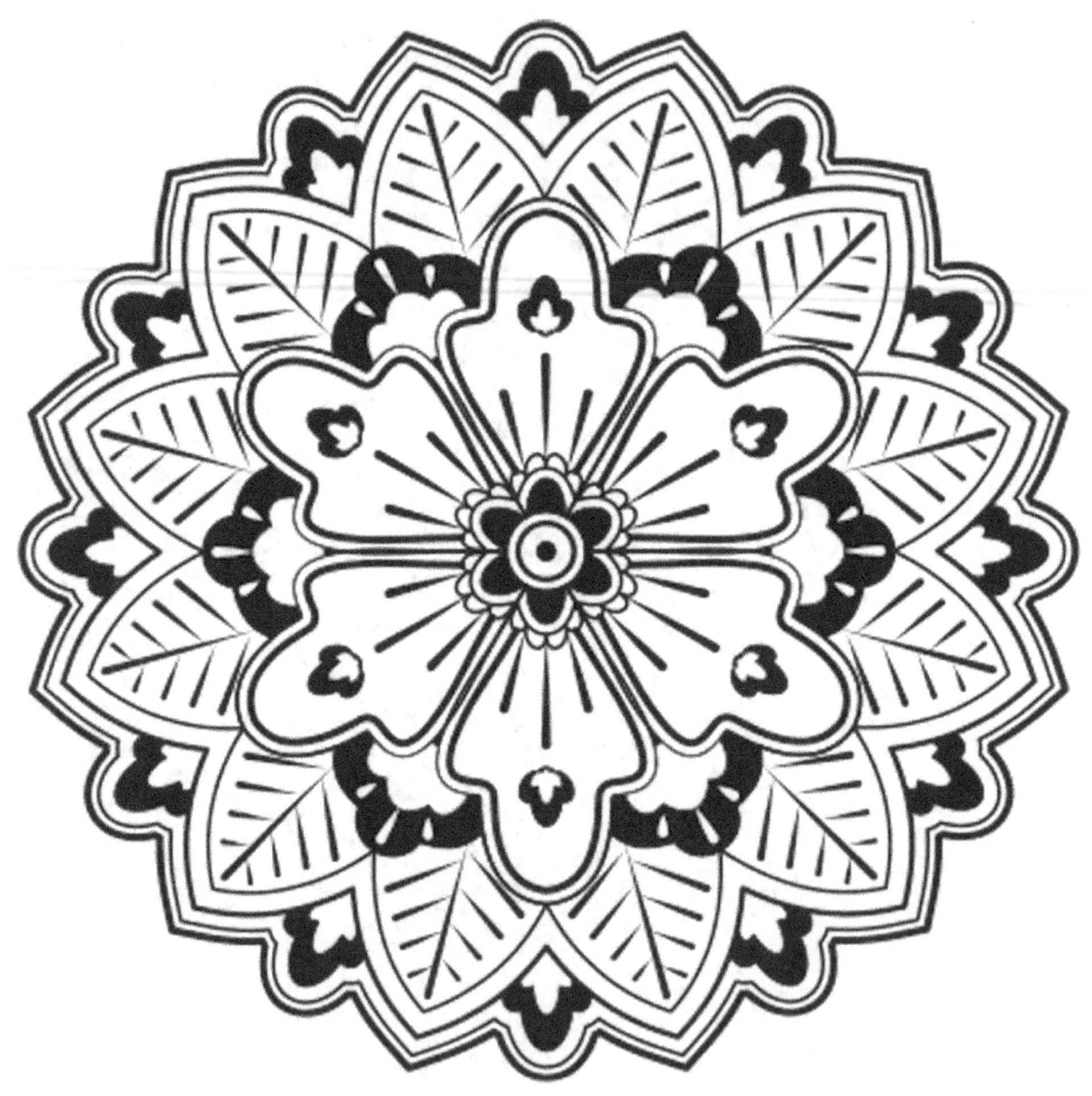

101bookclub.com

101 Flower Power

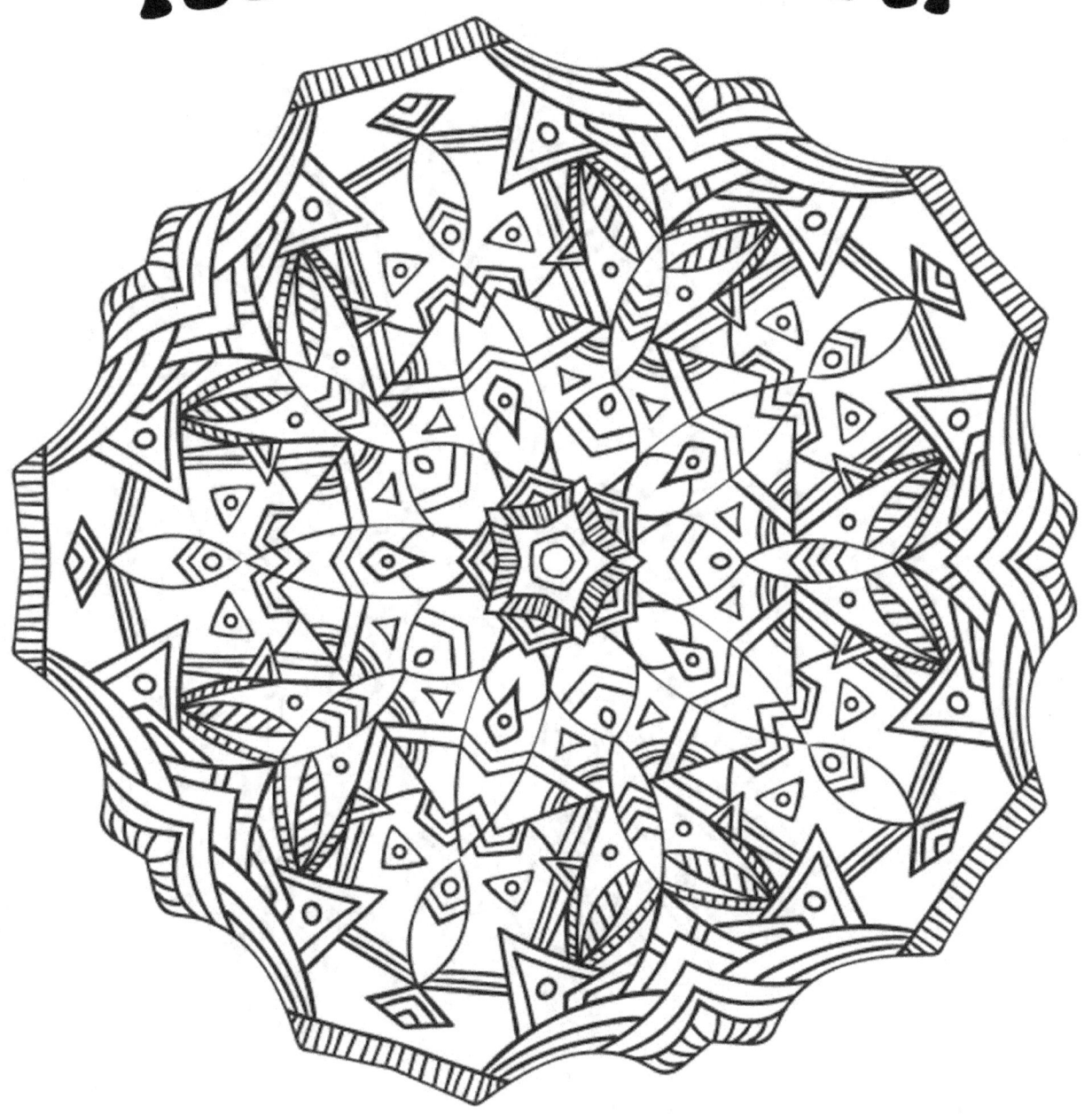

101bookclub.com

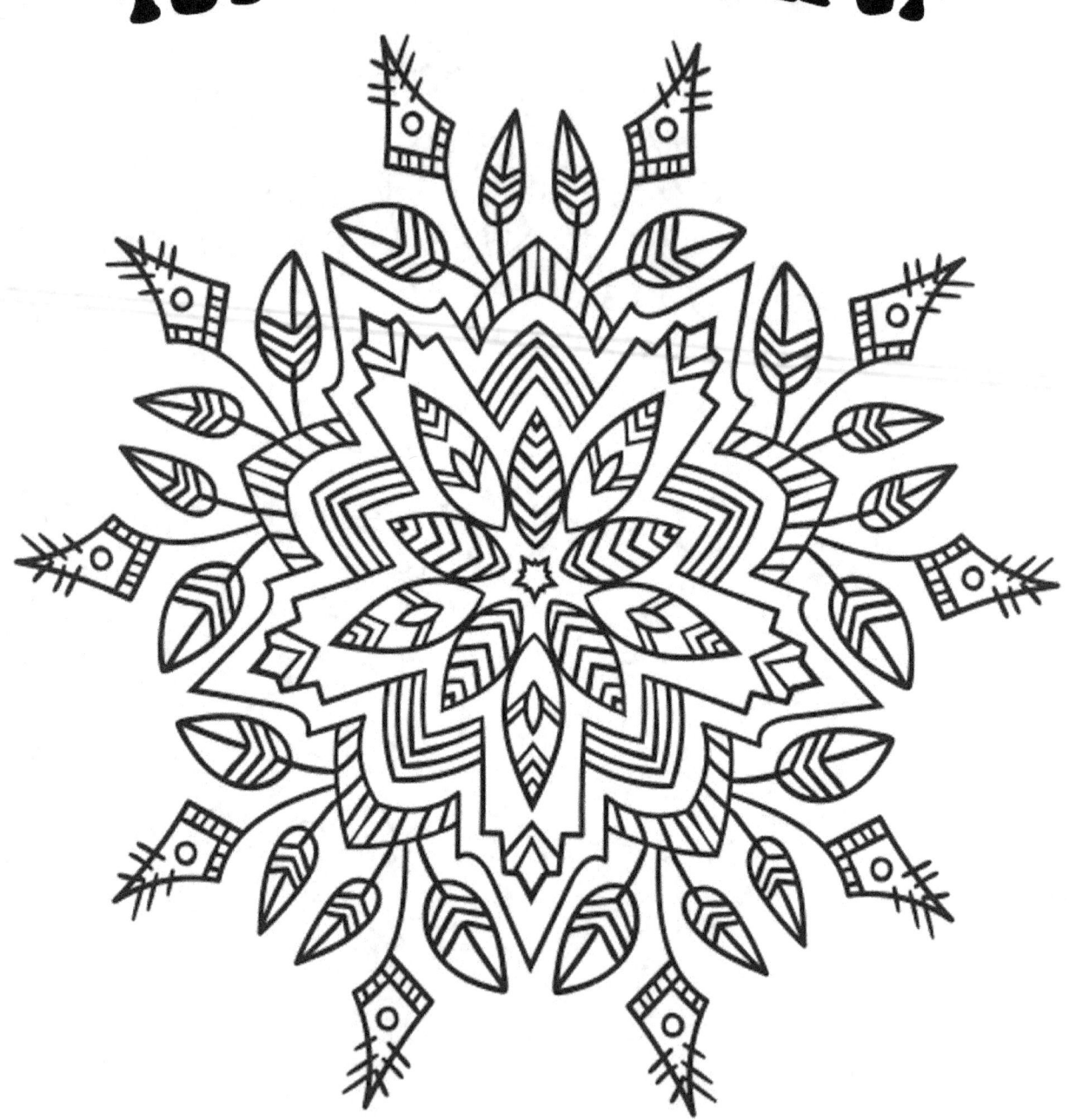

101 Flower Power

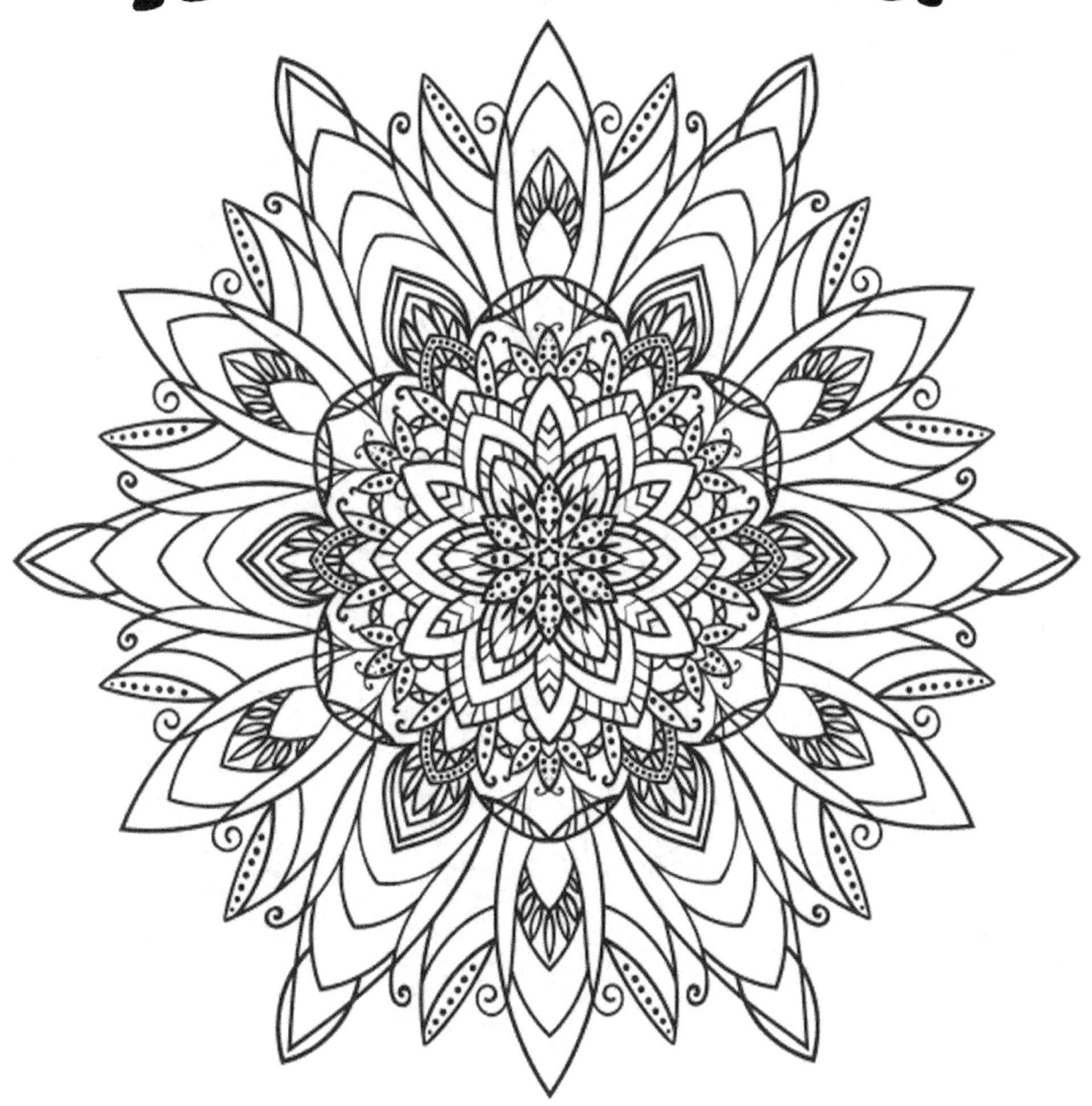

101bookclub.com

101 Flower Power

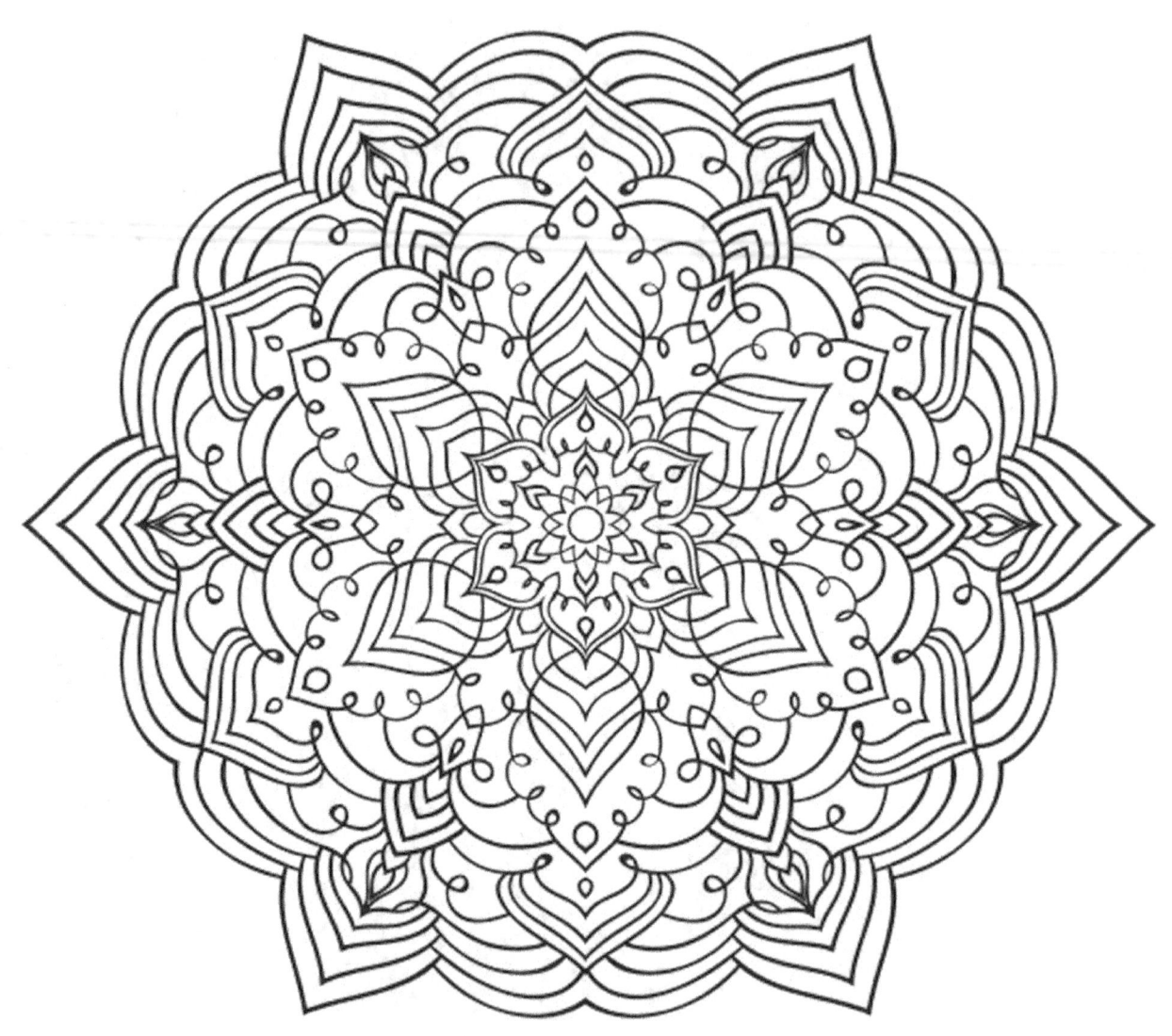

101bookclub.com

101 Flower Power

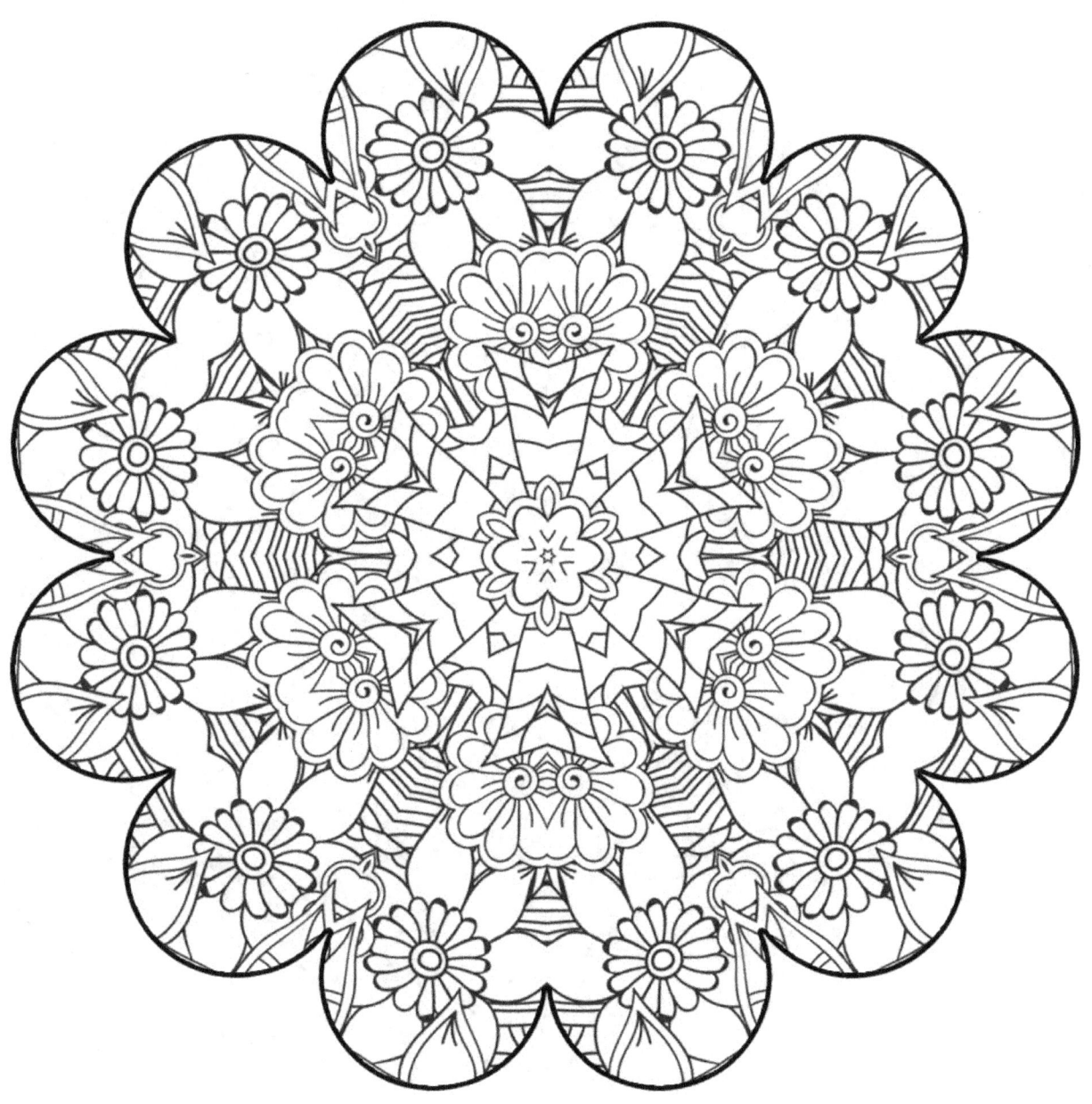

101bookclub.com

101 Flower Power

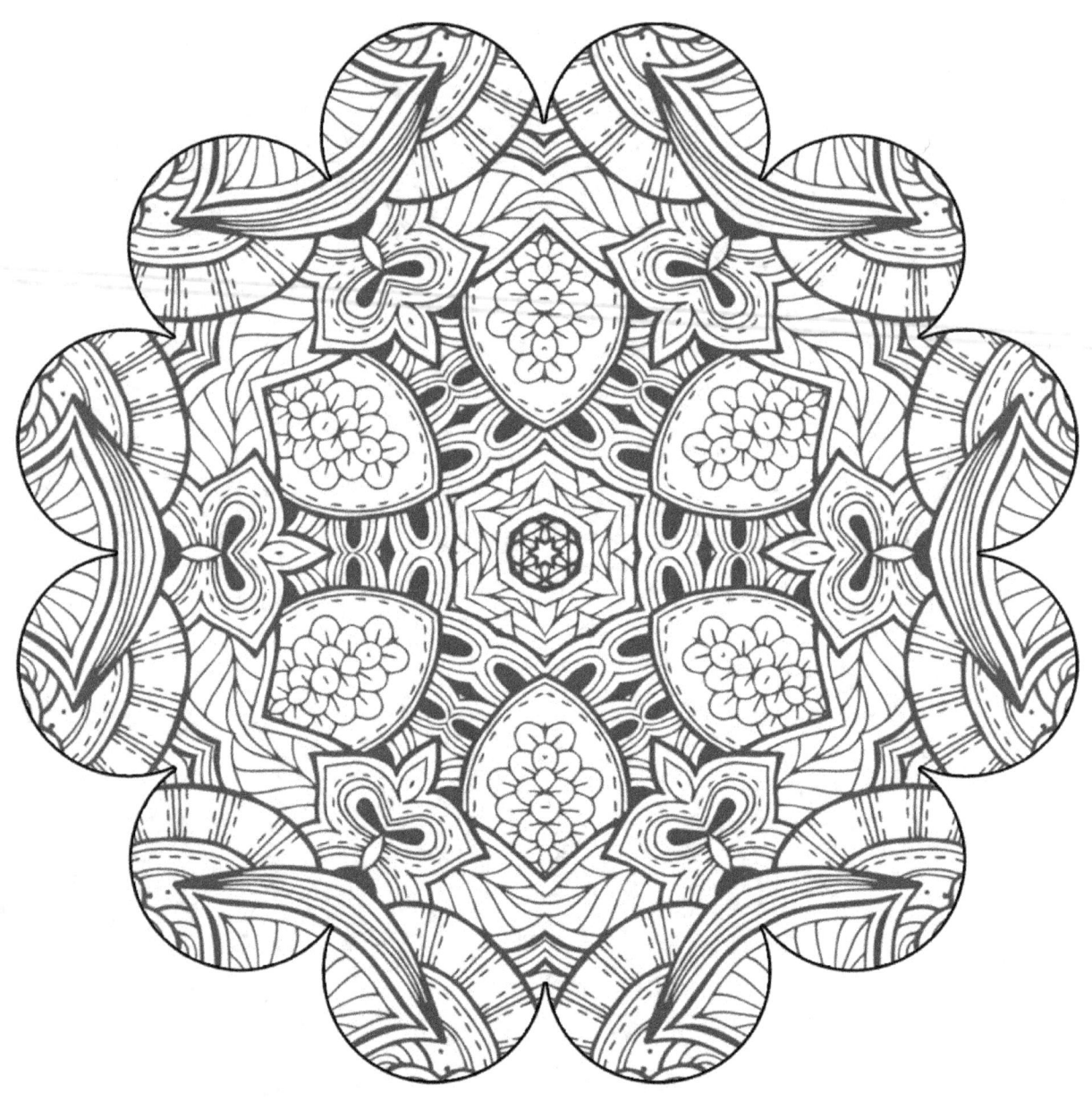

101bookclub.com

101 Flower Power

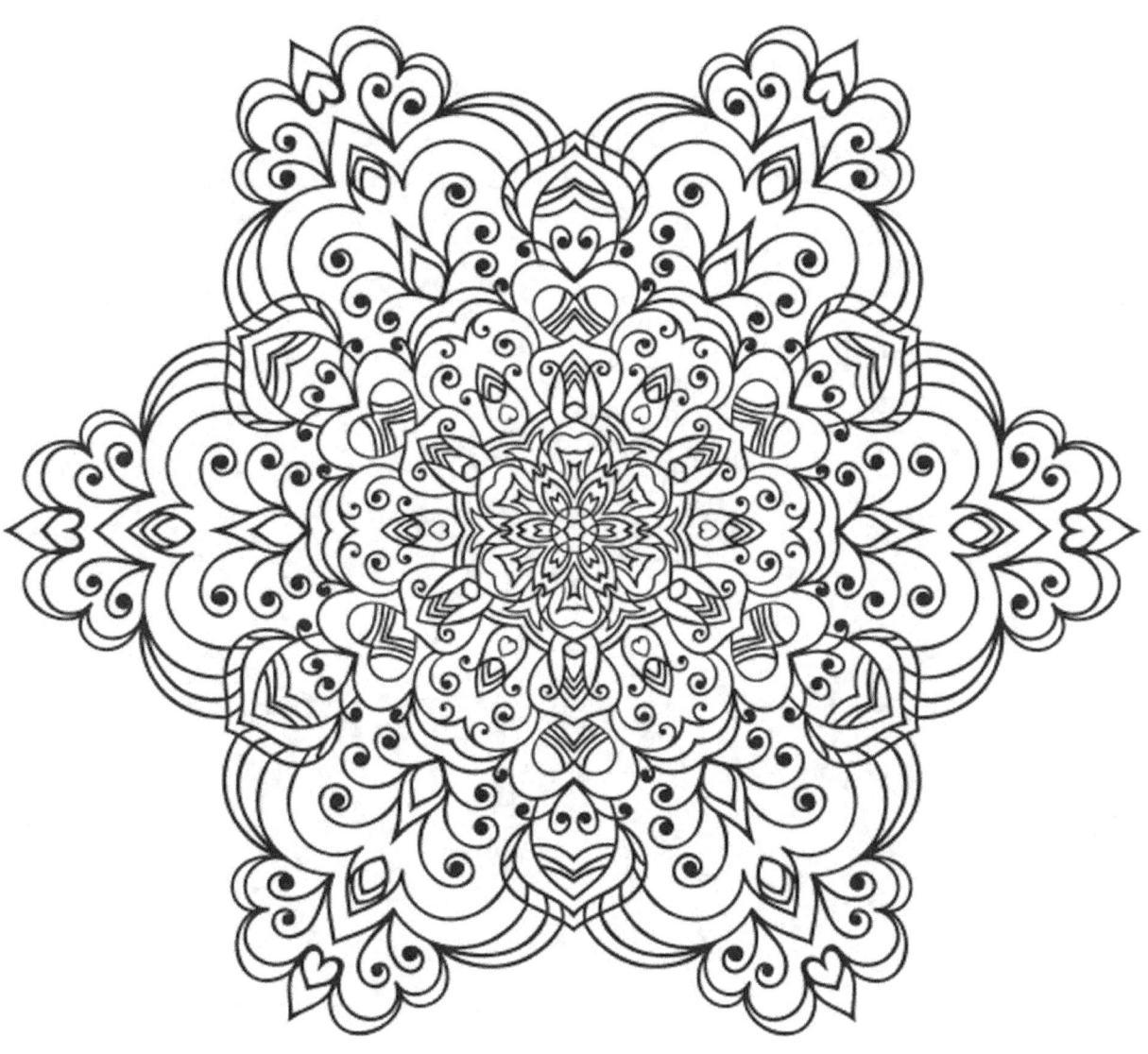

101bookclub.com

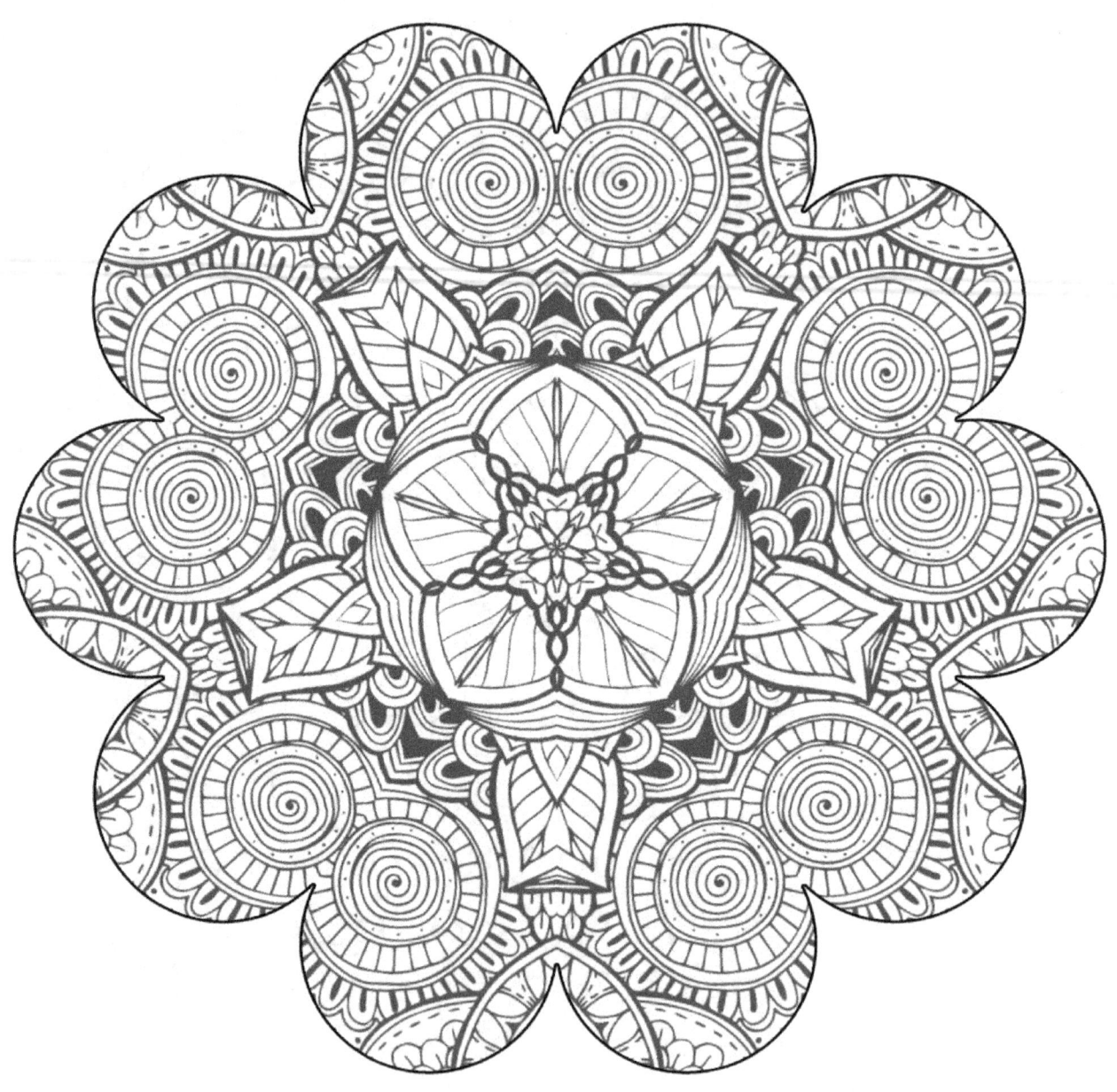

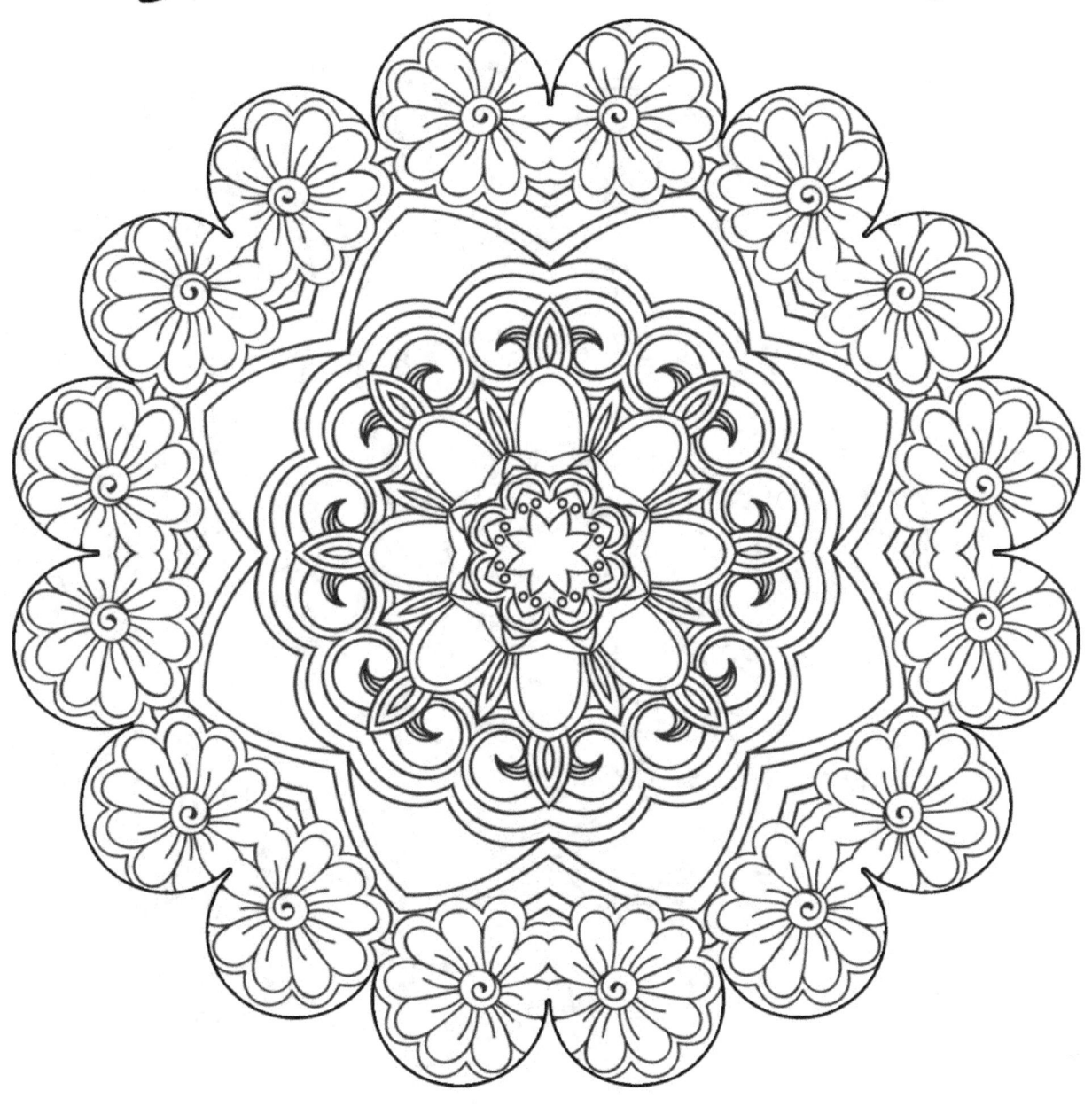

101 Flower Power

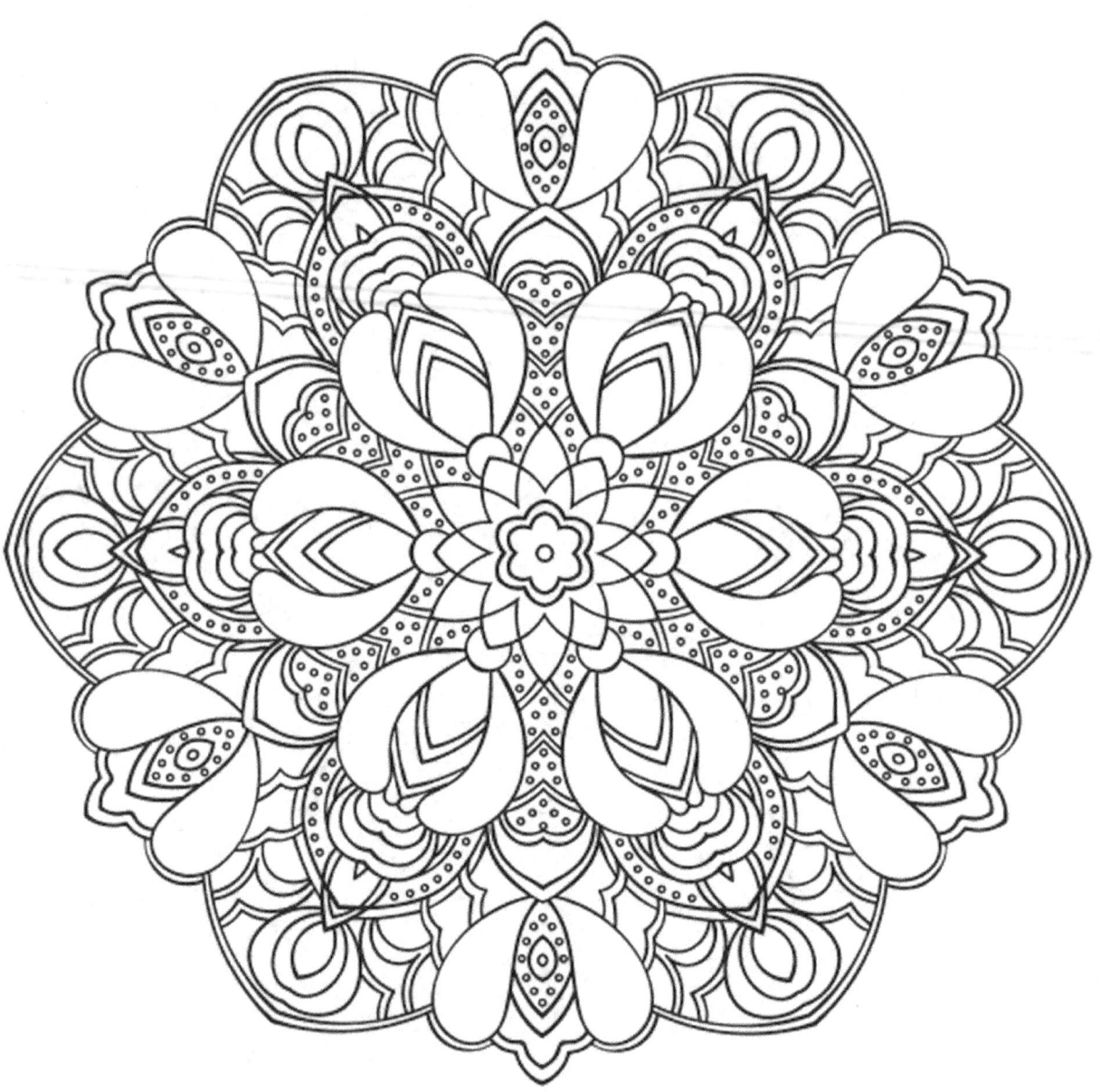

101bookclub.com

101 Flower Power

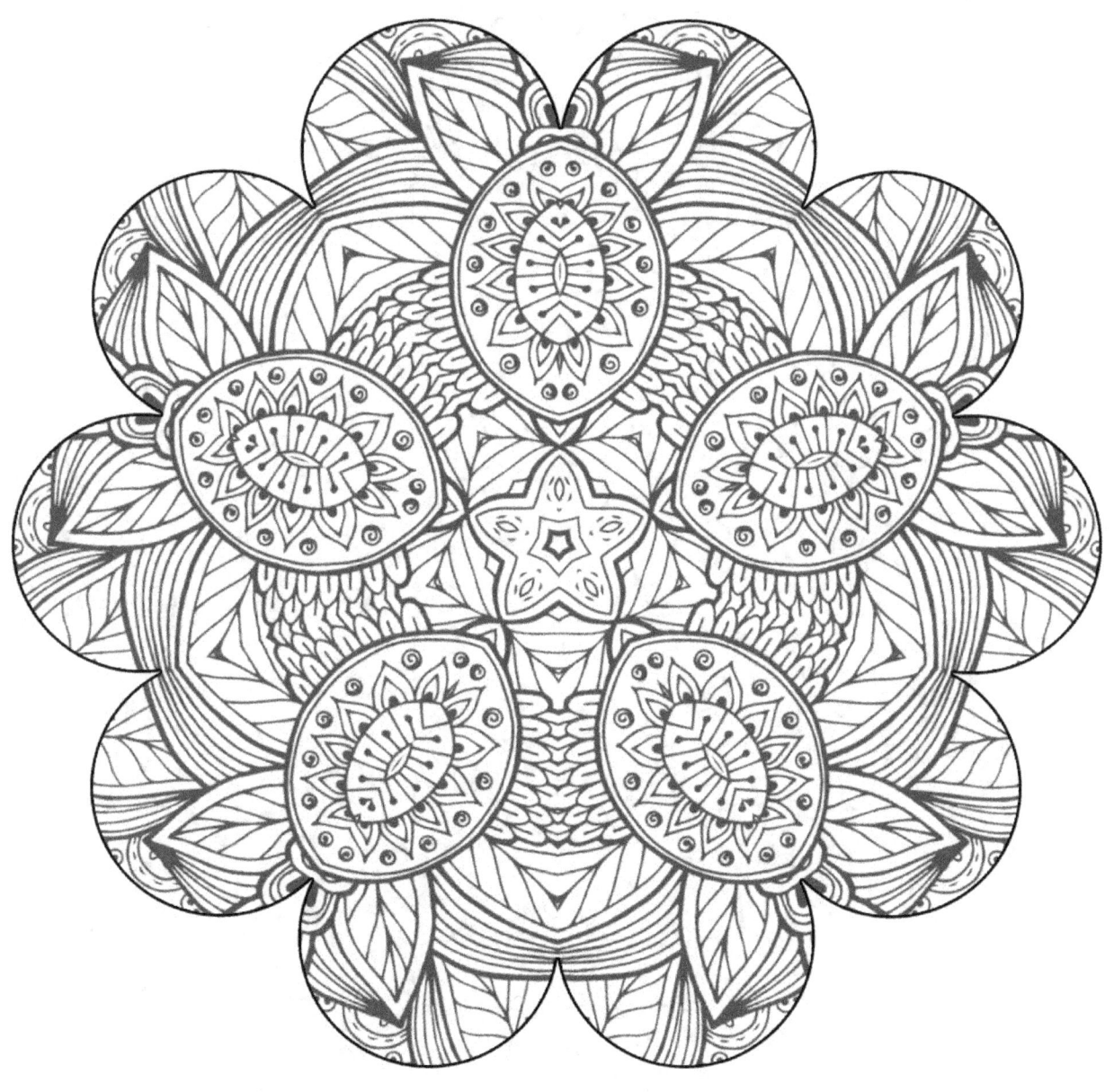

101bookclub.com

101 Flower Power

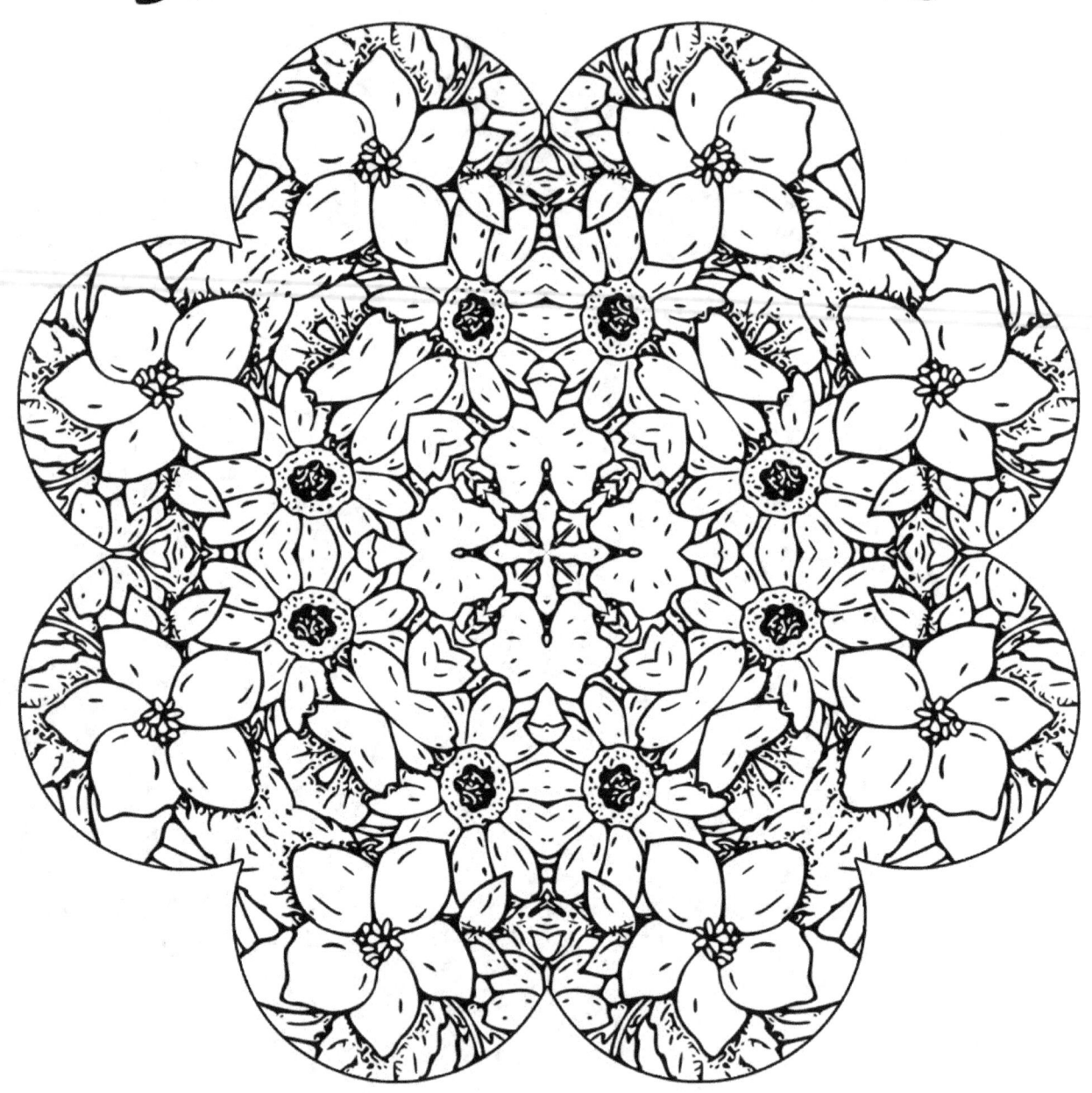

101bookclub.com

101 Flower Power

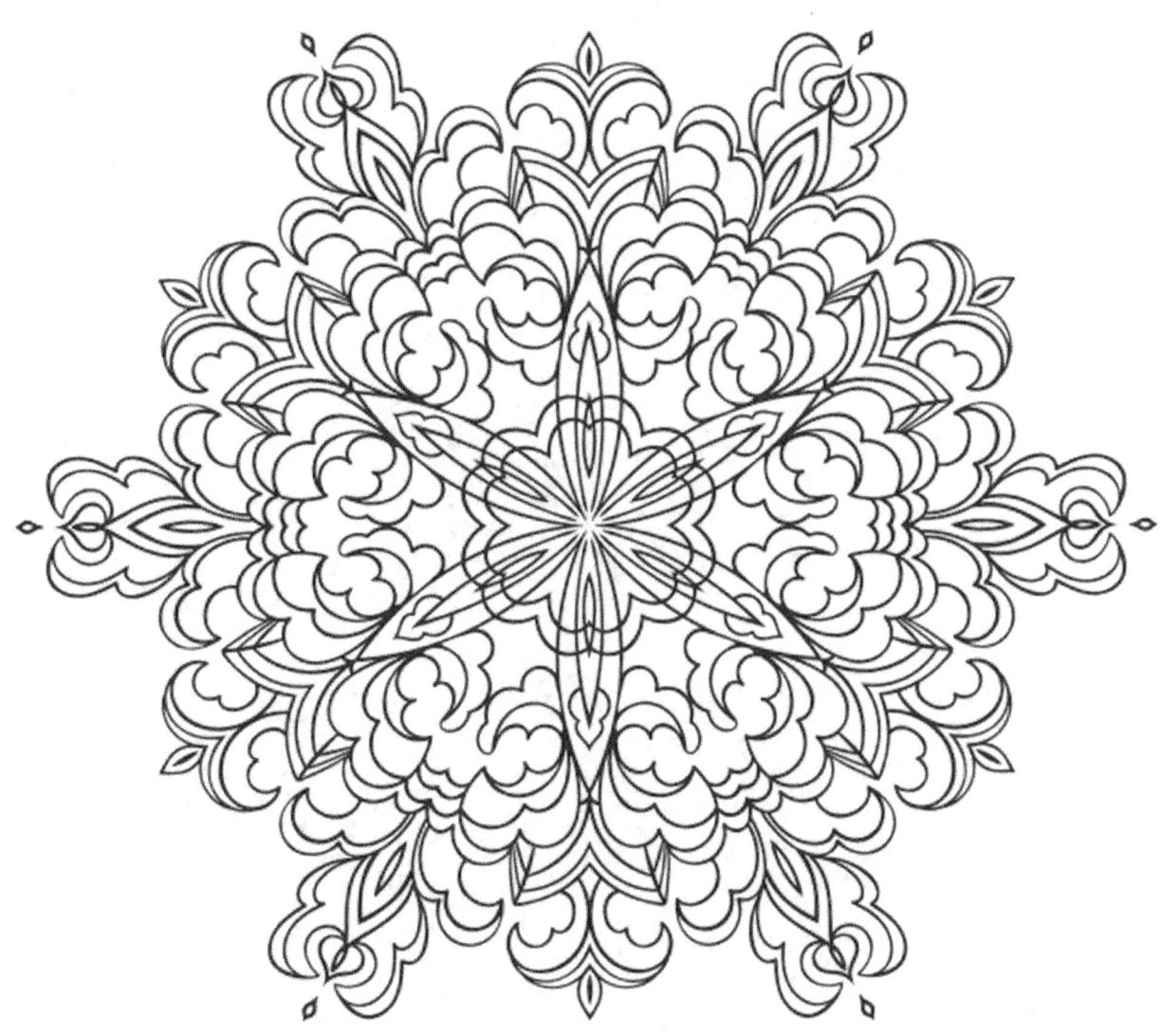

101bookclub.com

101 Flower Power

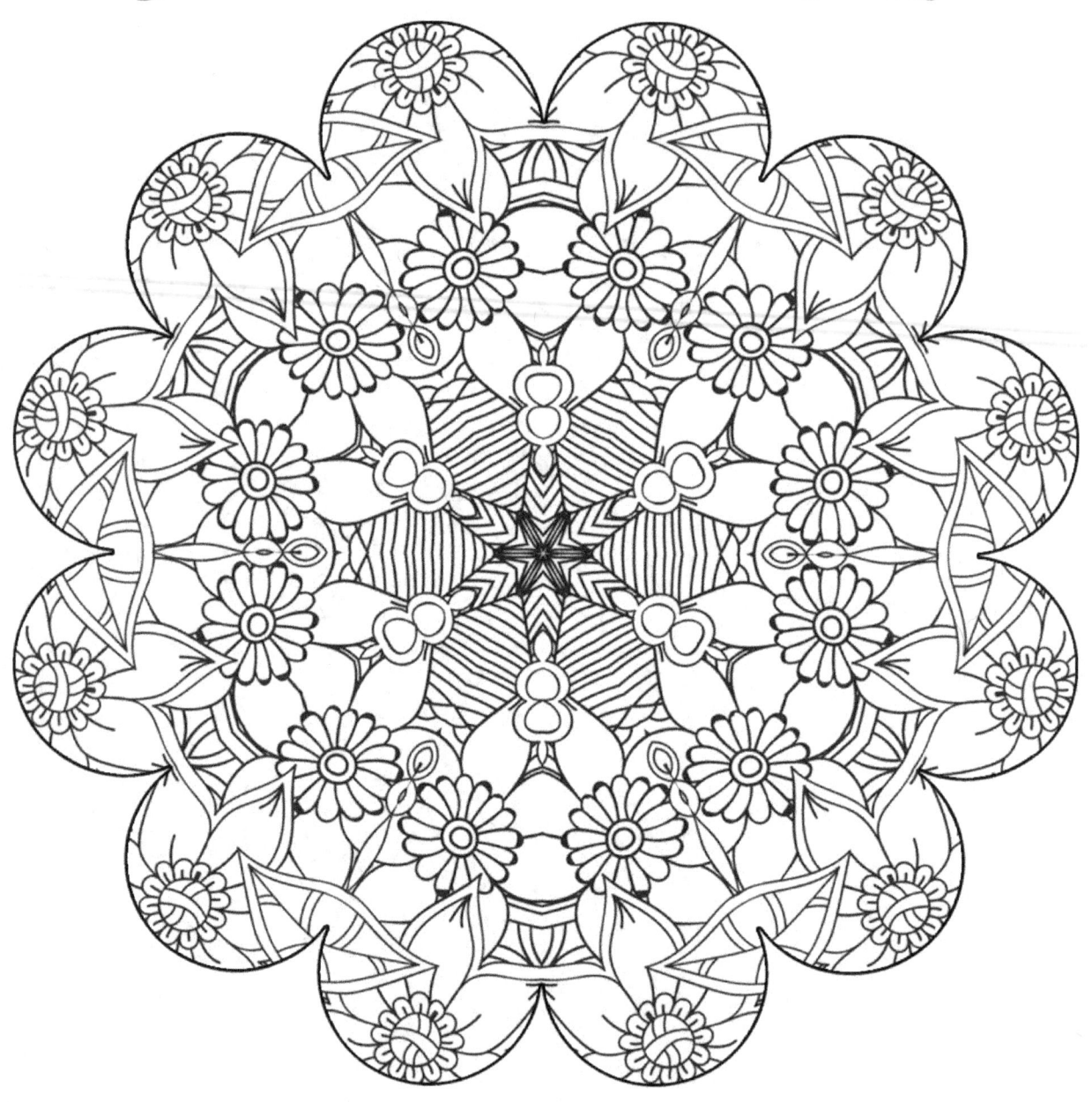

101bookclub.com

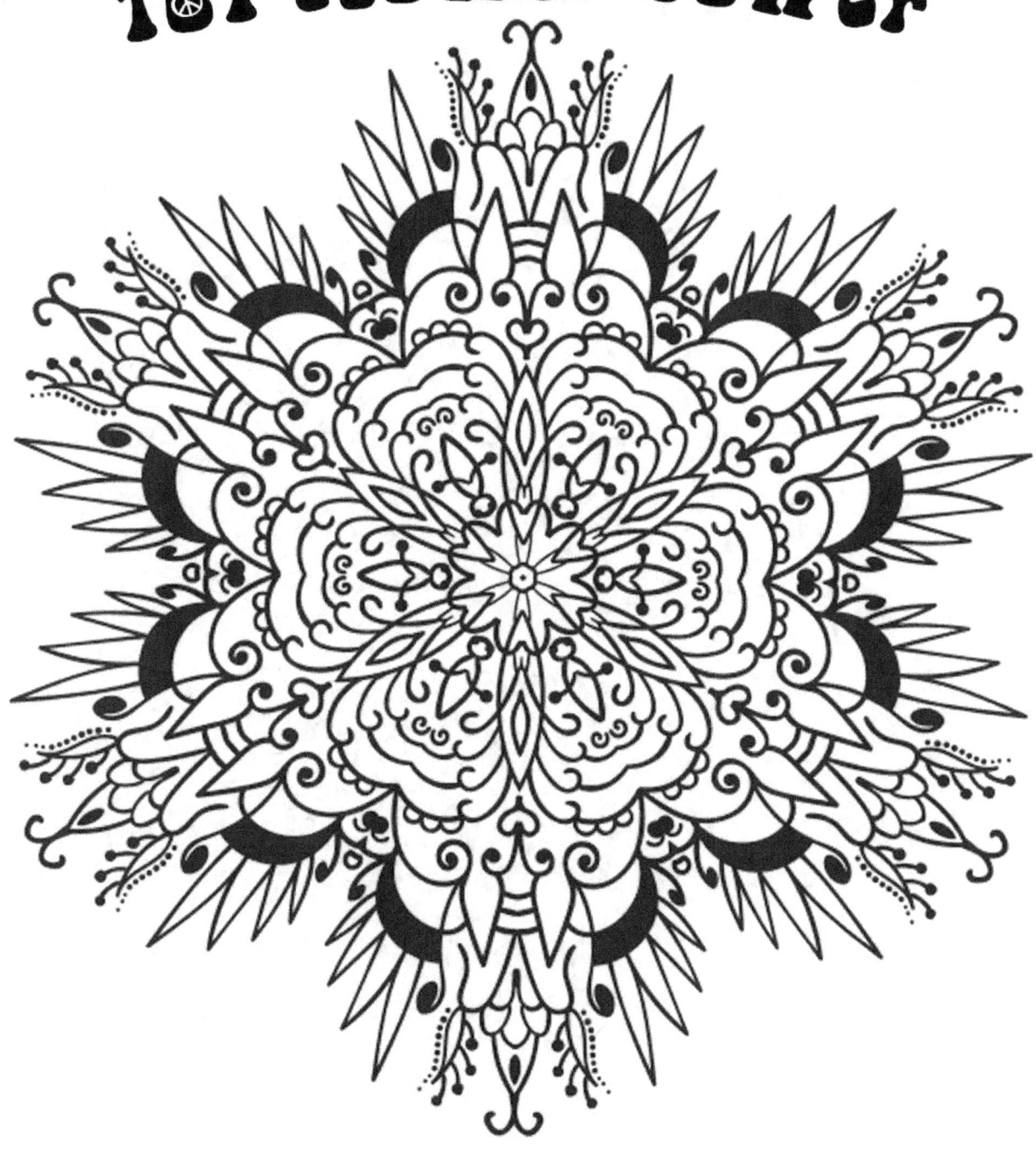

101 Flower Power

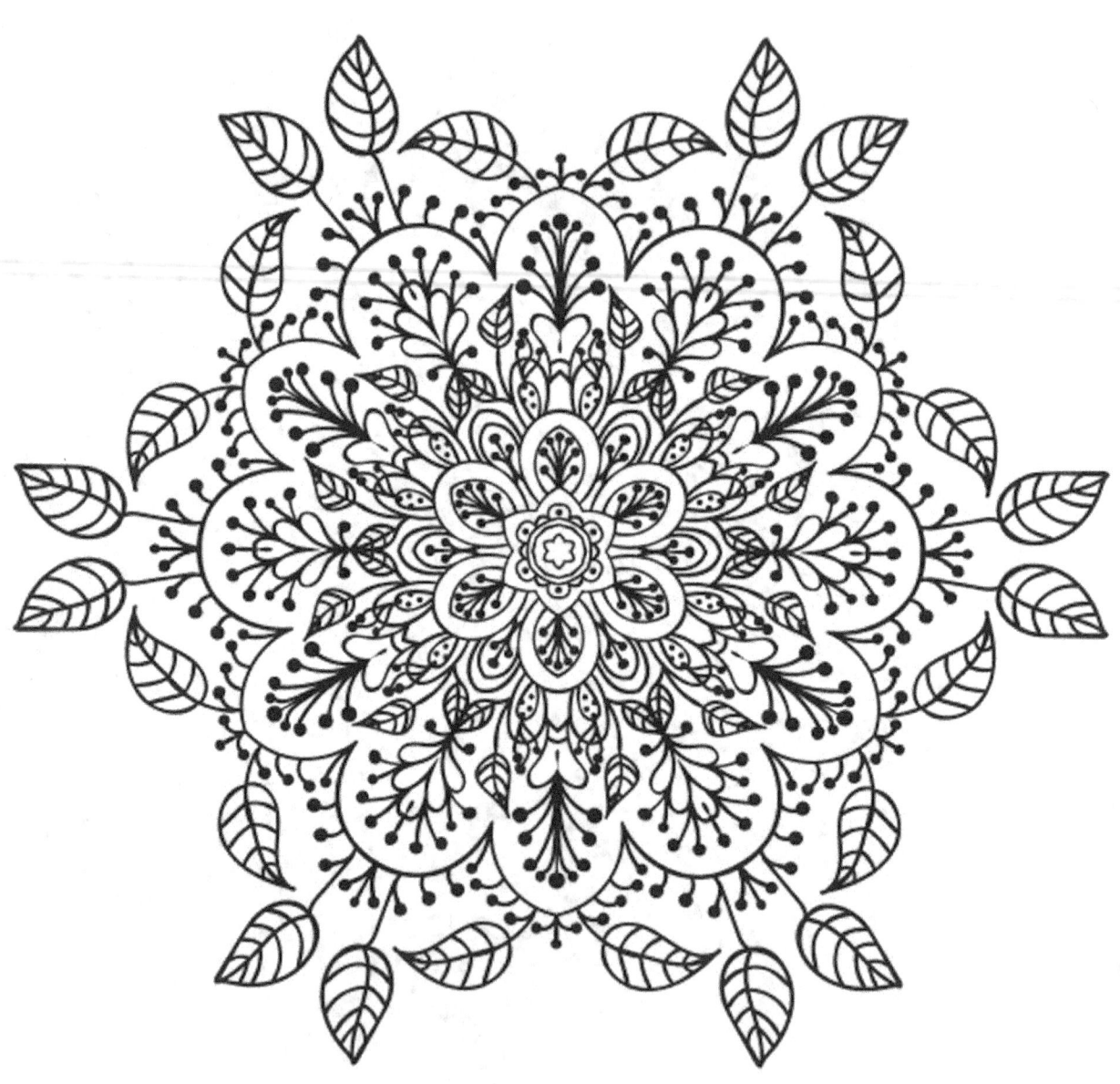

101bookclub.com

101 Flower Power

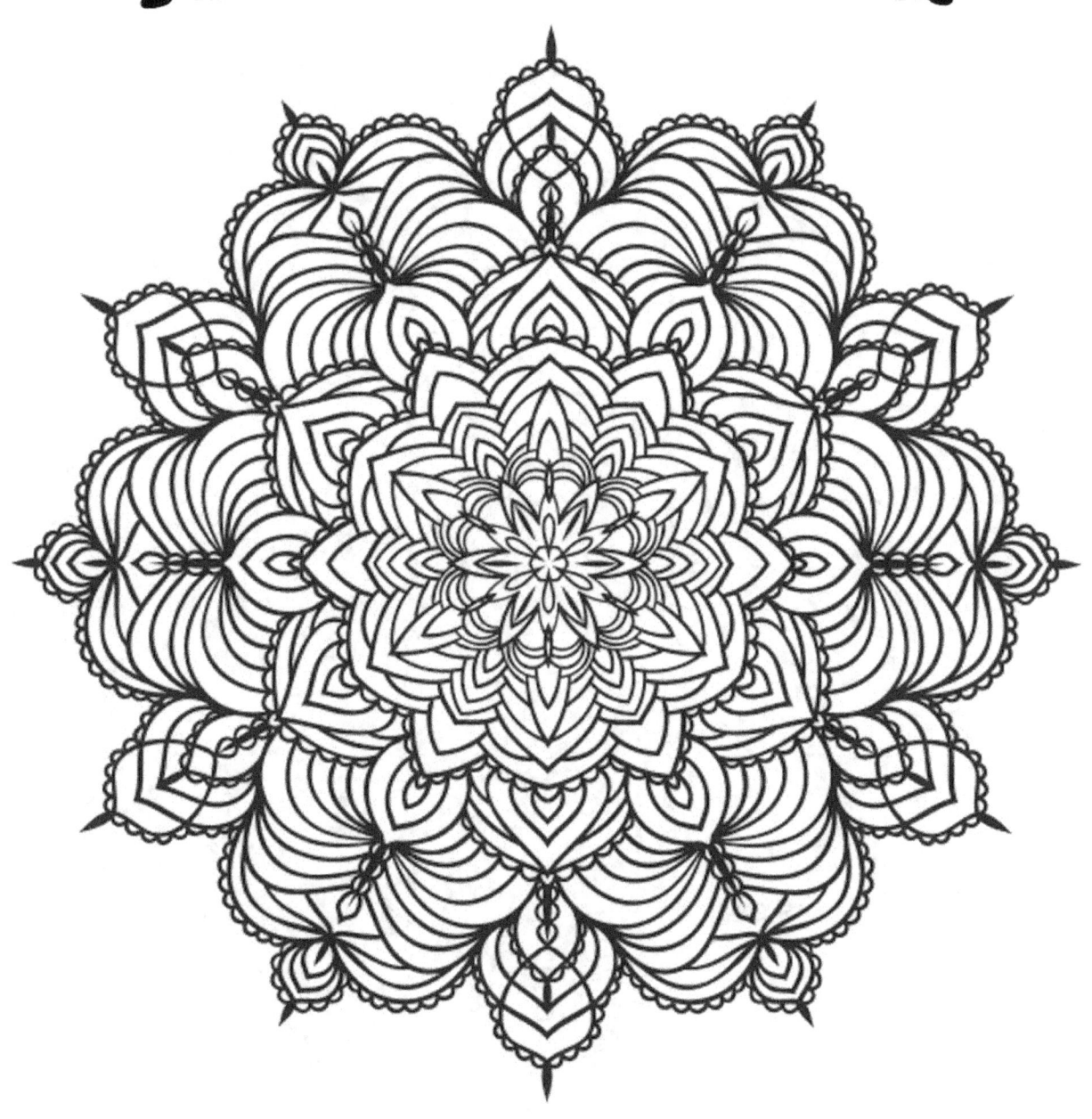

101bookclub.com

101 Flower Power

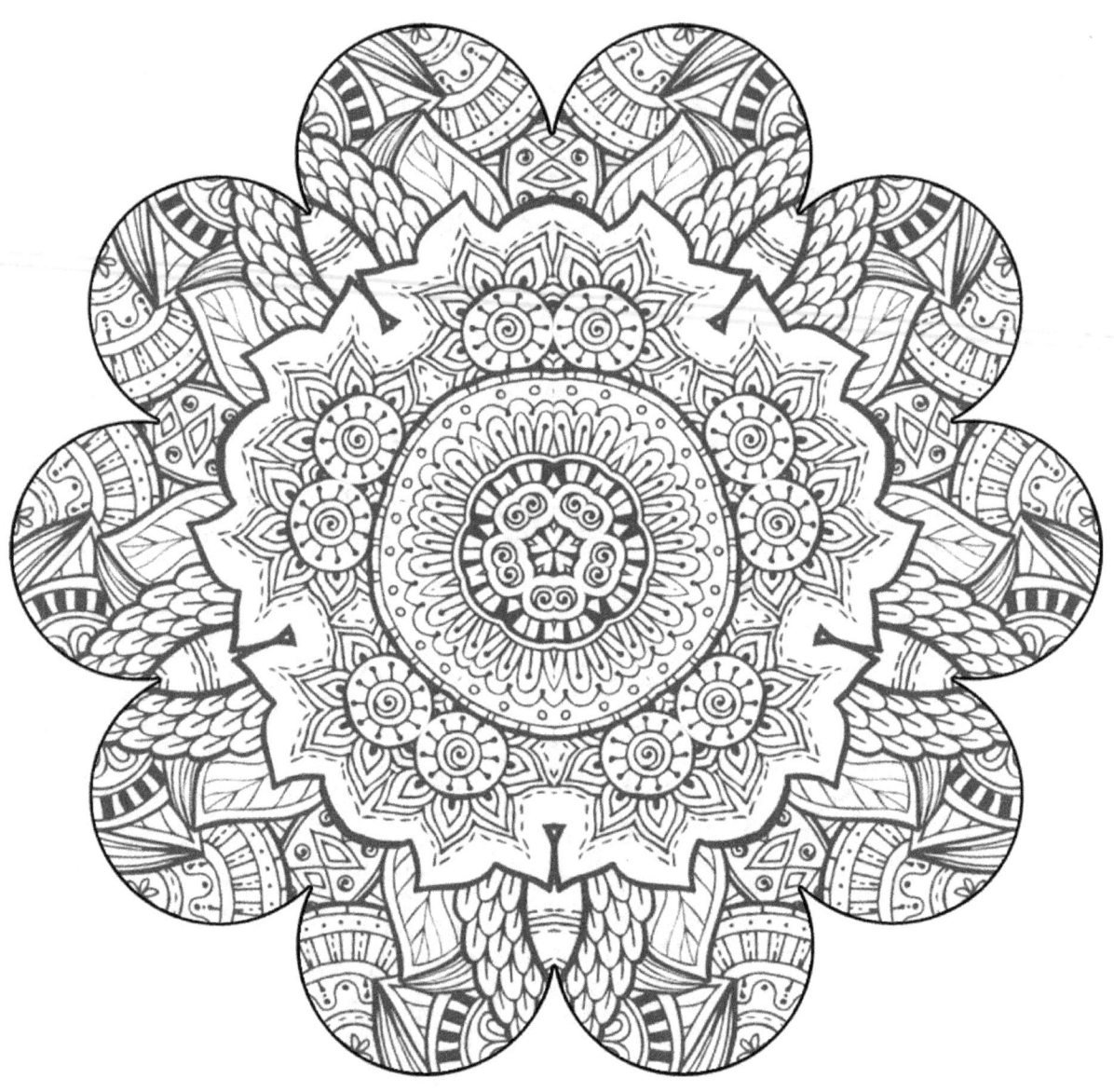

101bookclub.com

101 Flower Power

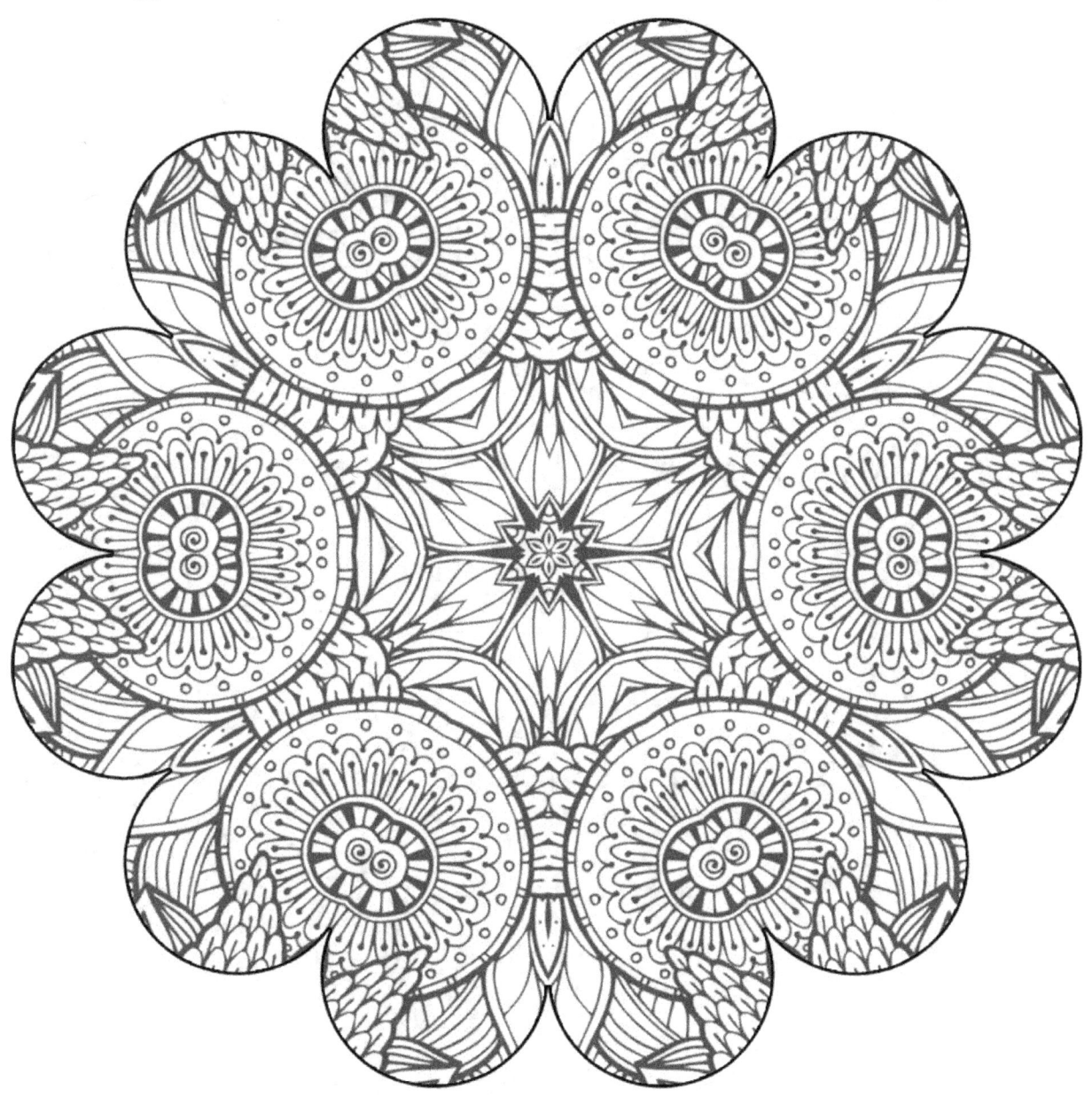

101bookclub.com

101 Flower Power

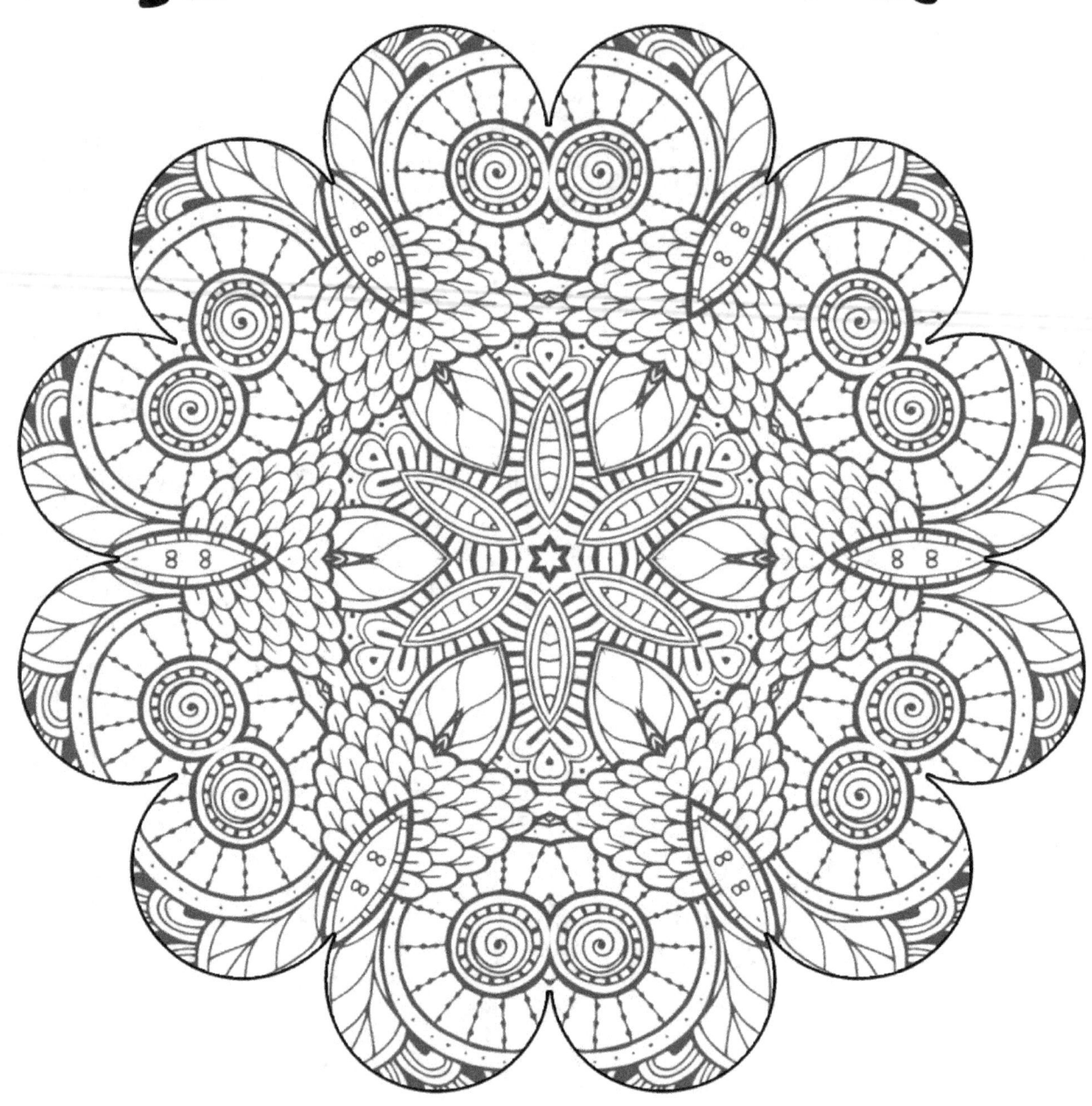

101bookclub.com

101 Flower Power

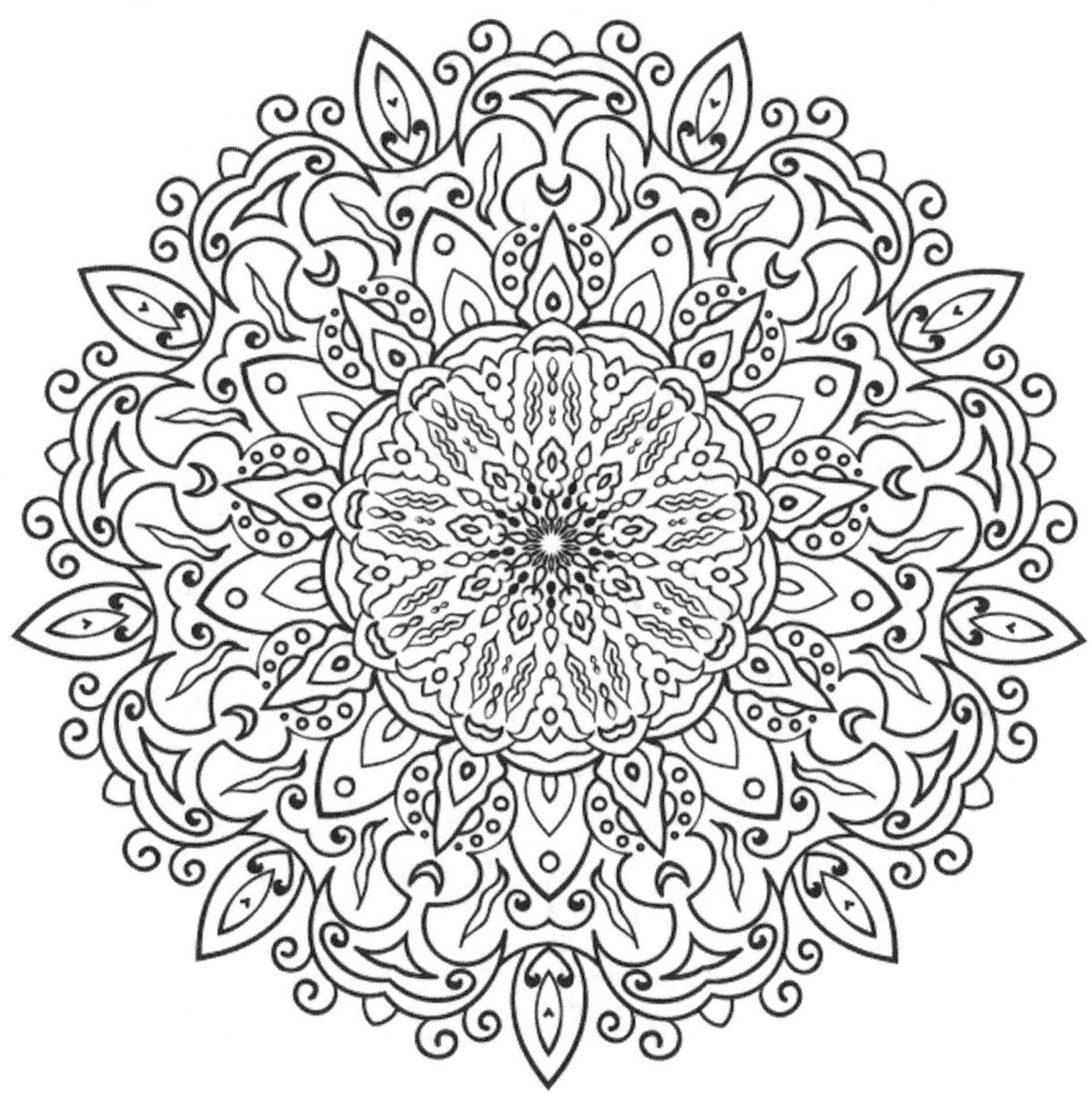

101bookclub.com

101 Flower Power

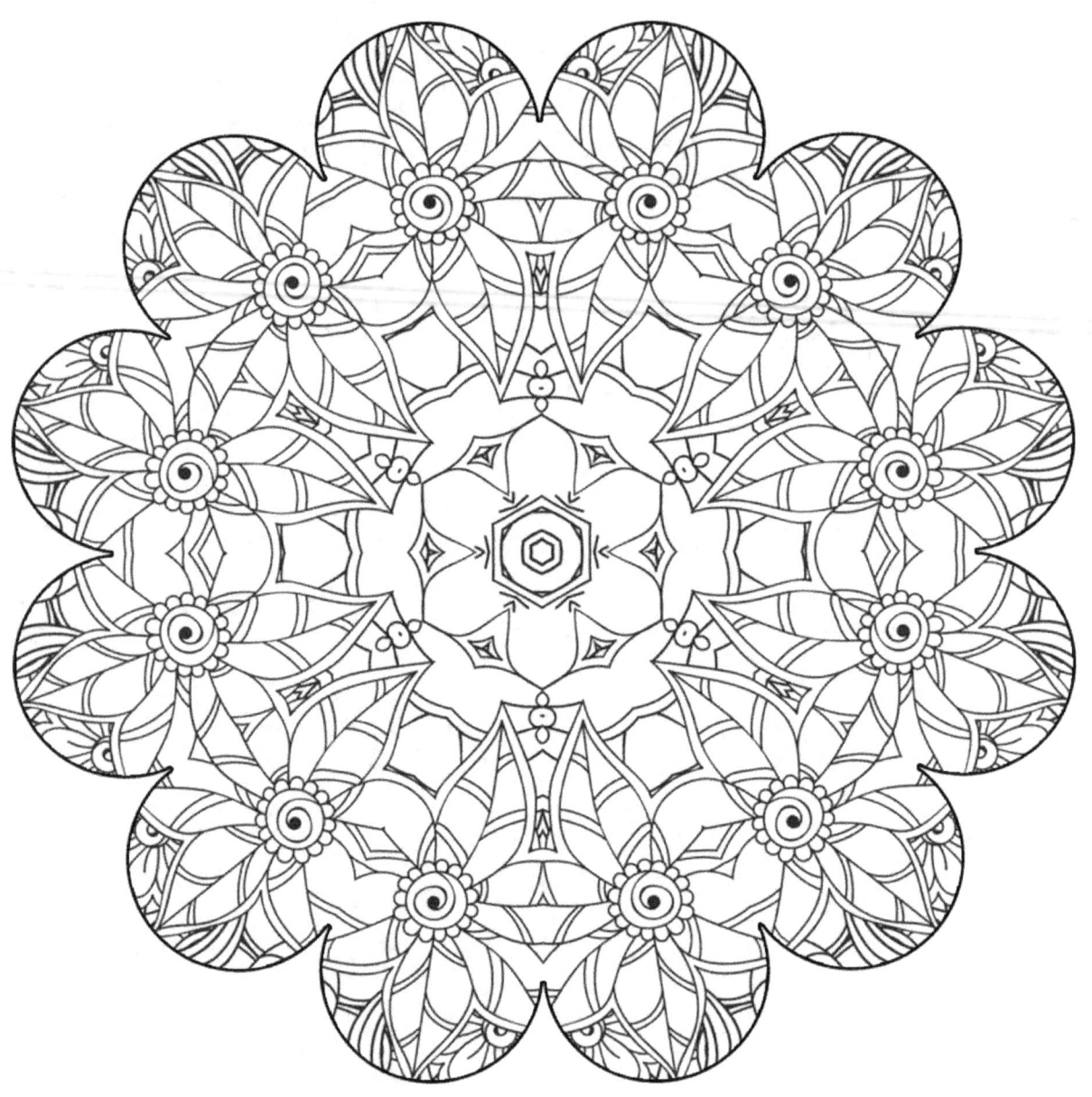

101bookclub.com

101 Flower Power

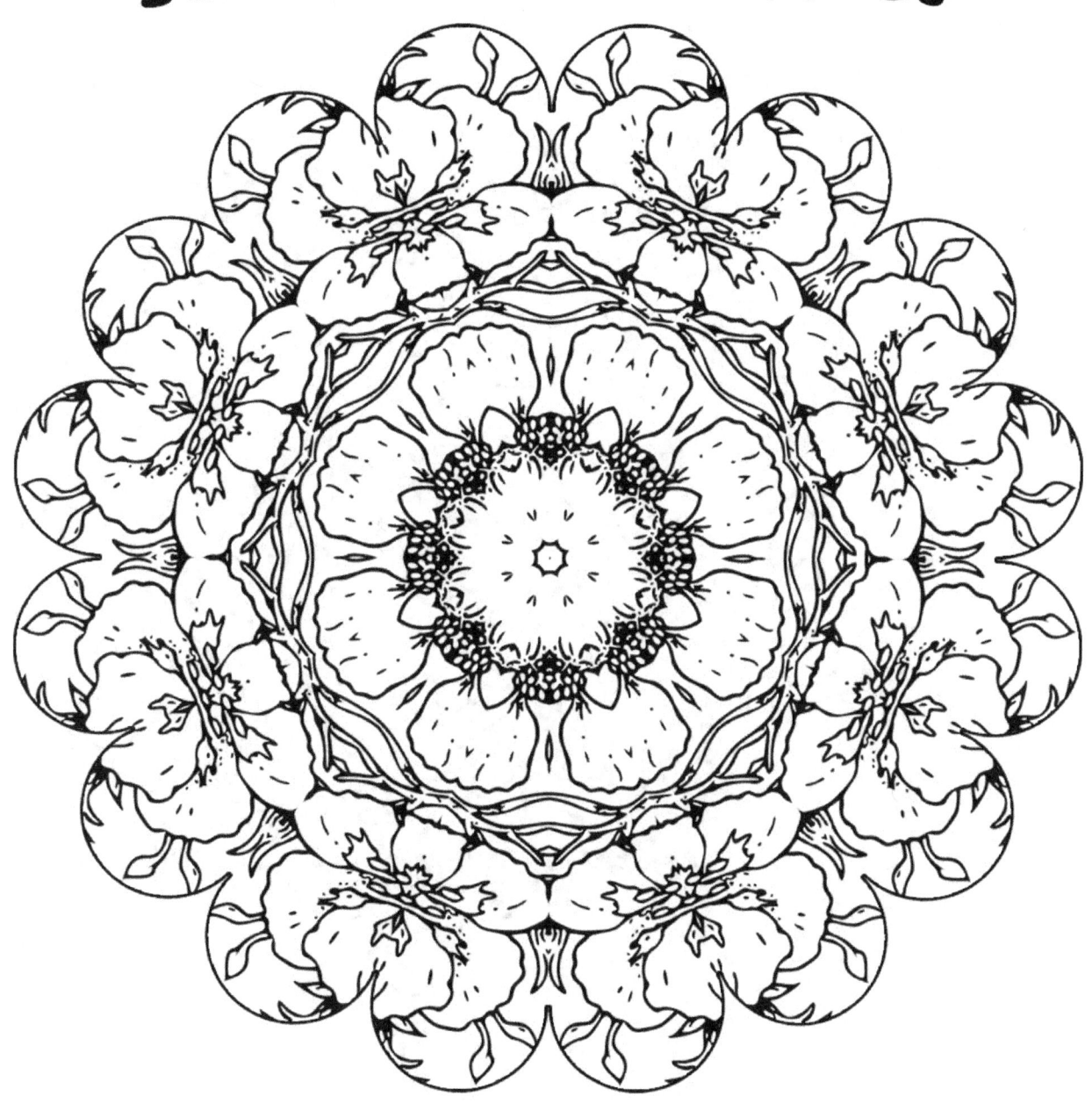

101bookclub.com

101 Flower Power

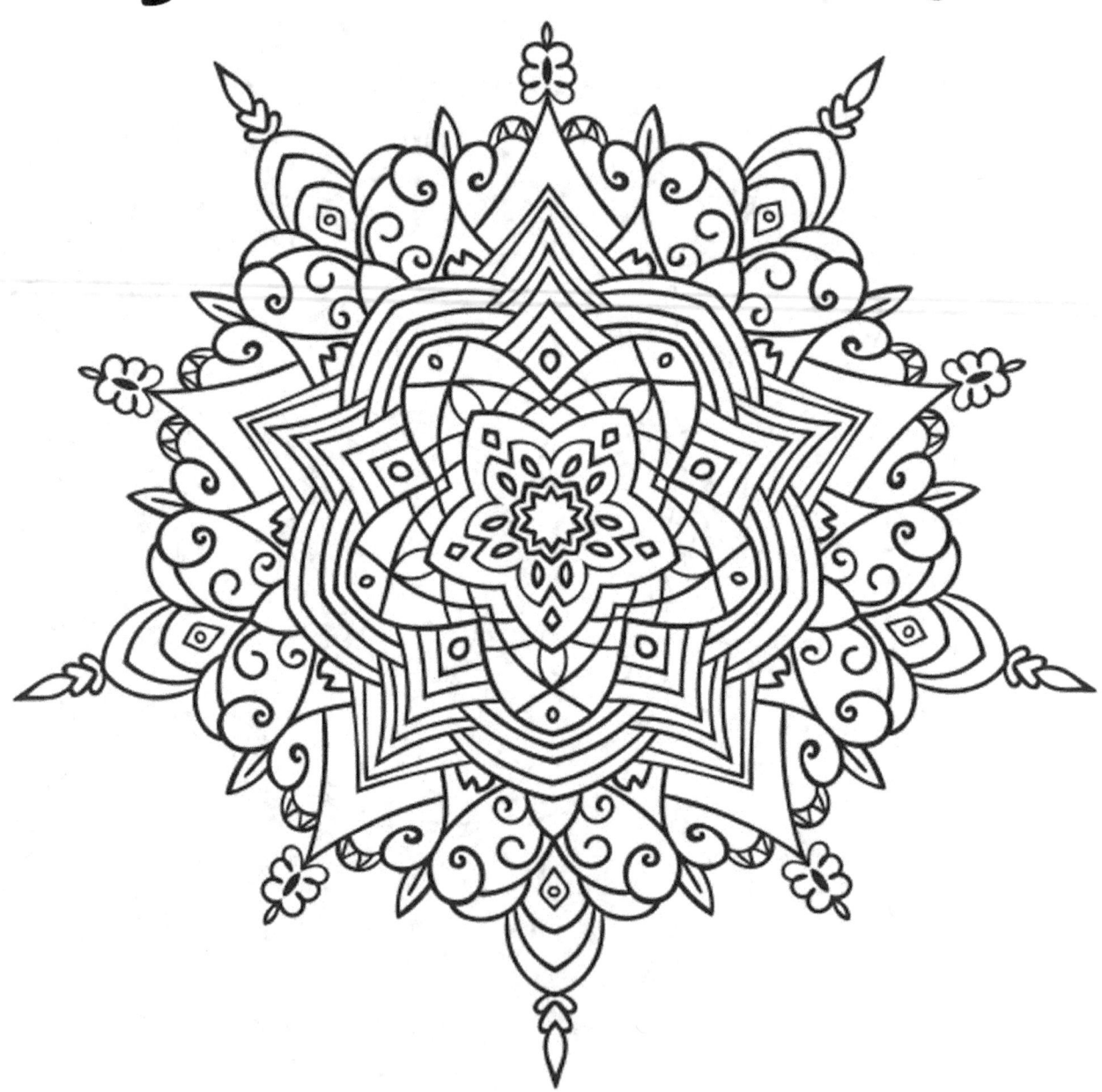

101bookclub.com

101 Flower Power

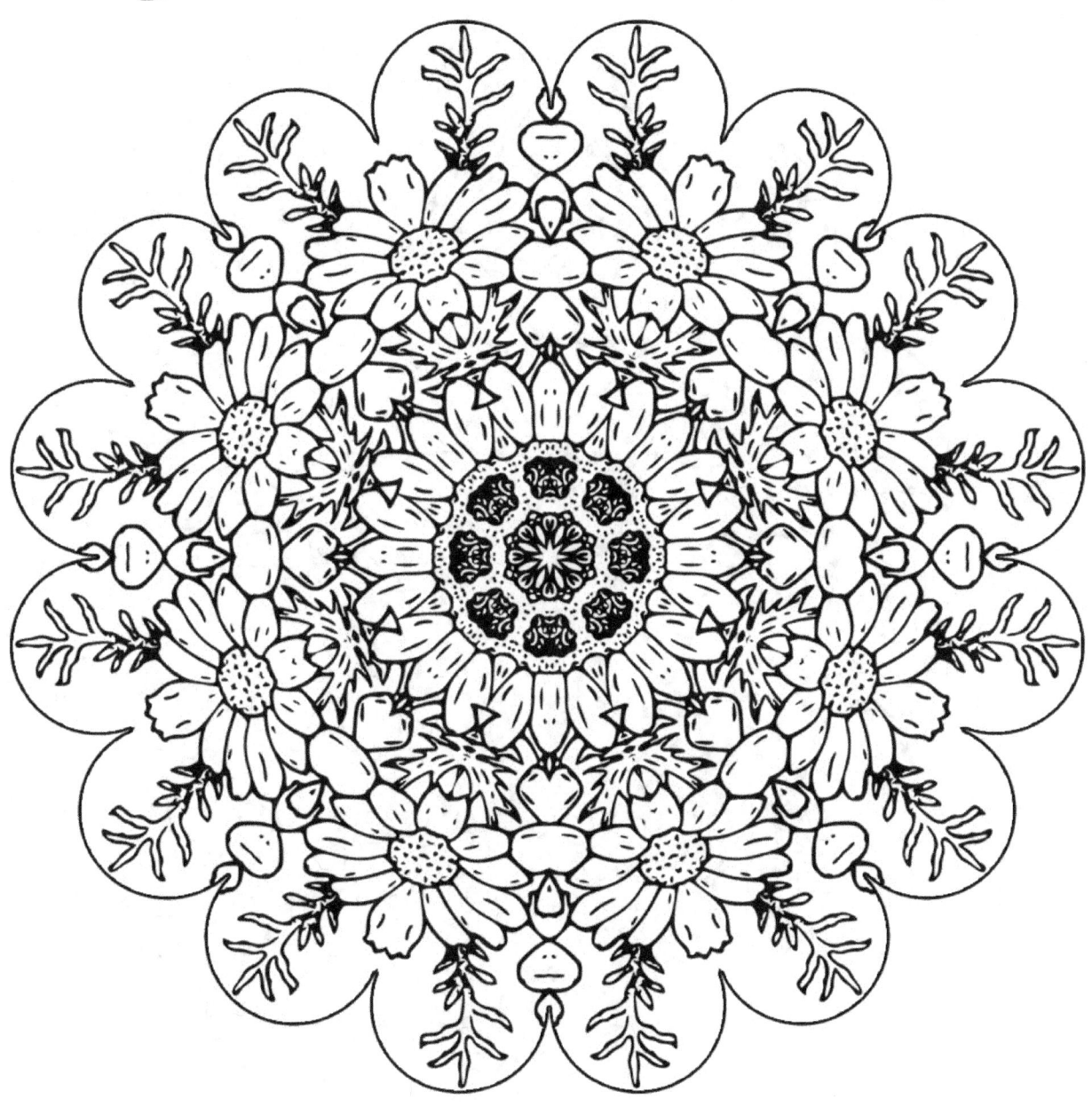

101bookclub.com

101 Flower Power

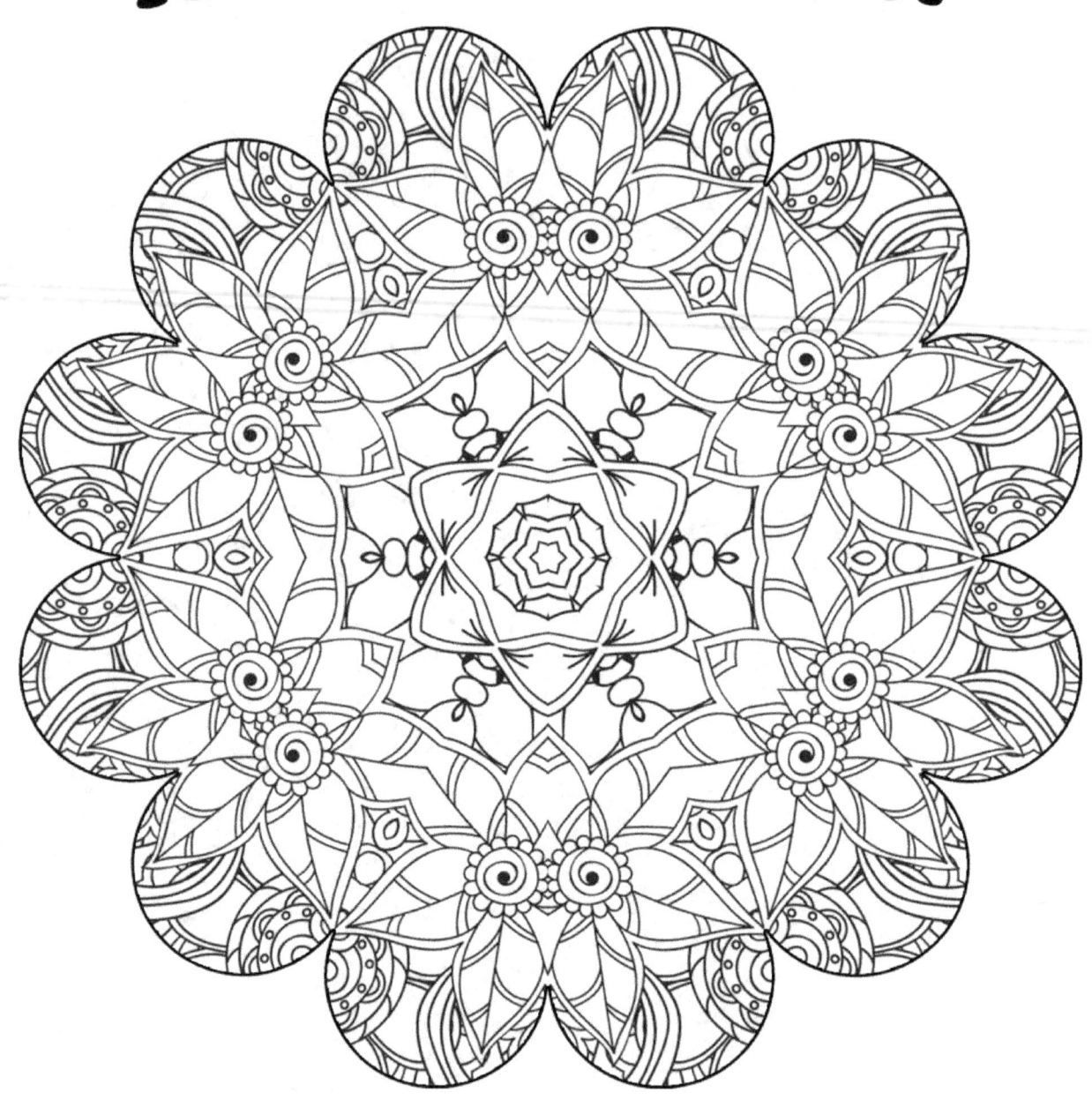

101bookclub.com

101 Flower Power

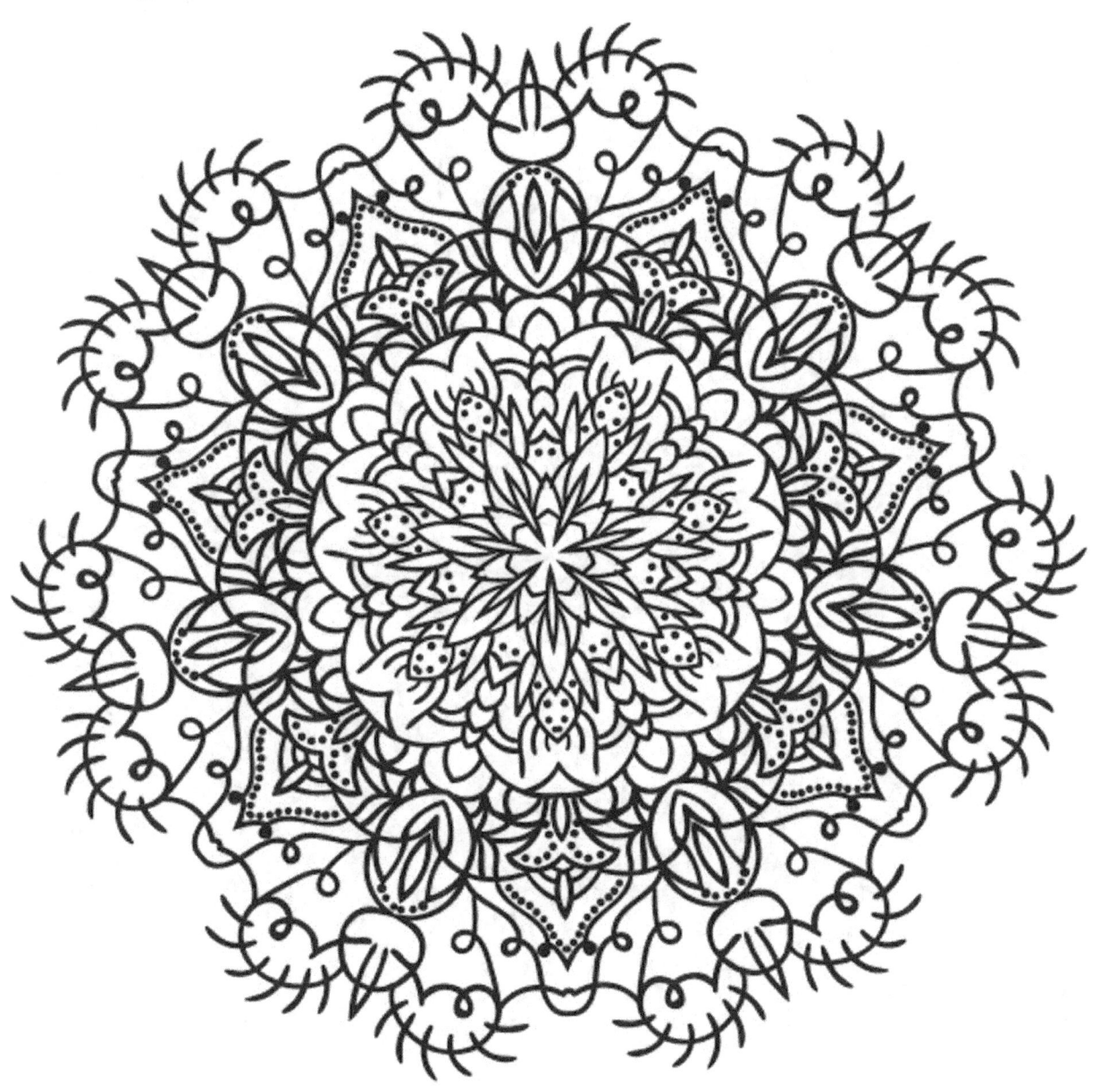

101bookclub.com

101 Flower Power

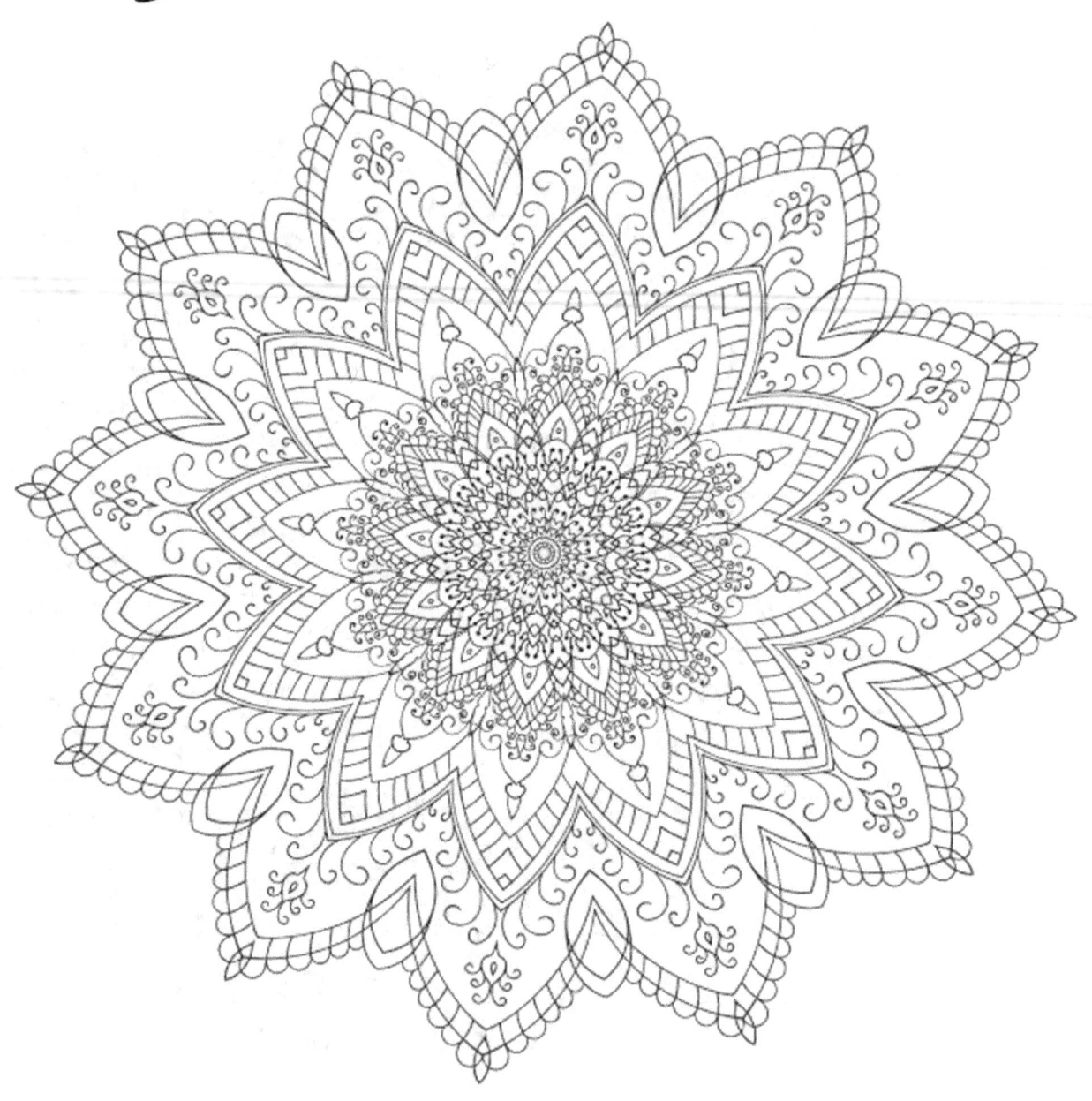

101bookclub.com

101 Flower Power

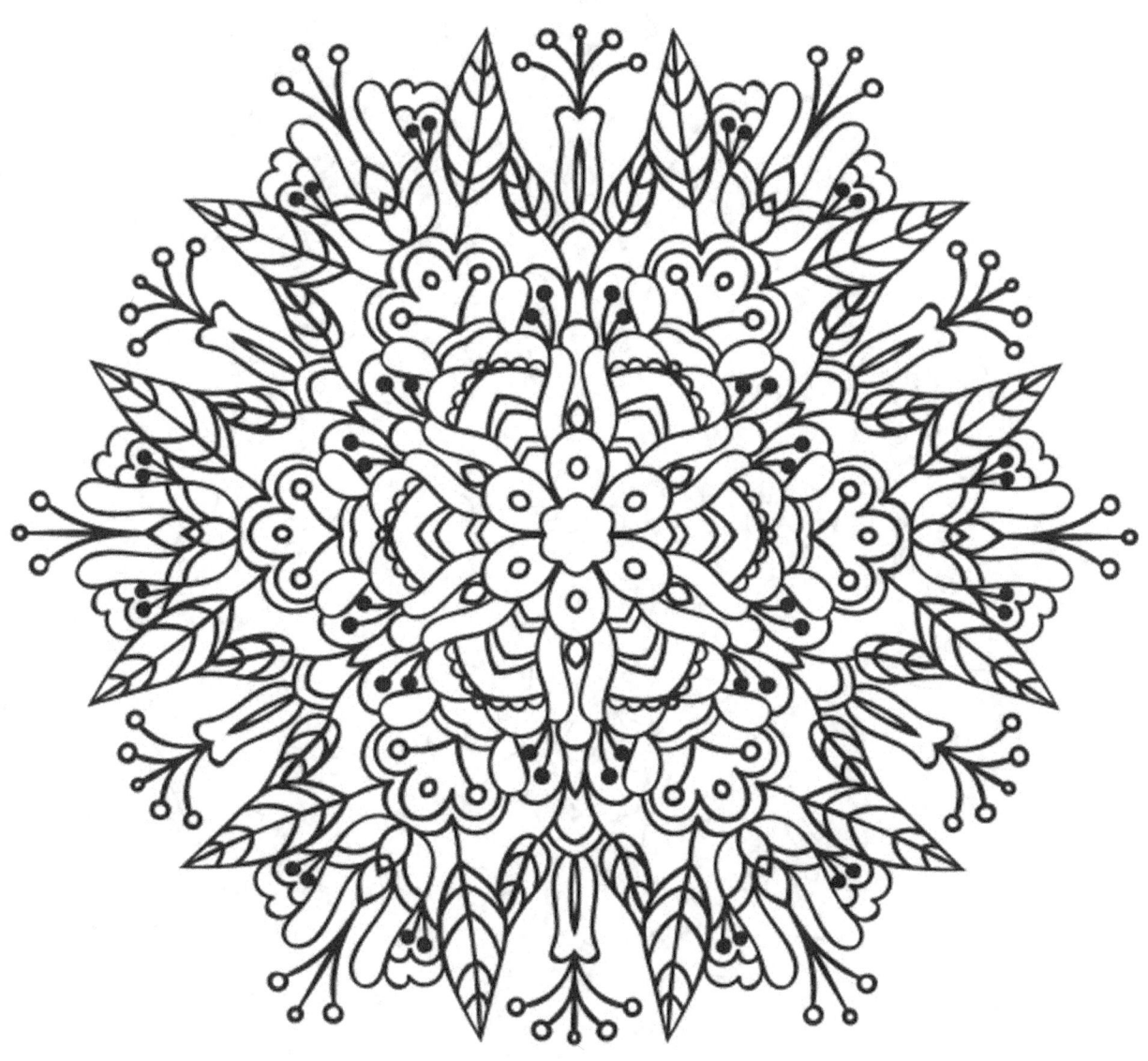

101bookclub.com

101 Flower Power

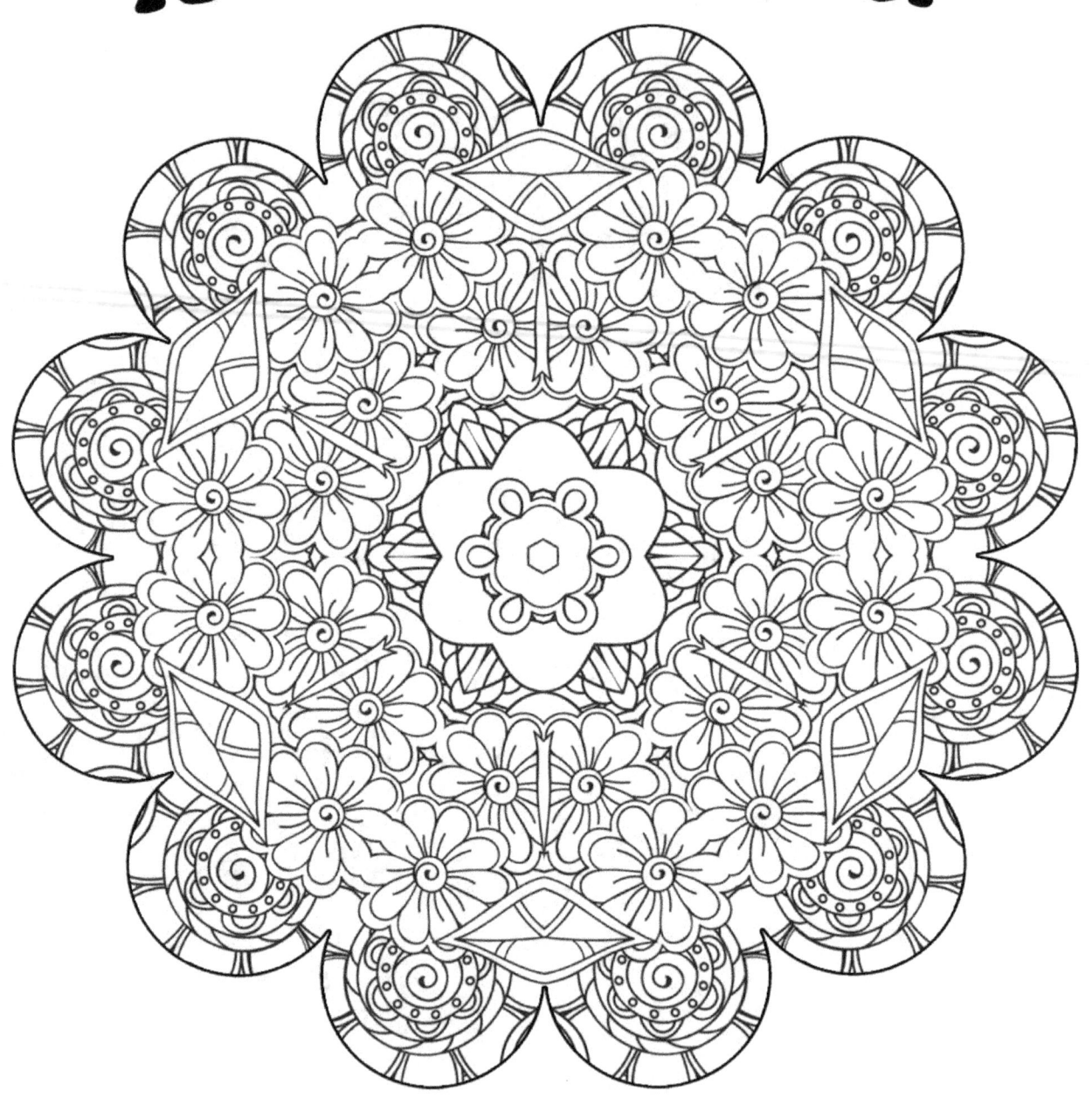

101bookclub.com

101 Flower Power

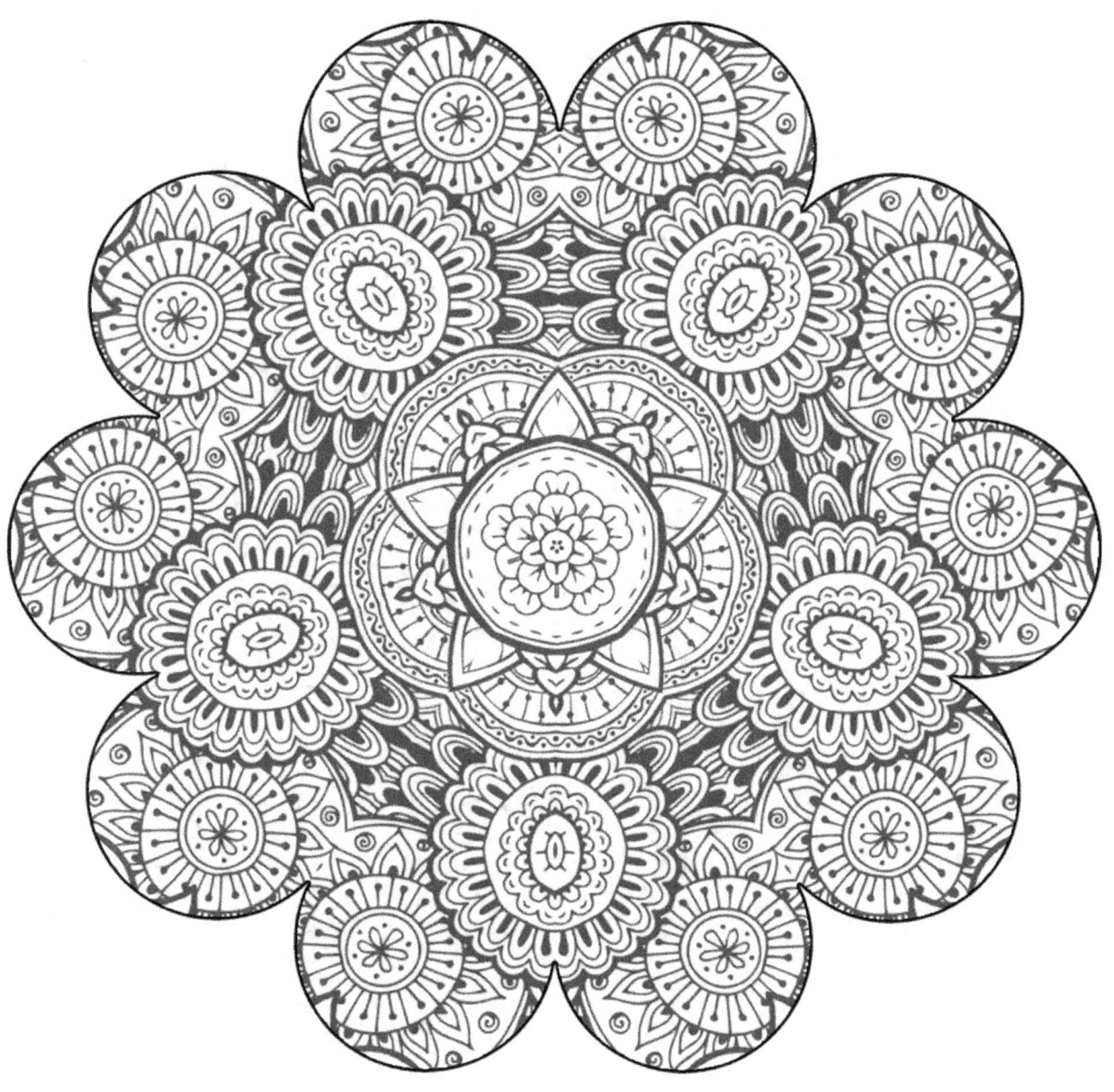

101bookclub.com

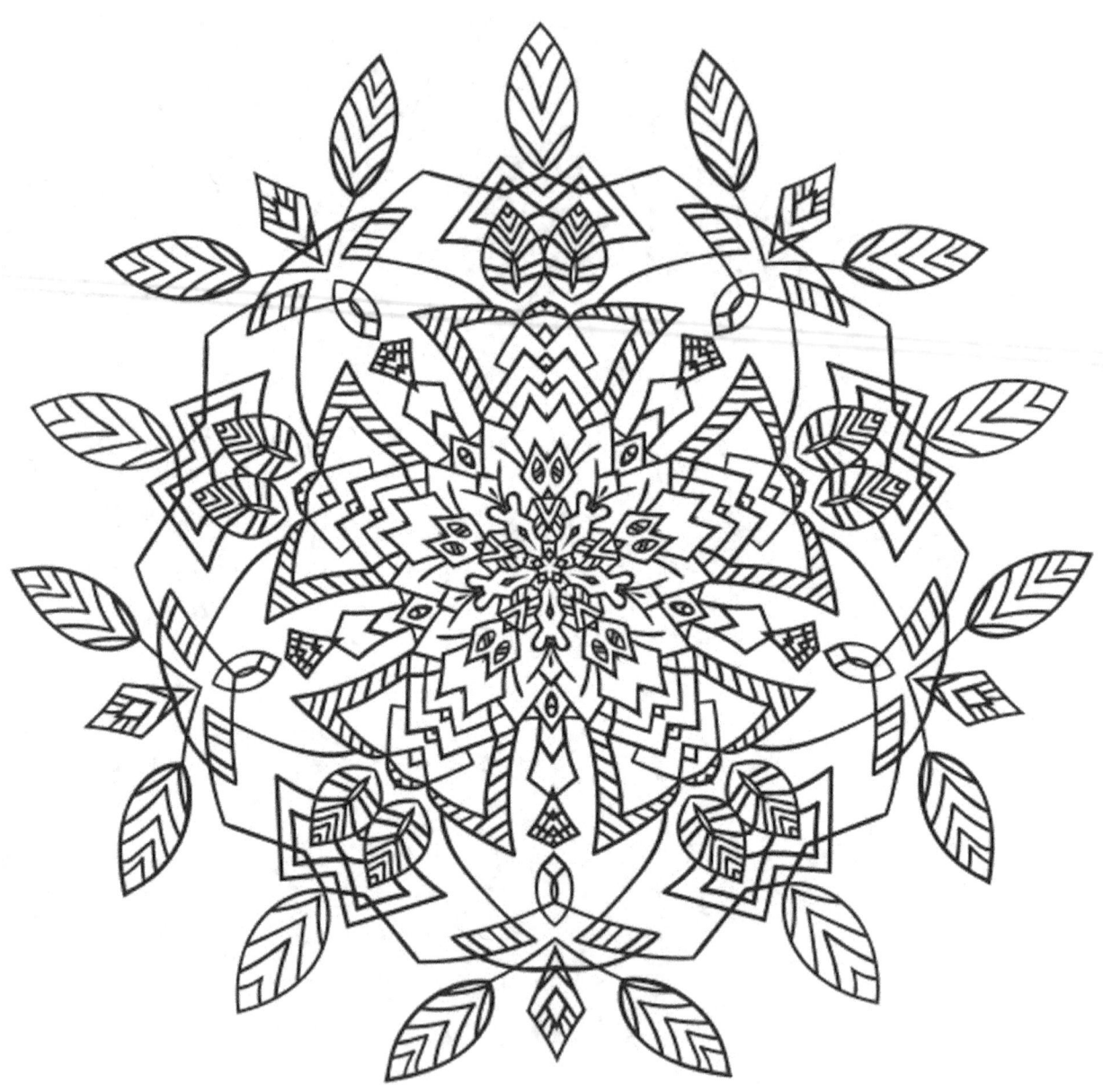

101 Flower Power

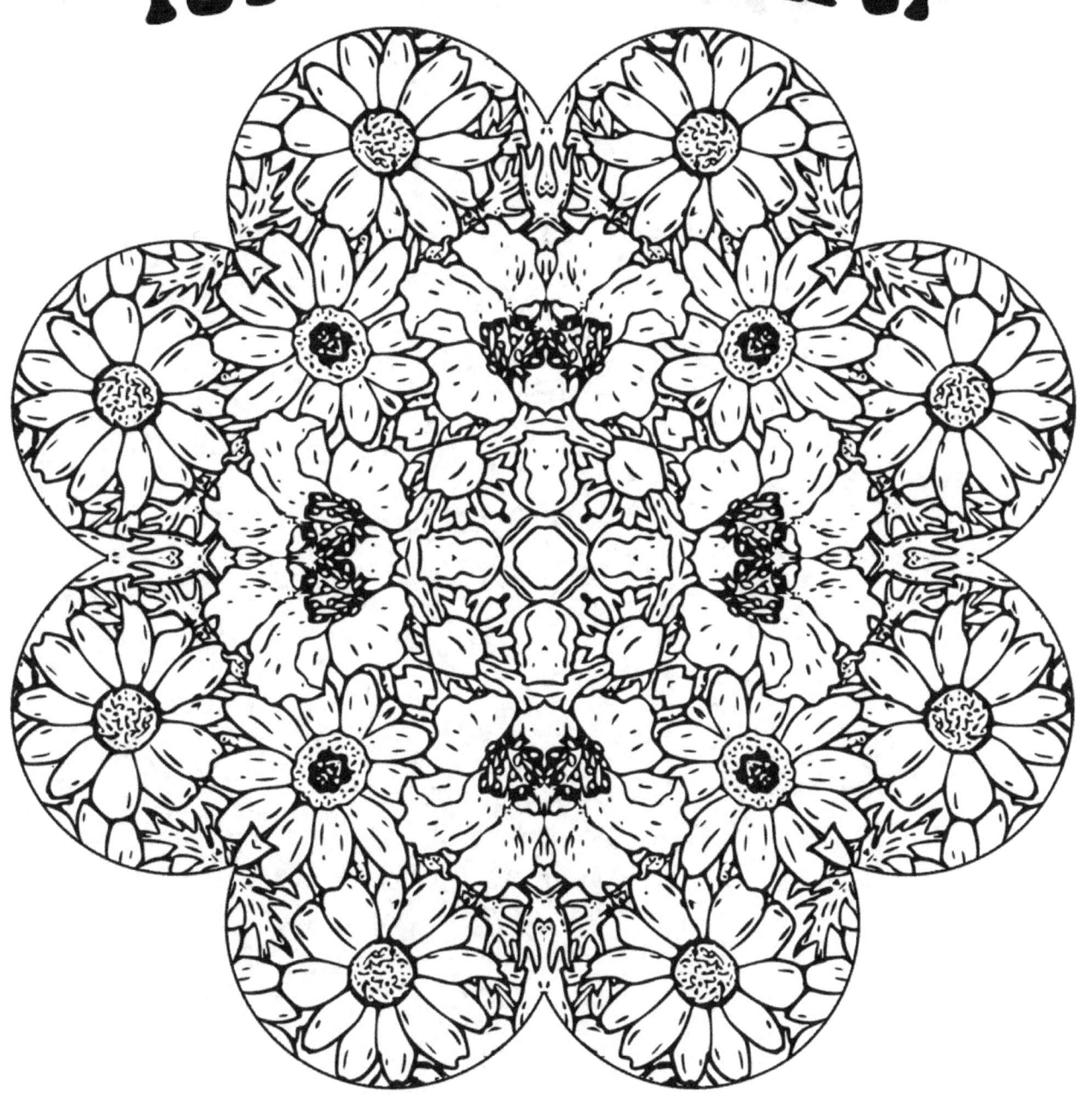

101bookclub.com

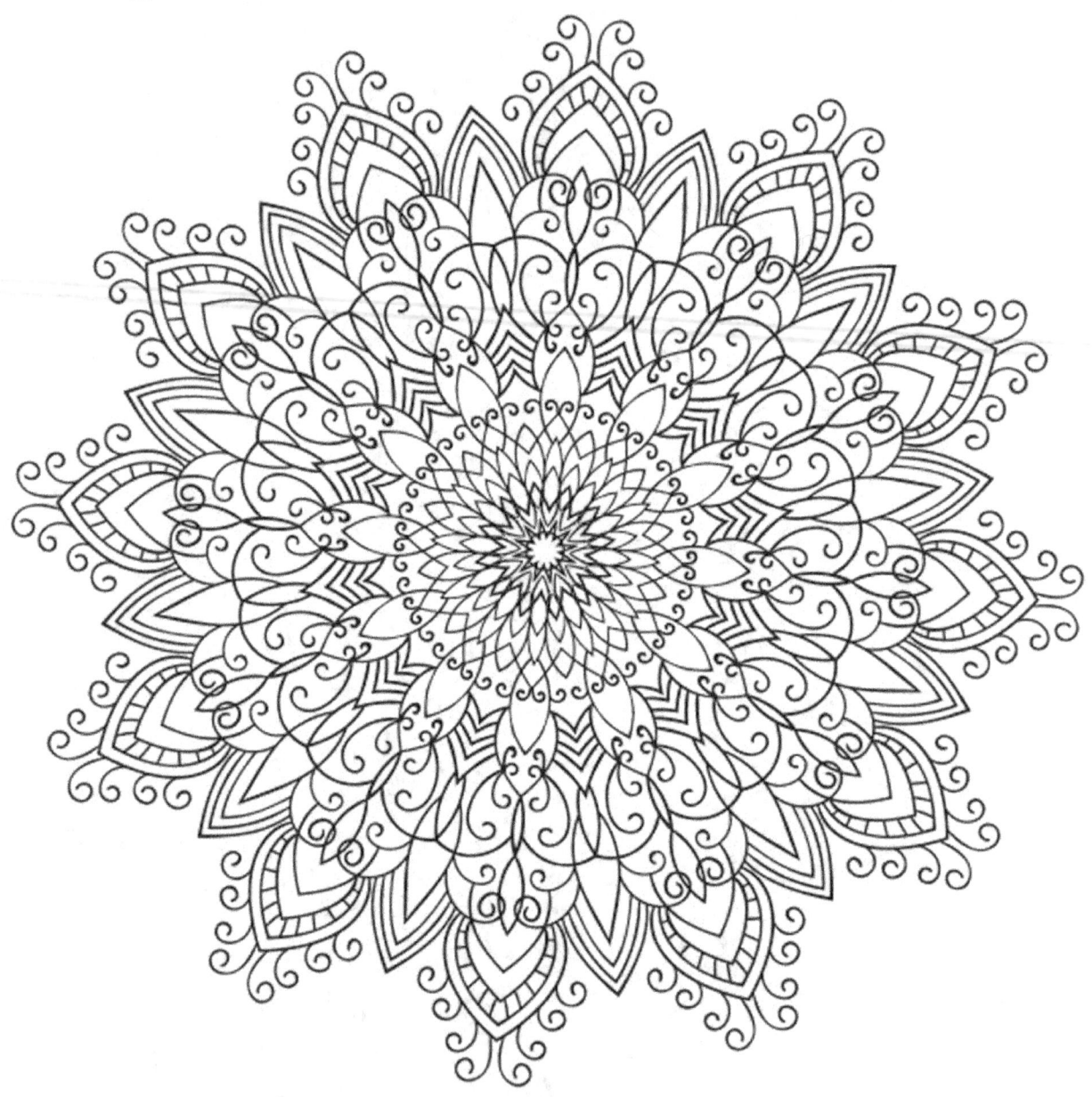

101 Flower Power

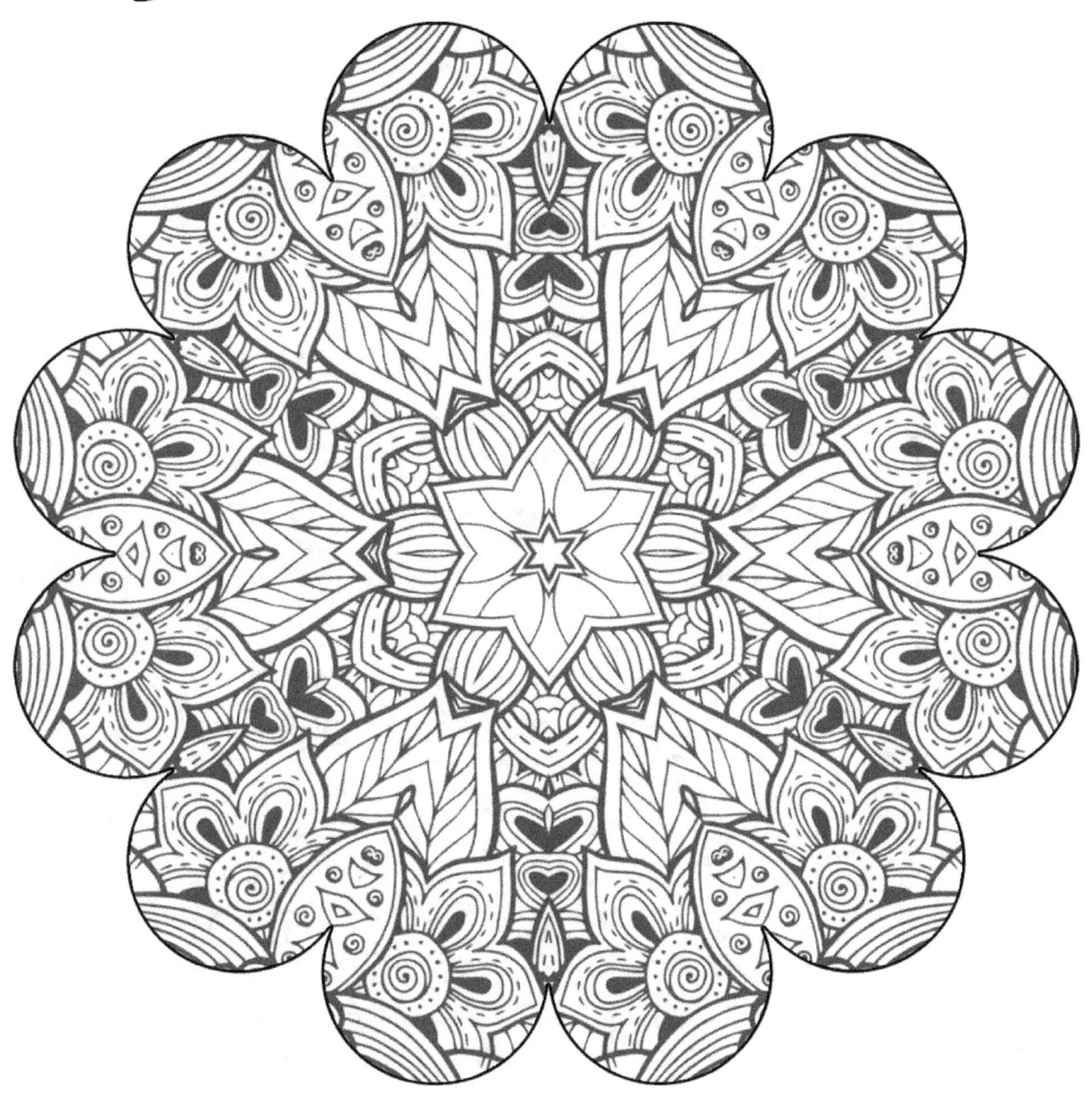

101bookclub.com

101 Flower Power

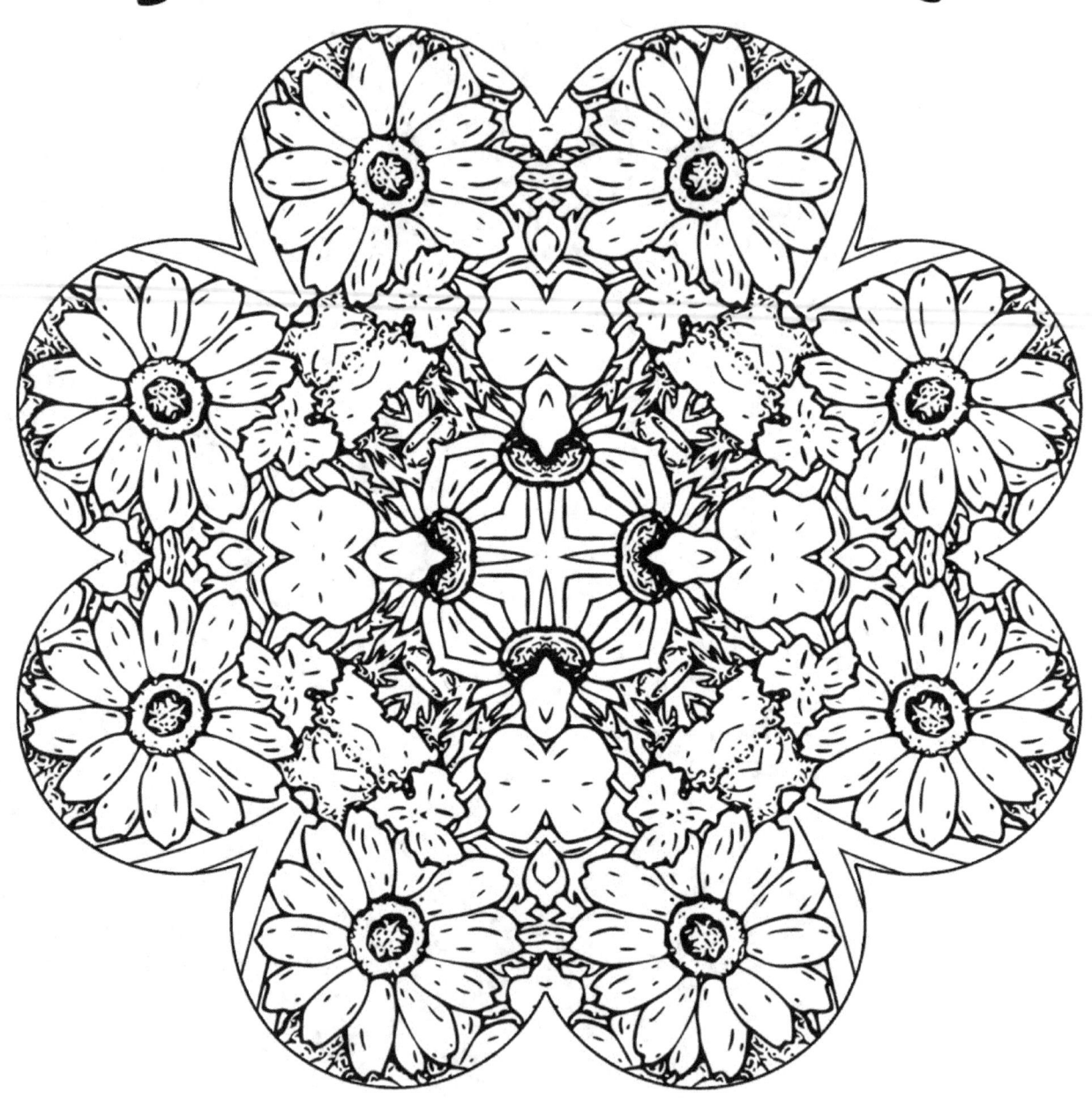

101bookclub.com

101 Flower Power

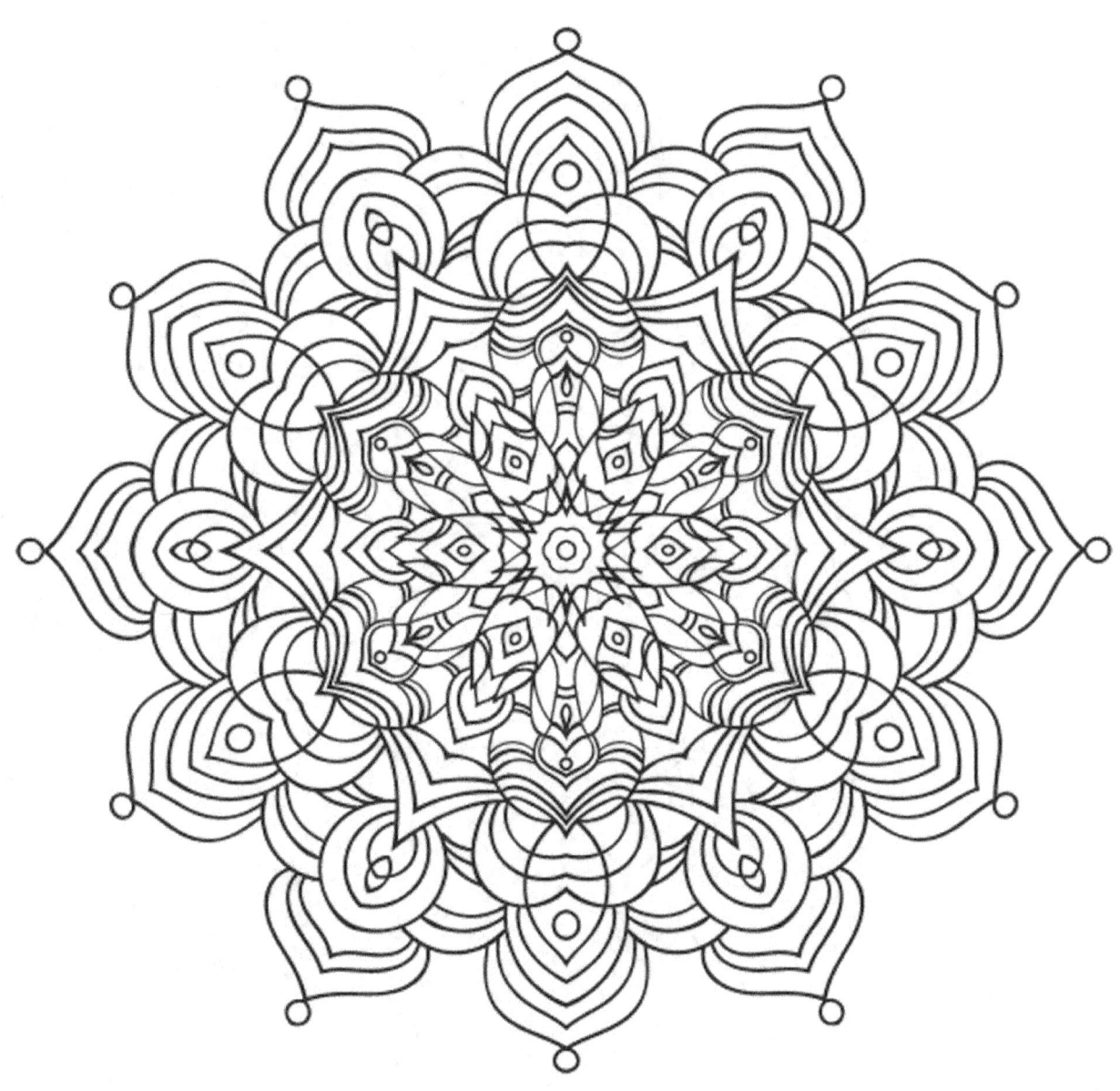

101bookclub.com

101 Flower Power

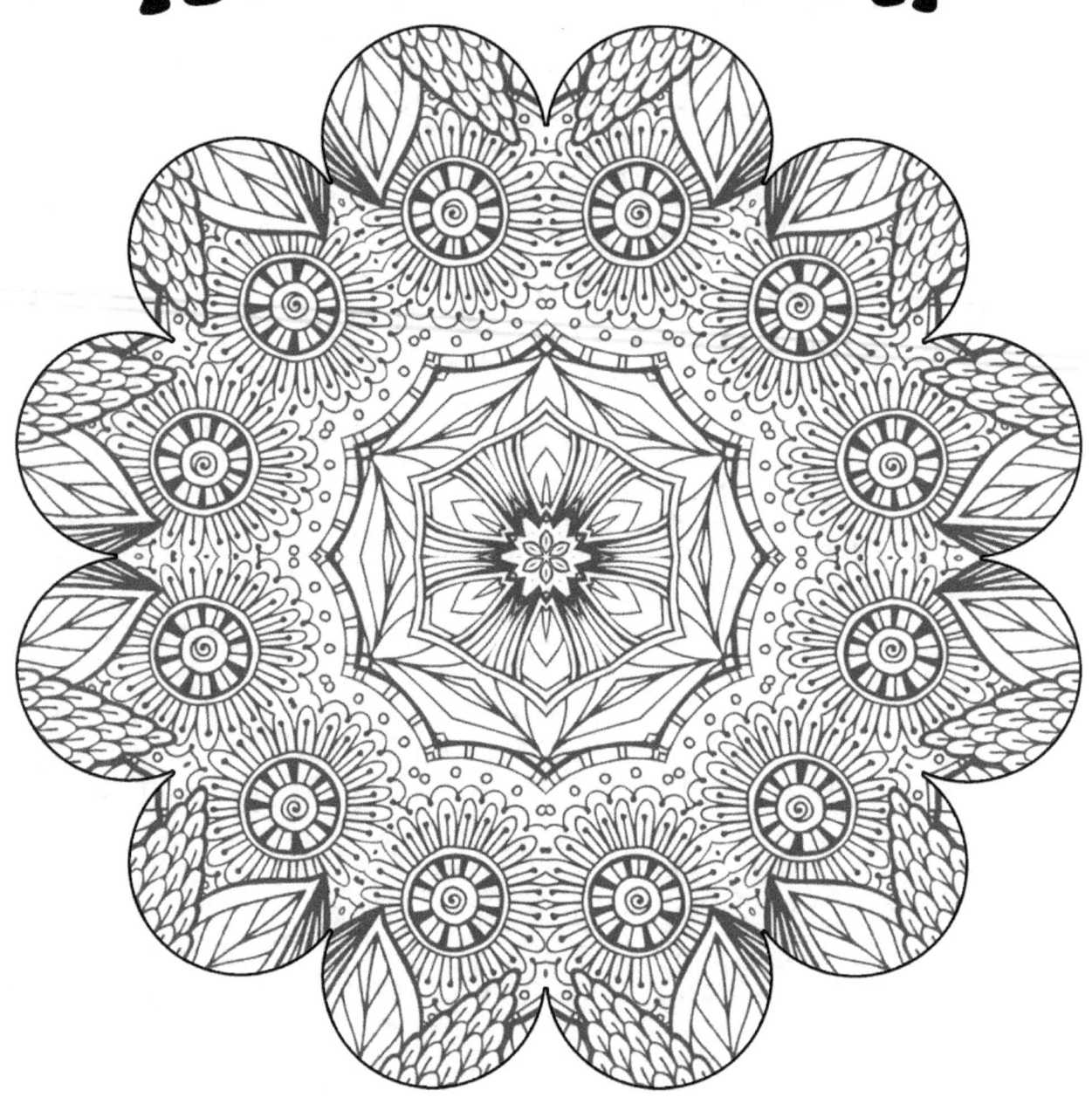

101bookclub.com

101 Flower Power

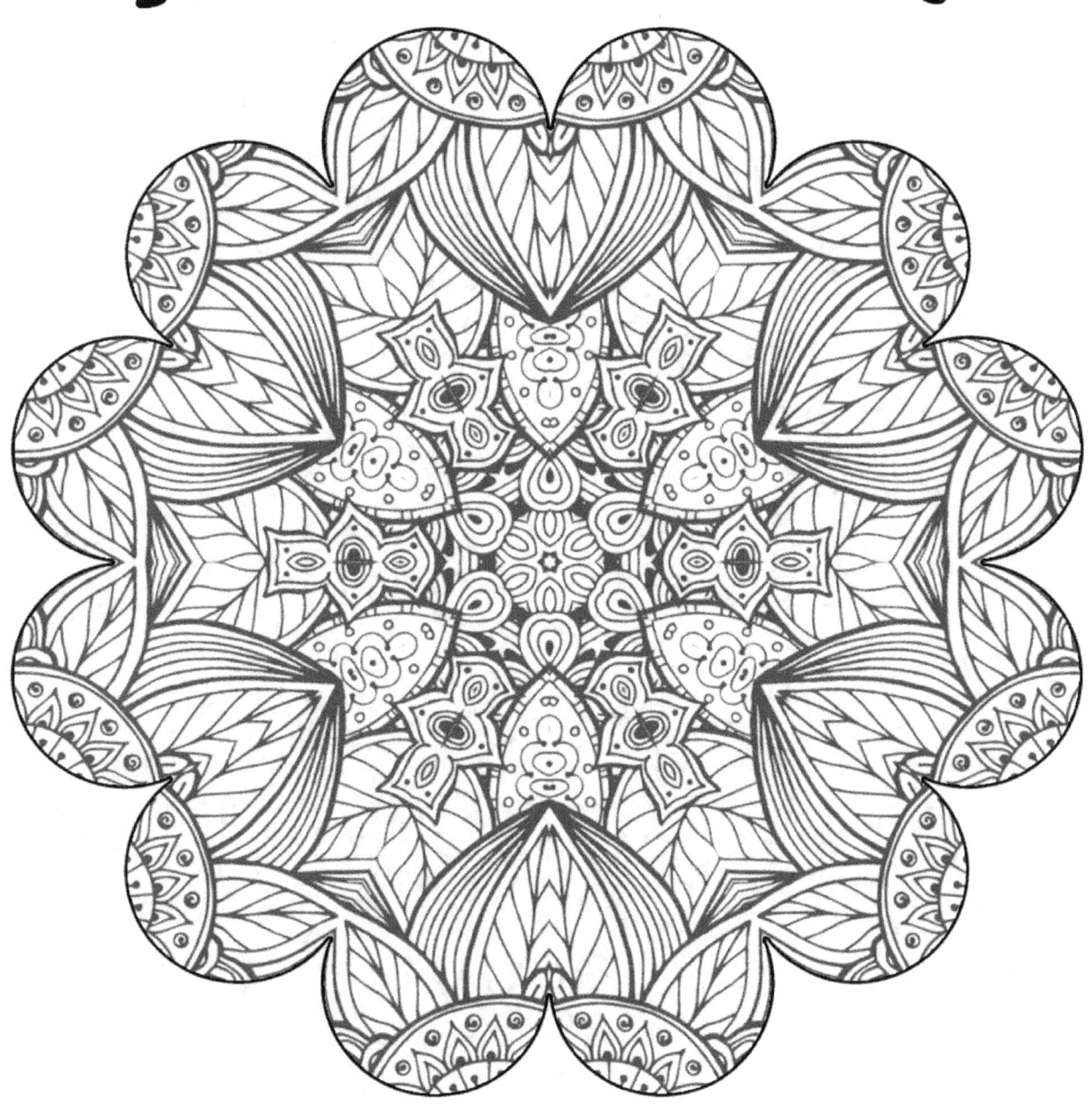

101bookclub.com

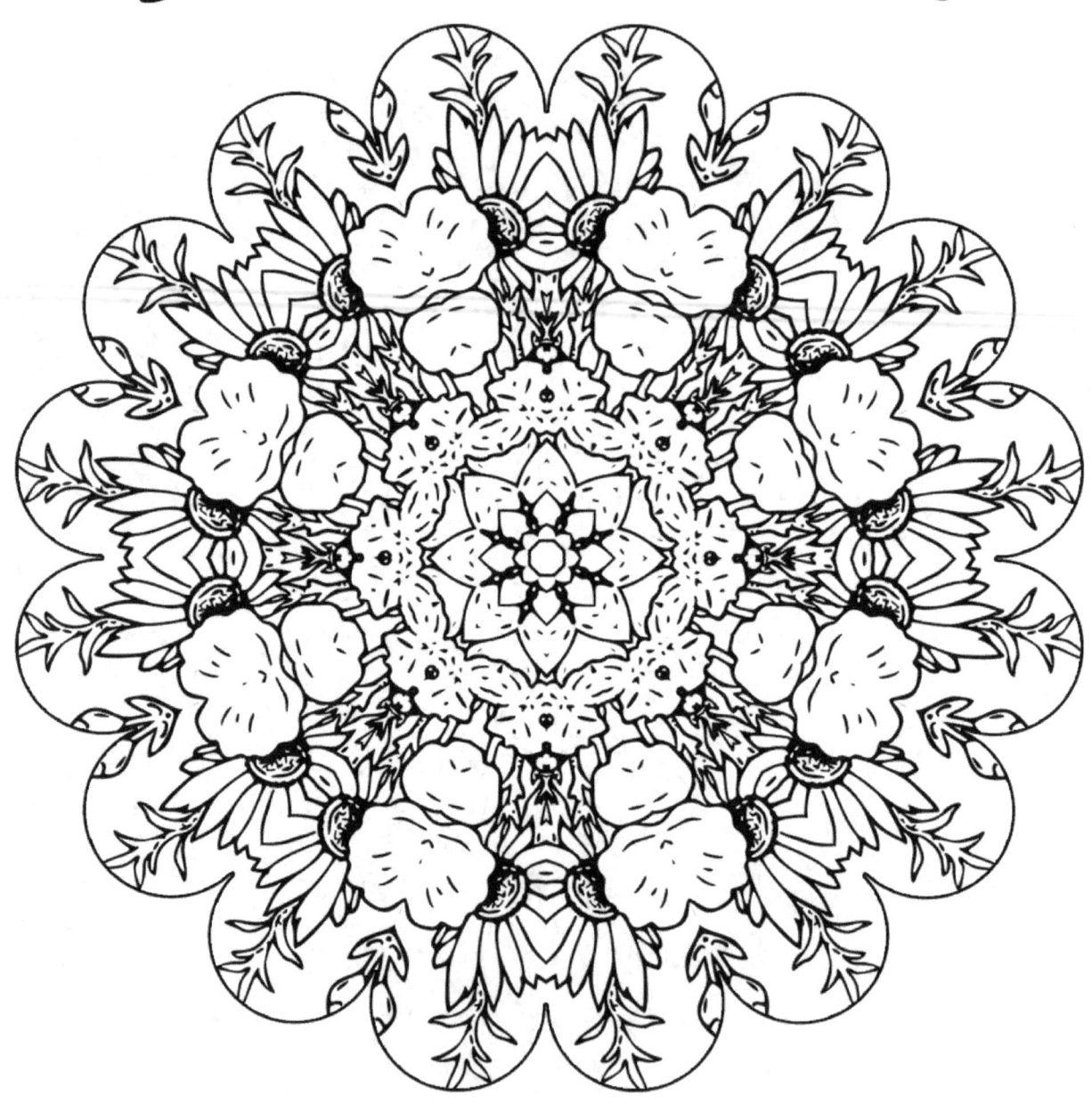

101 Flower Power

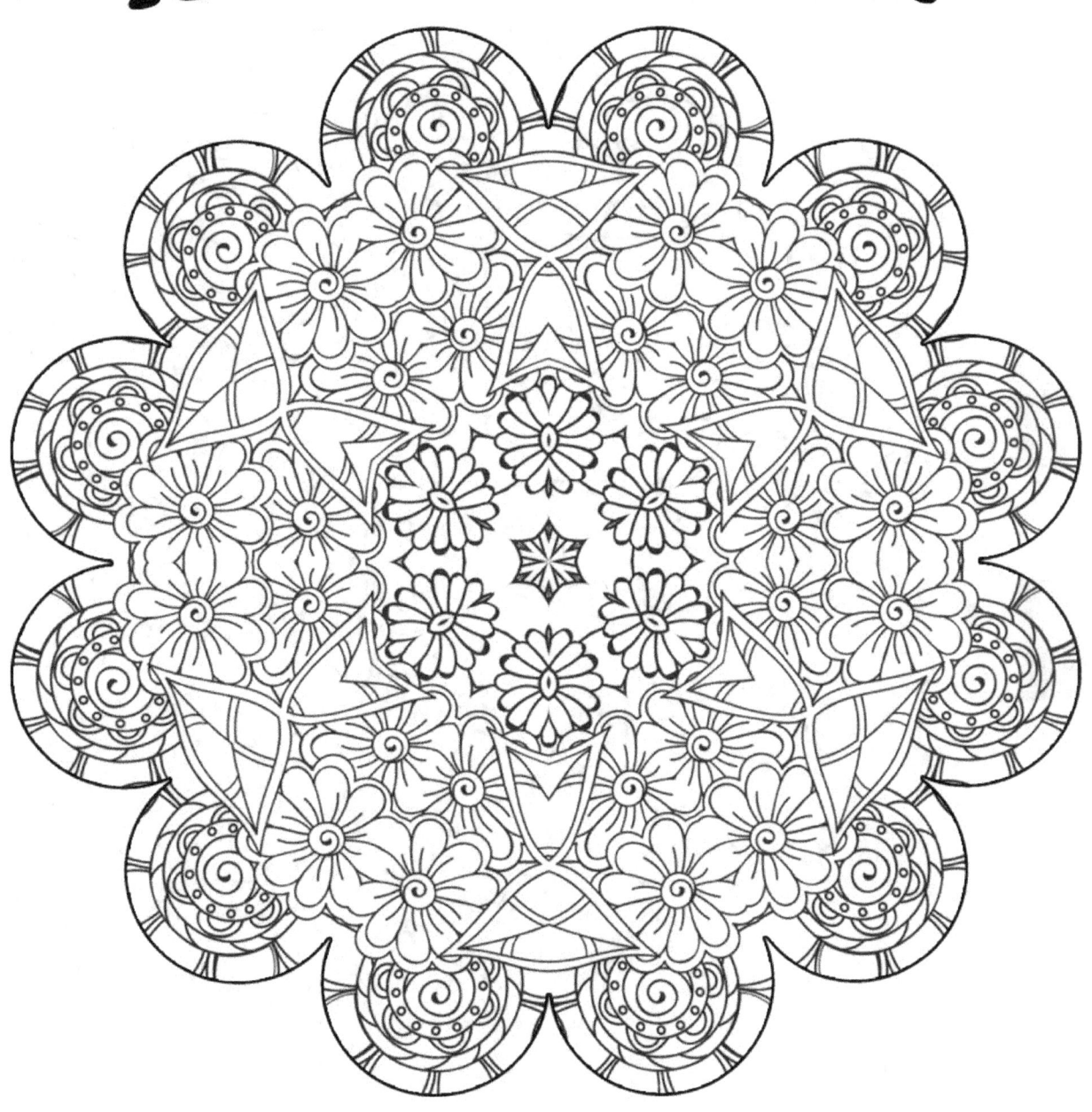

101bookclub.com

101 Flower Power

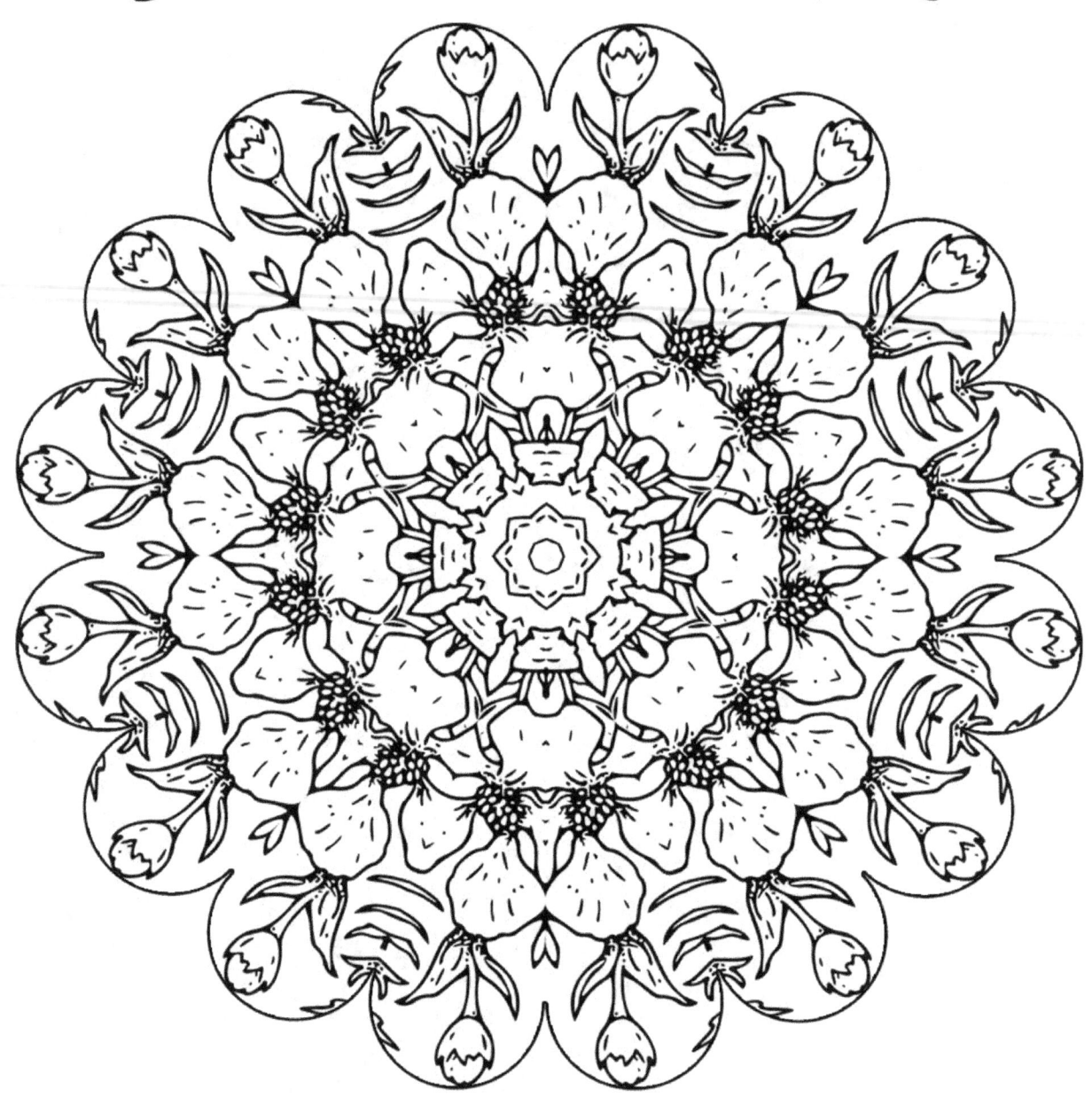

101bookclub.com

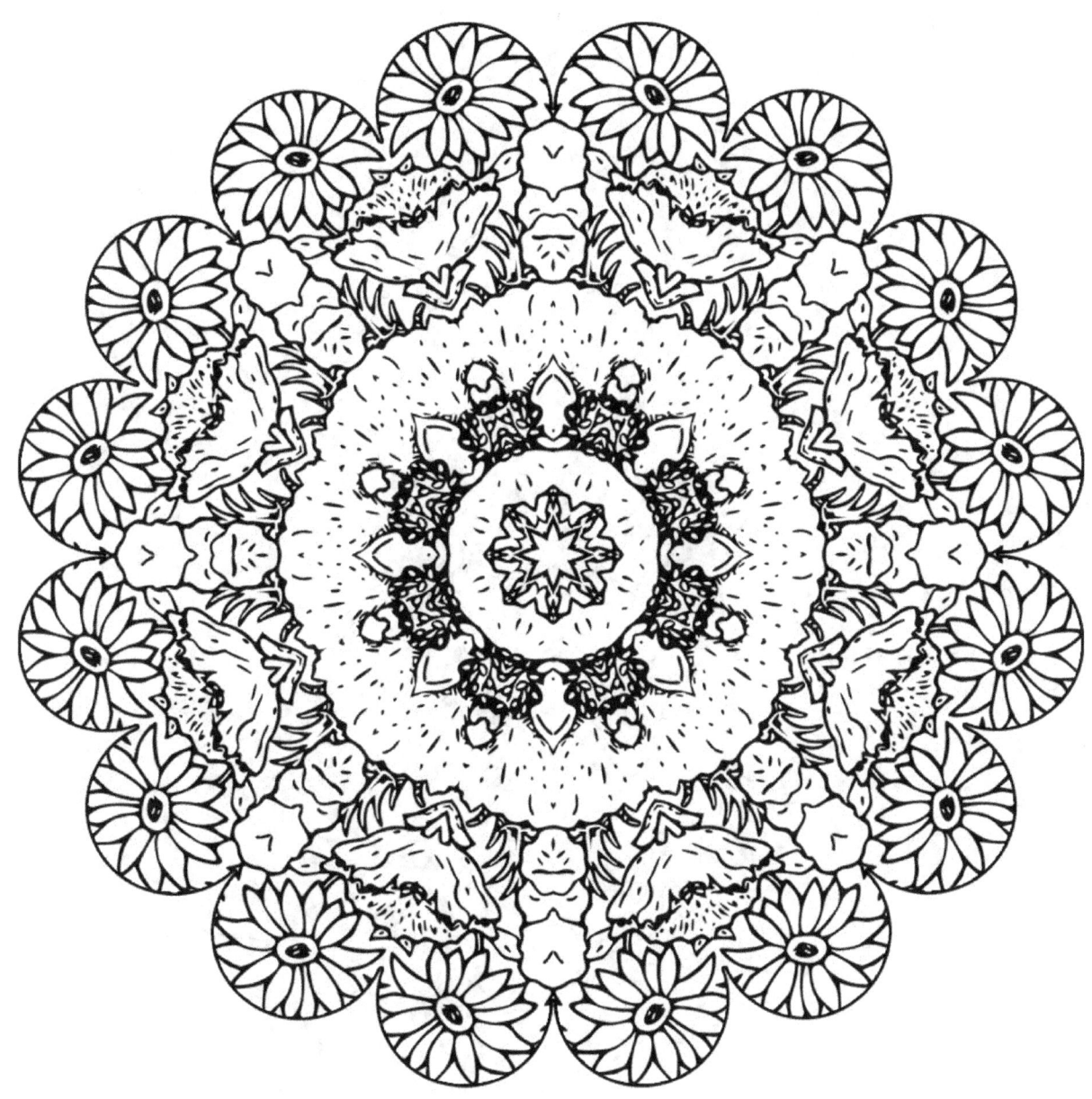

101 Flower Power

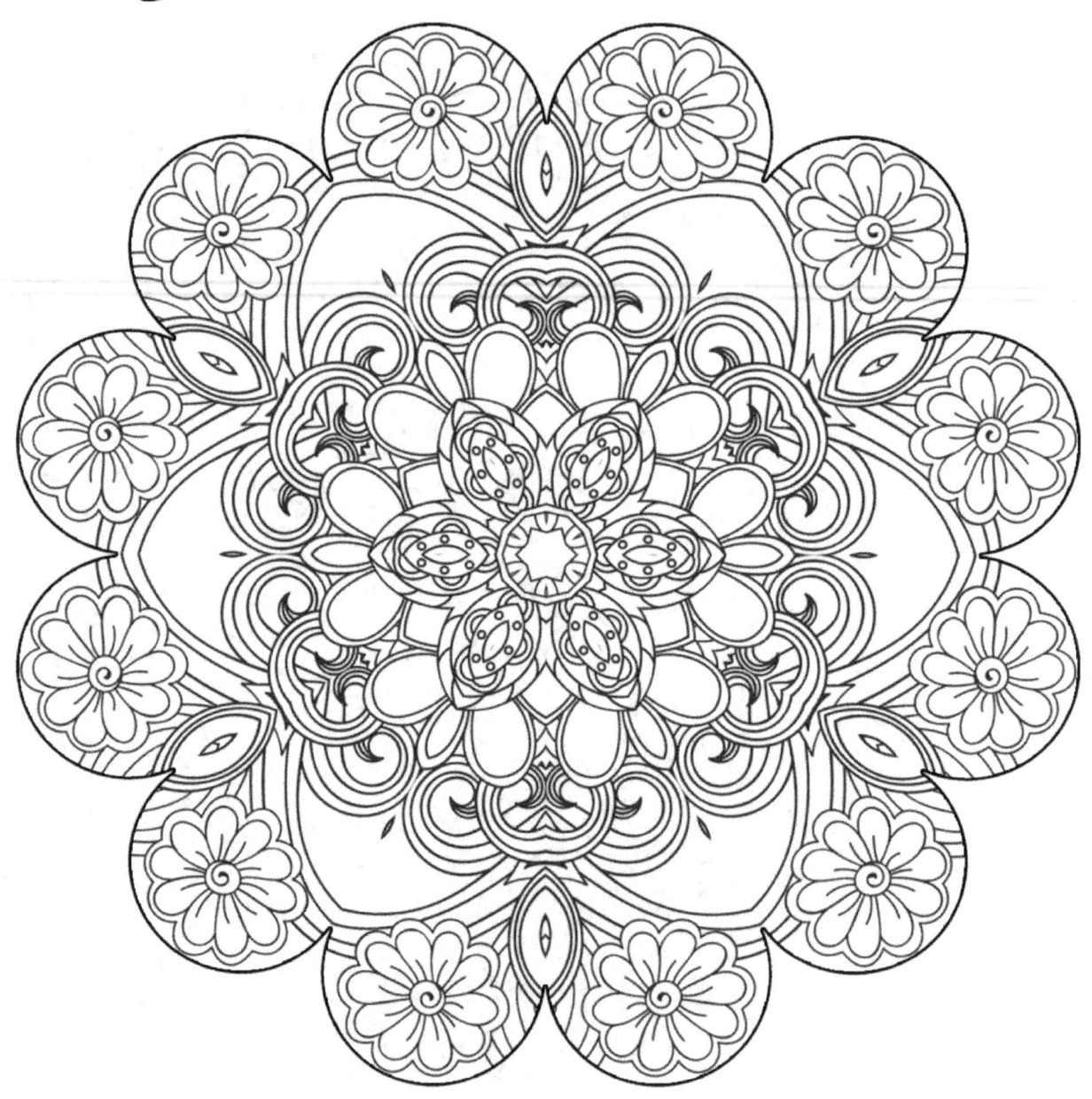

101bookclub.com

101 Flower Power

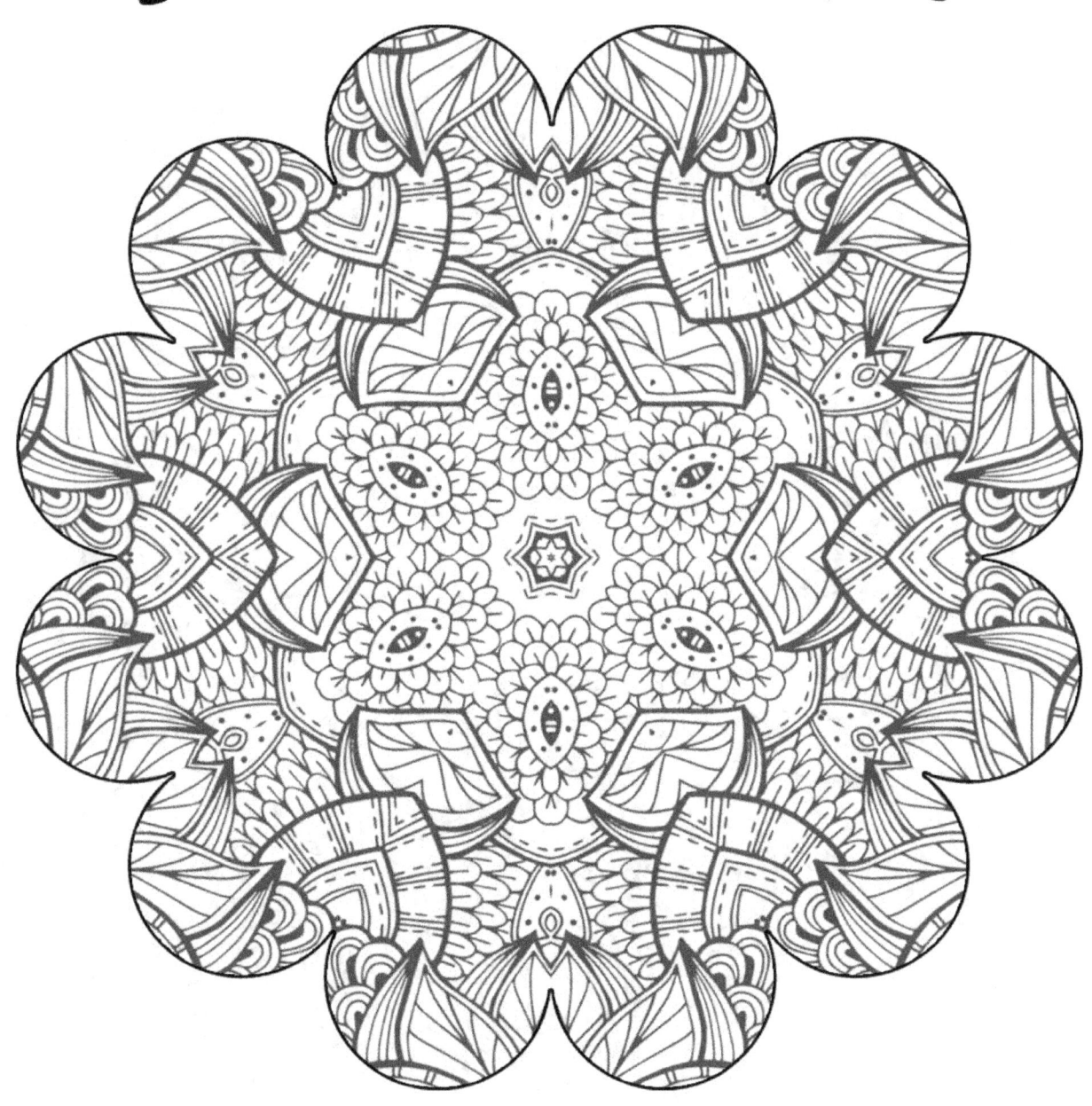

101bookclub.com

101 Flower Power

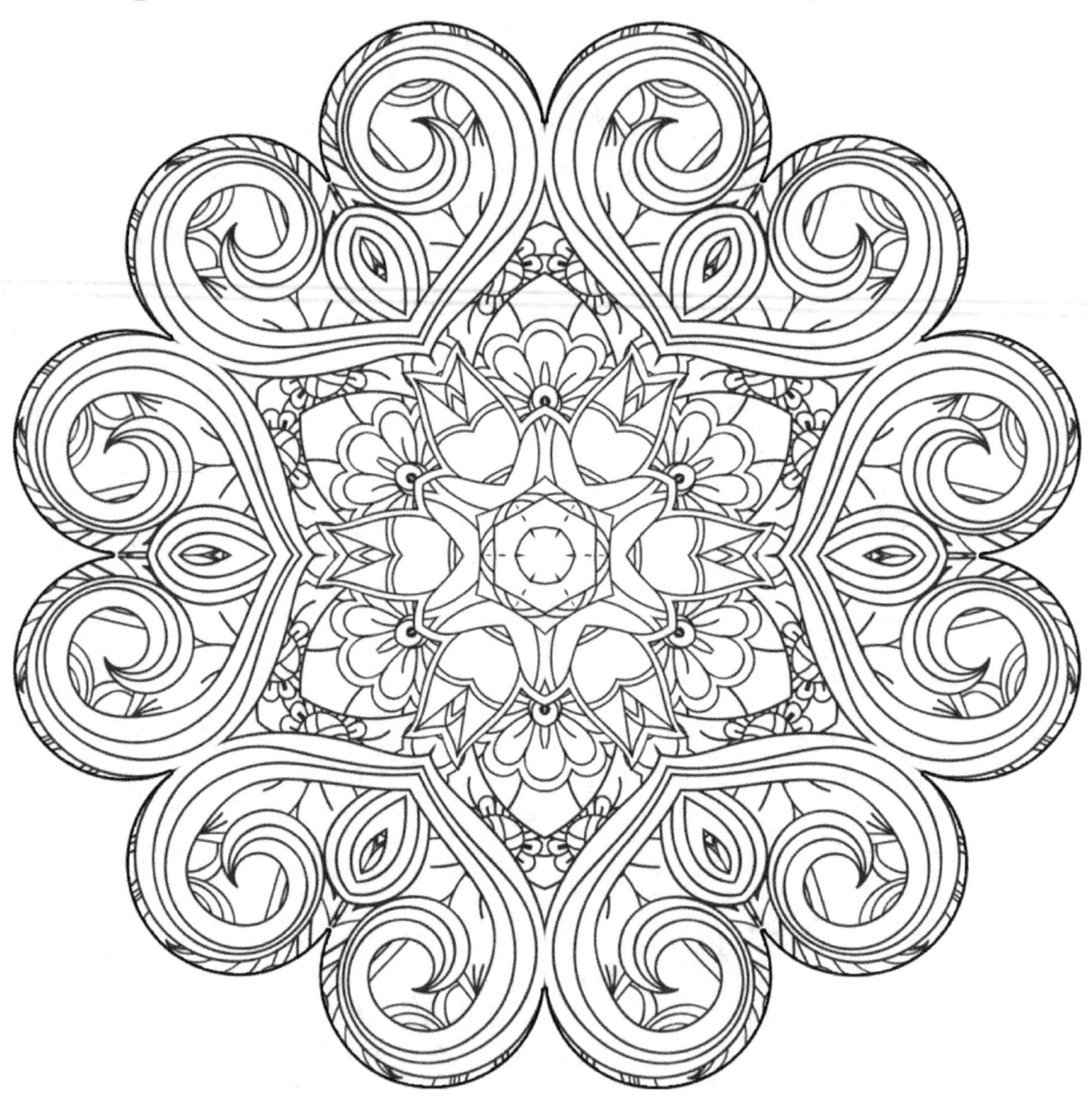

101bookclub.com

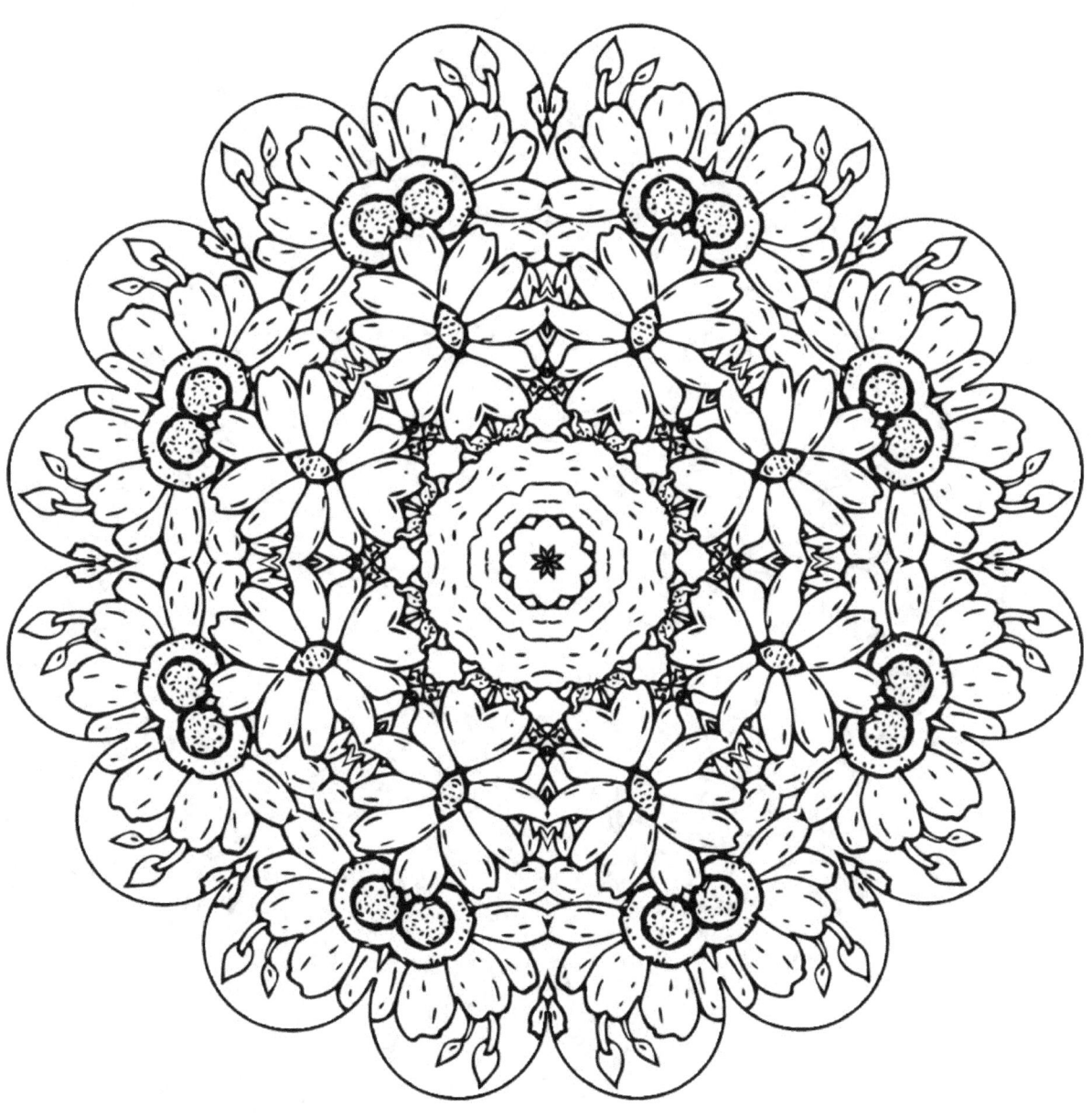

101 Flower Power

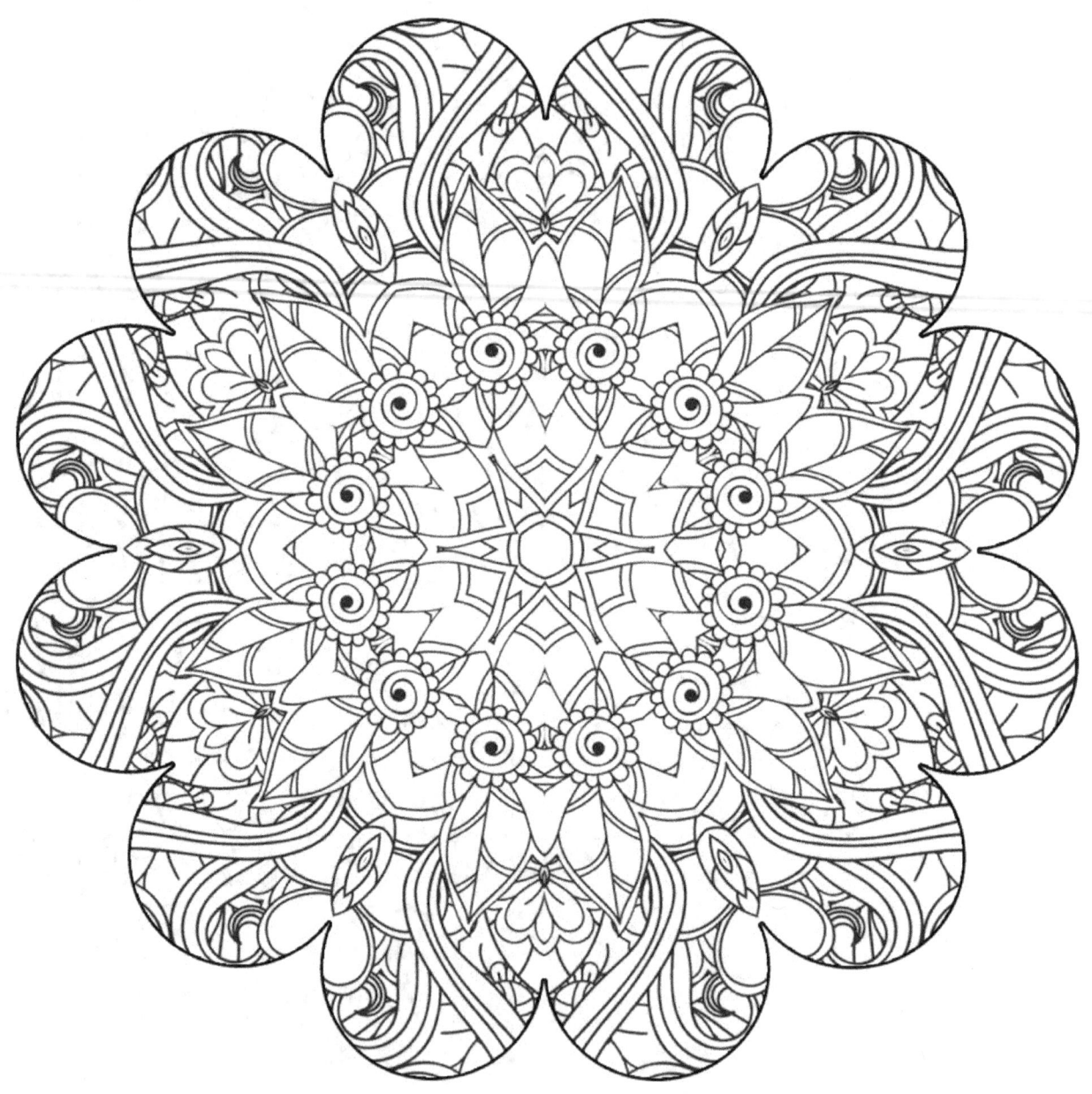

101bookclub.com

101 Flower Power

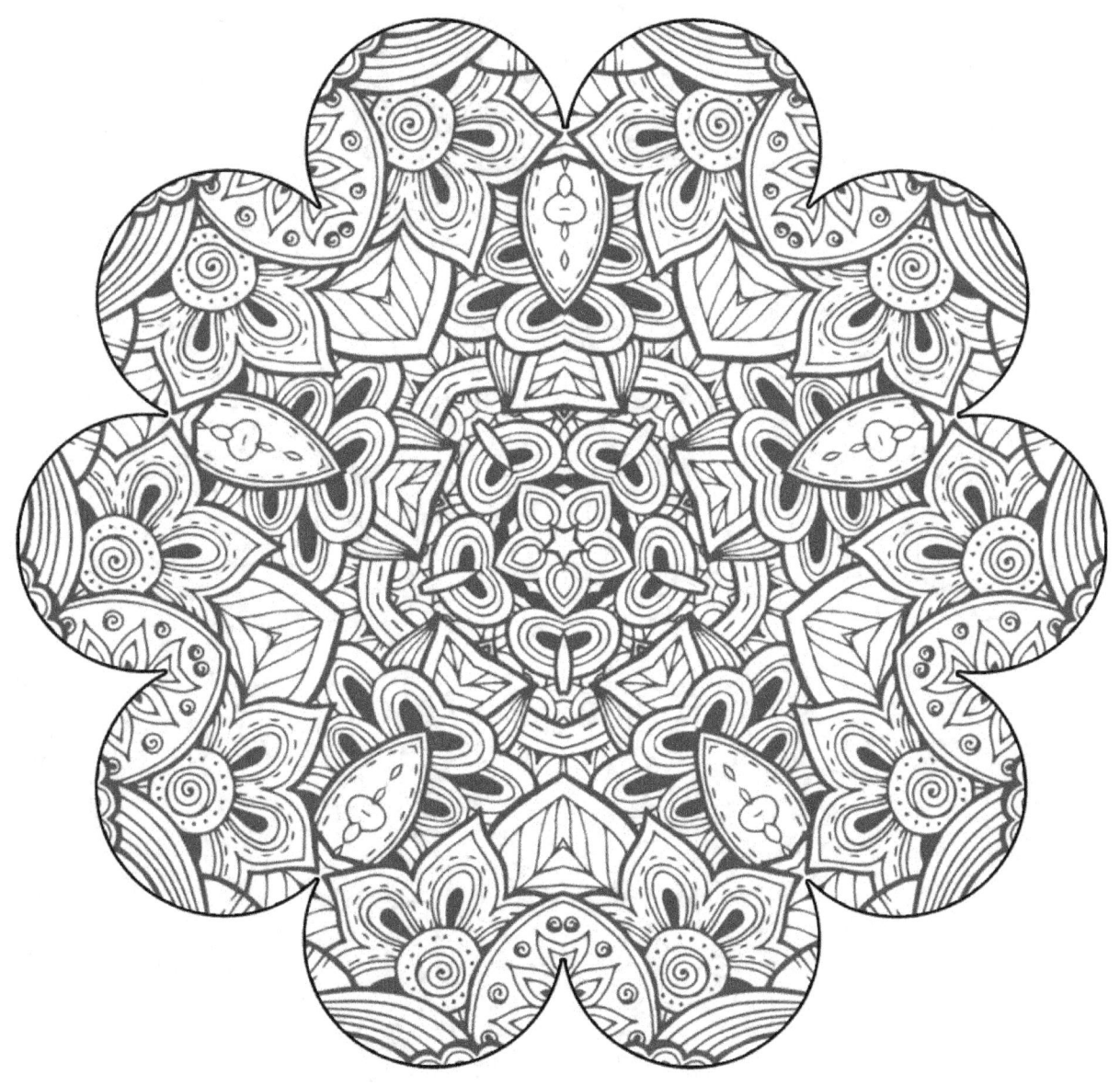

101bookclub.com

101 Flower Power

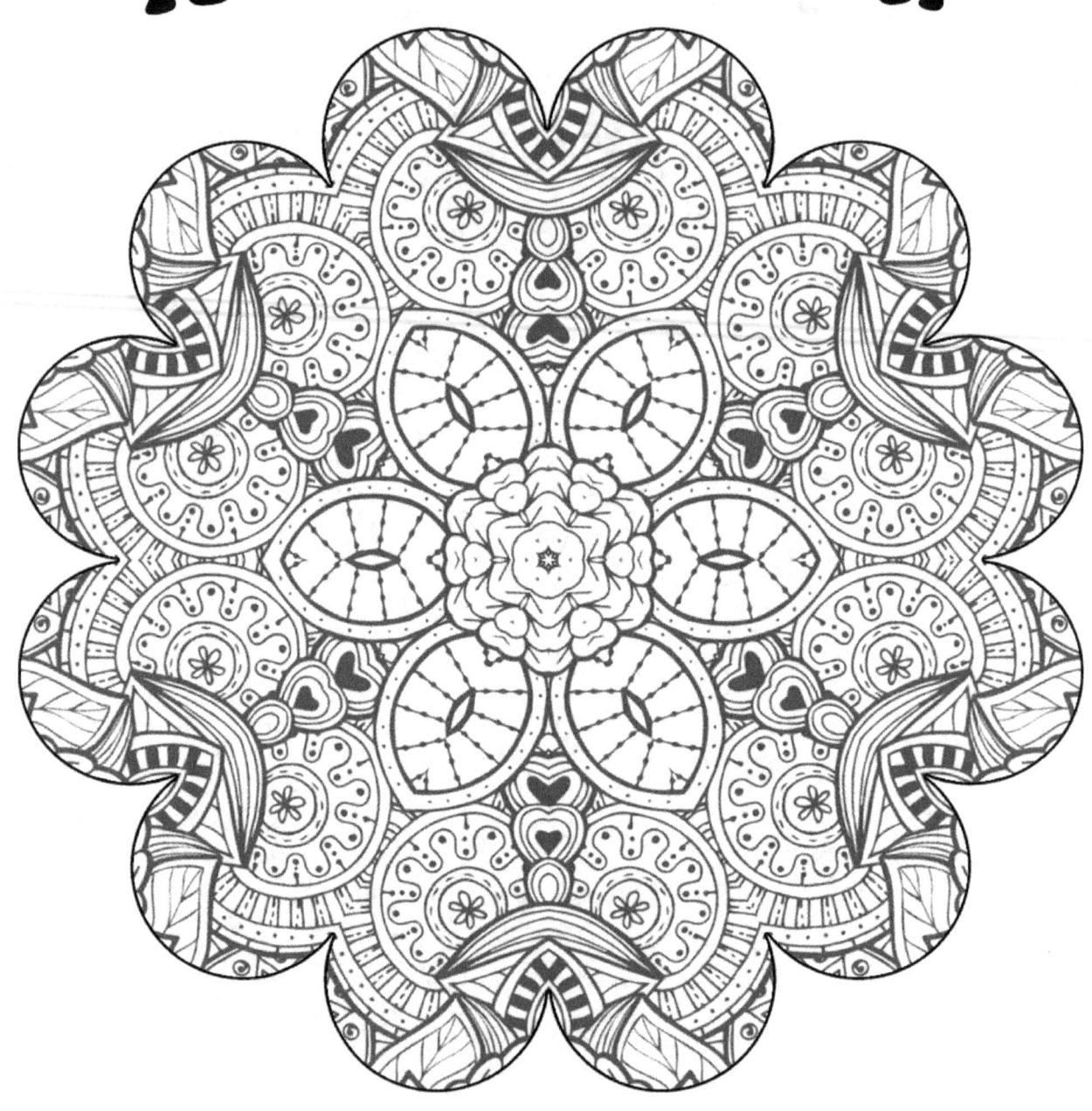

101bookclub.com

101 Flower Power

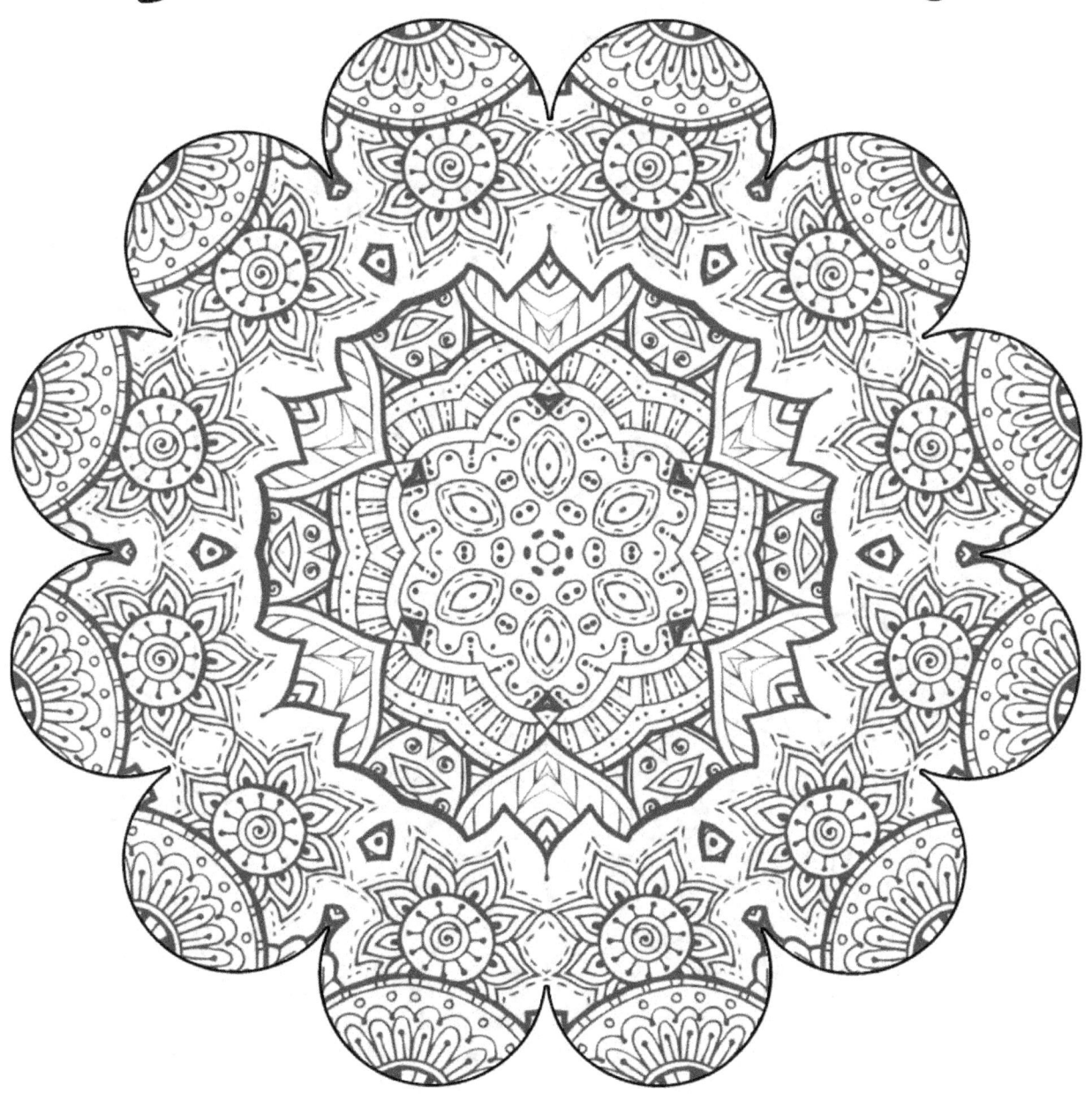

101bookclub.com

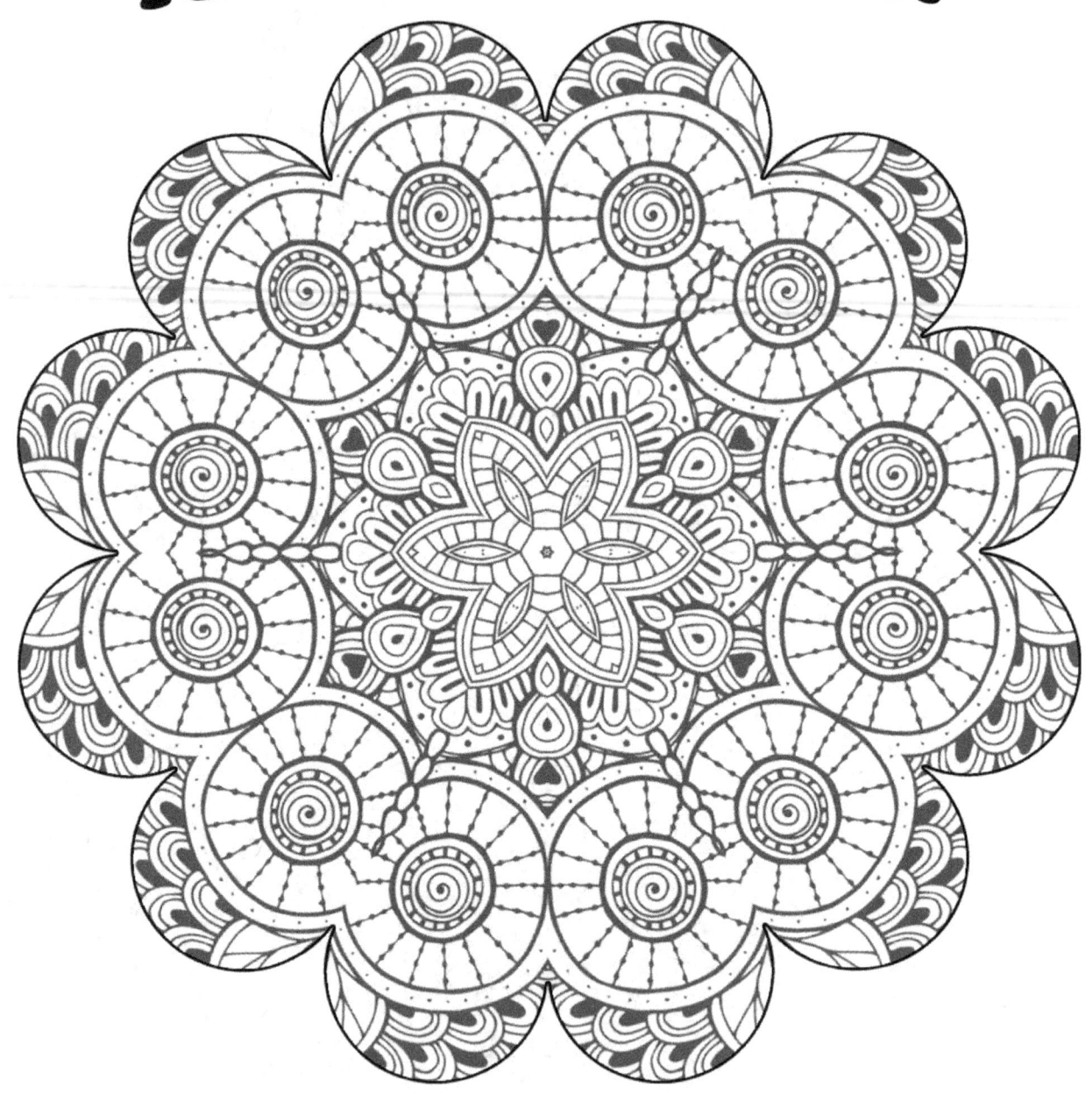

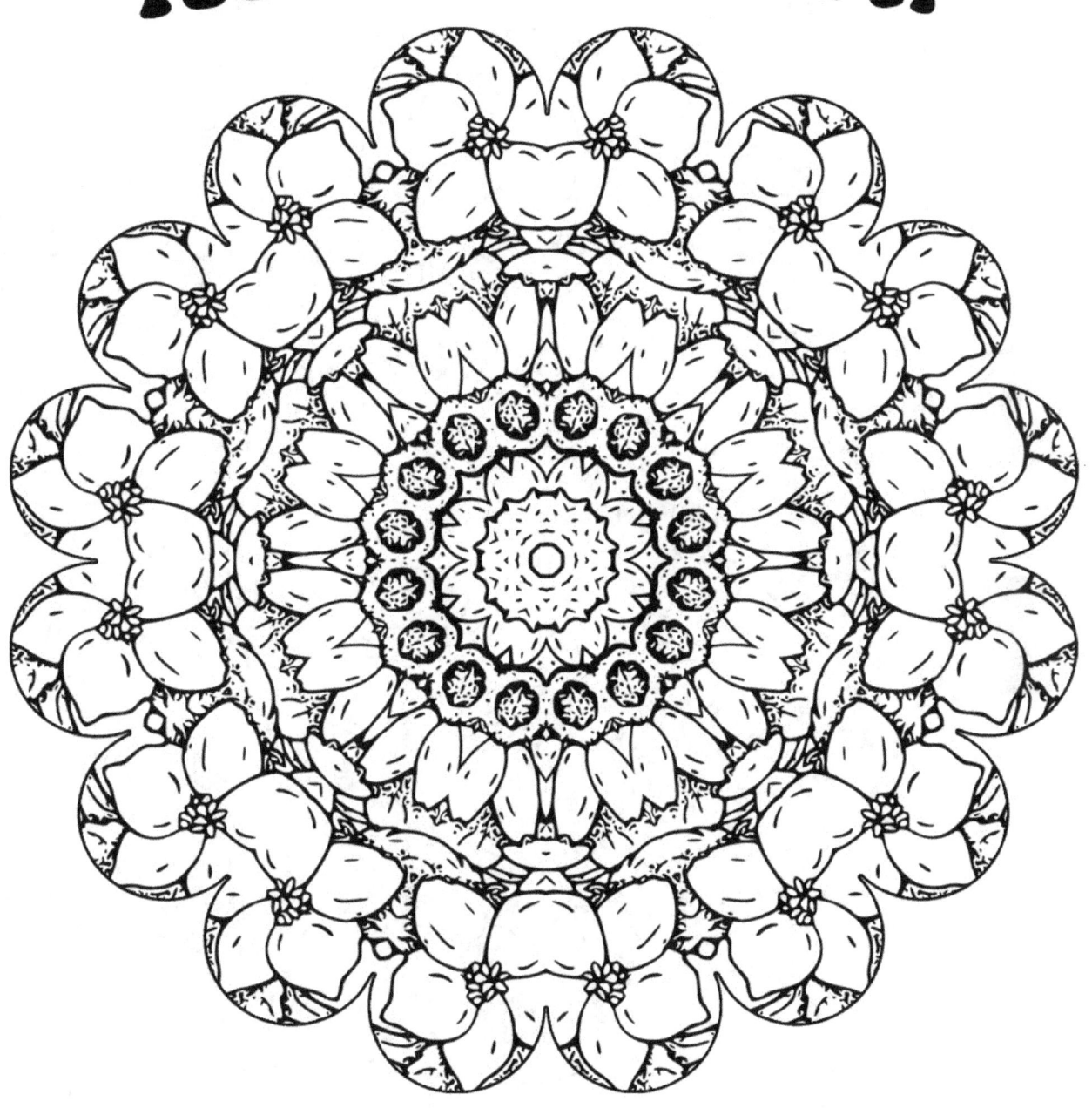

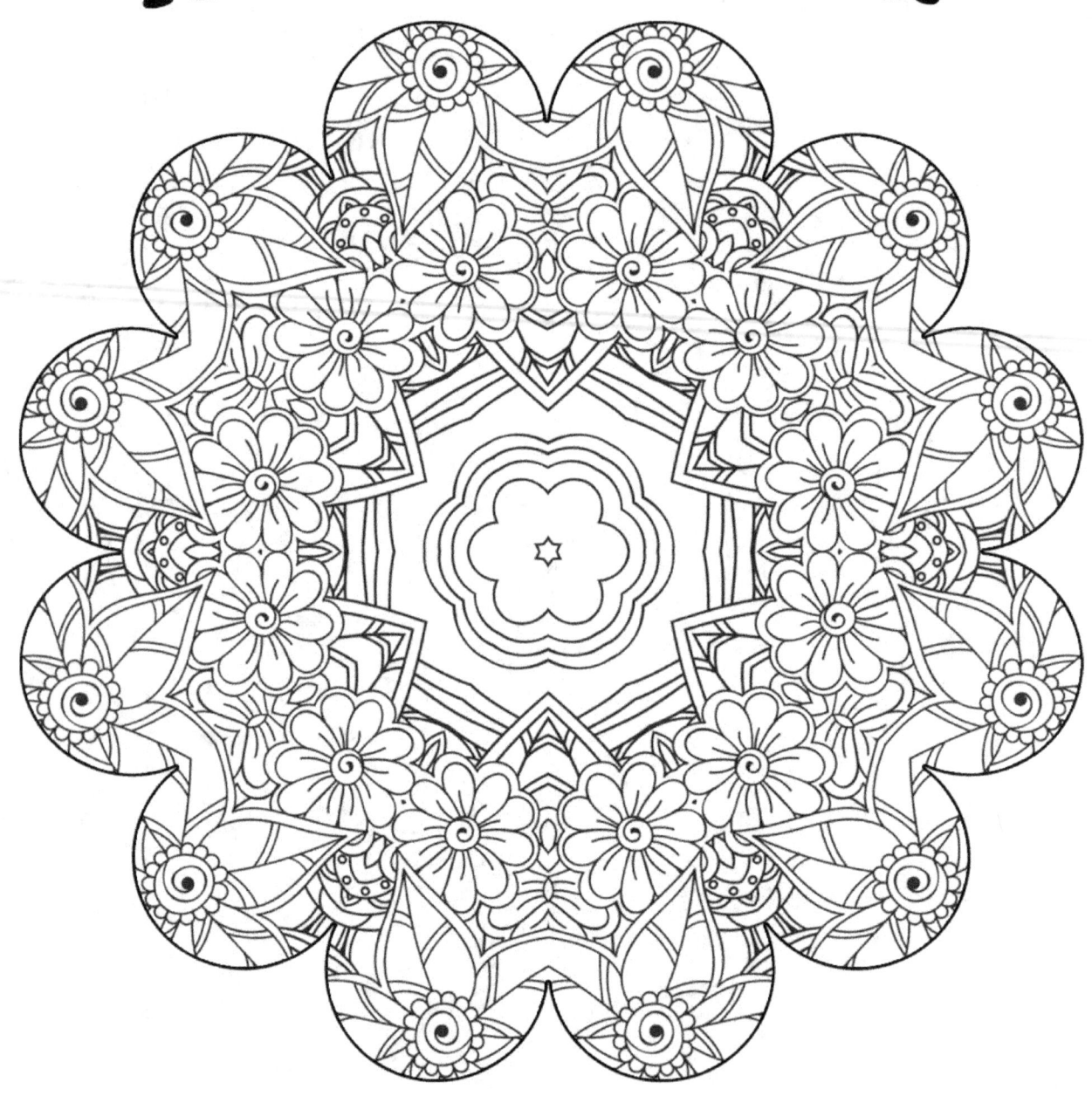

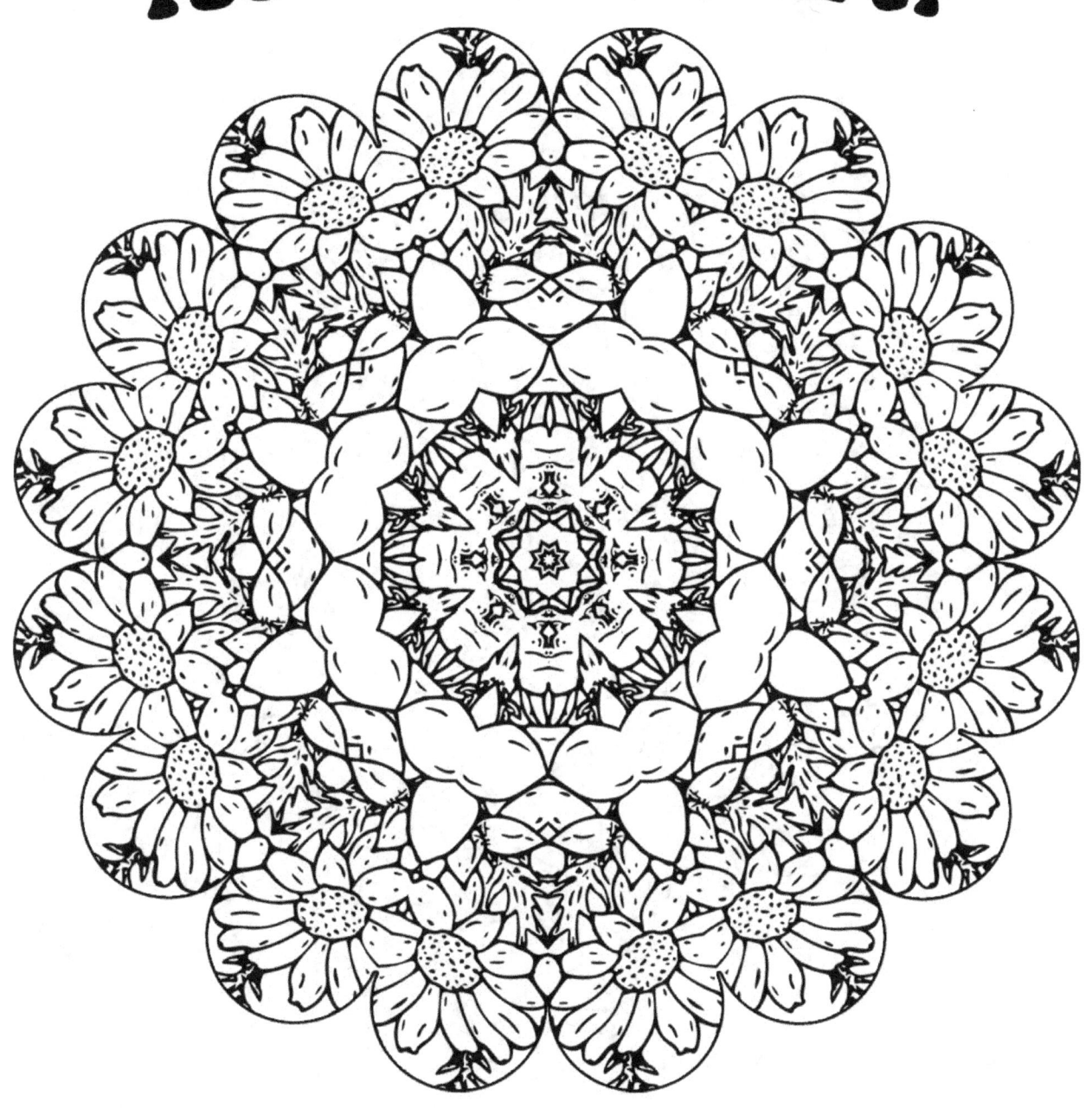

101 Flower Power

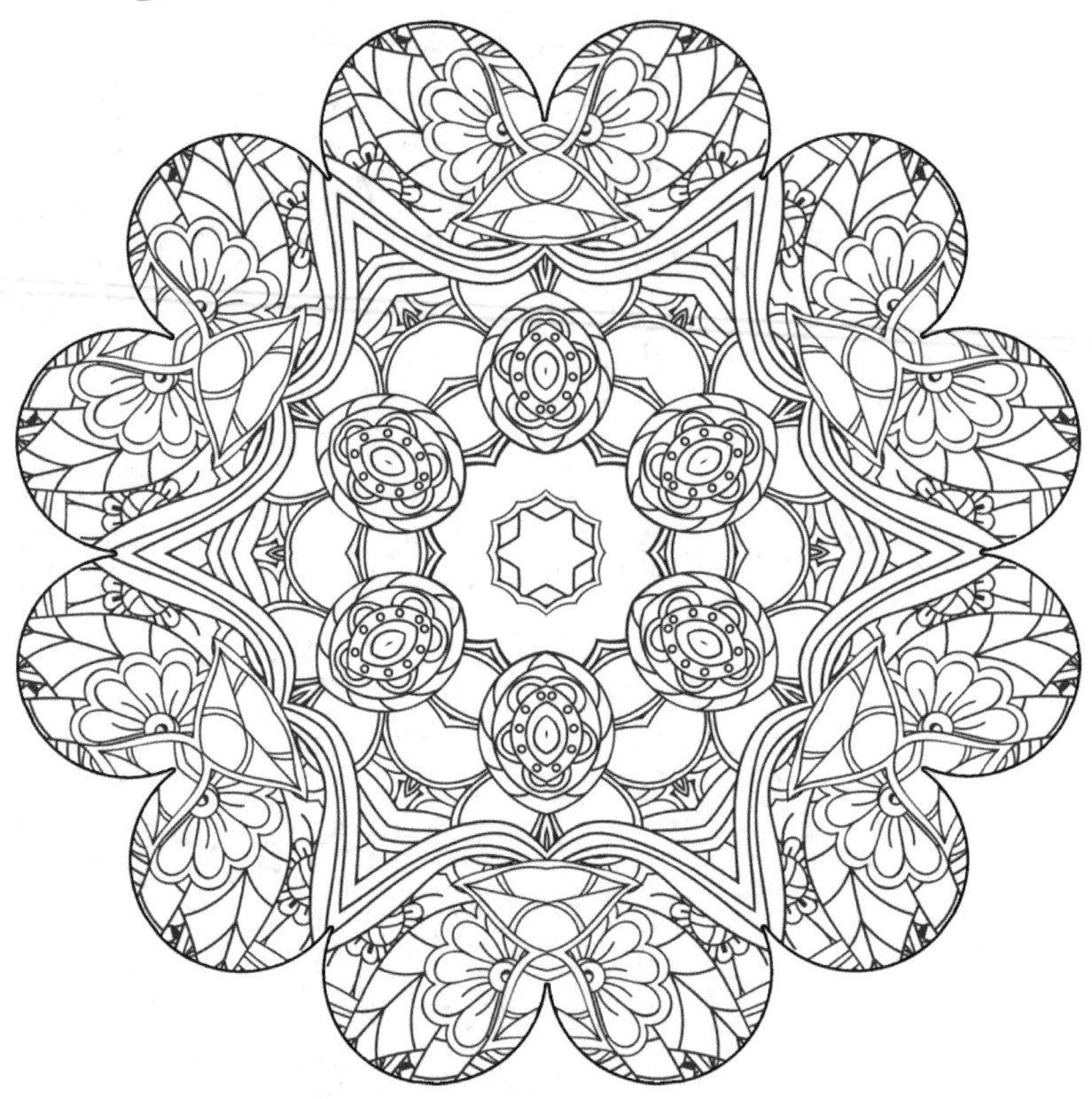

101bookclub.com

101 Flower Power

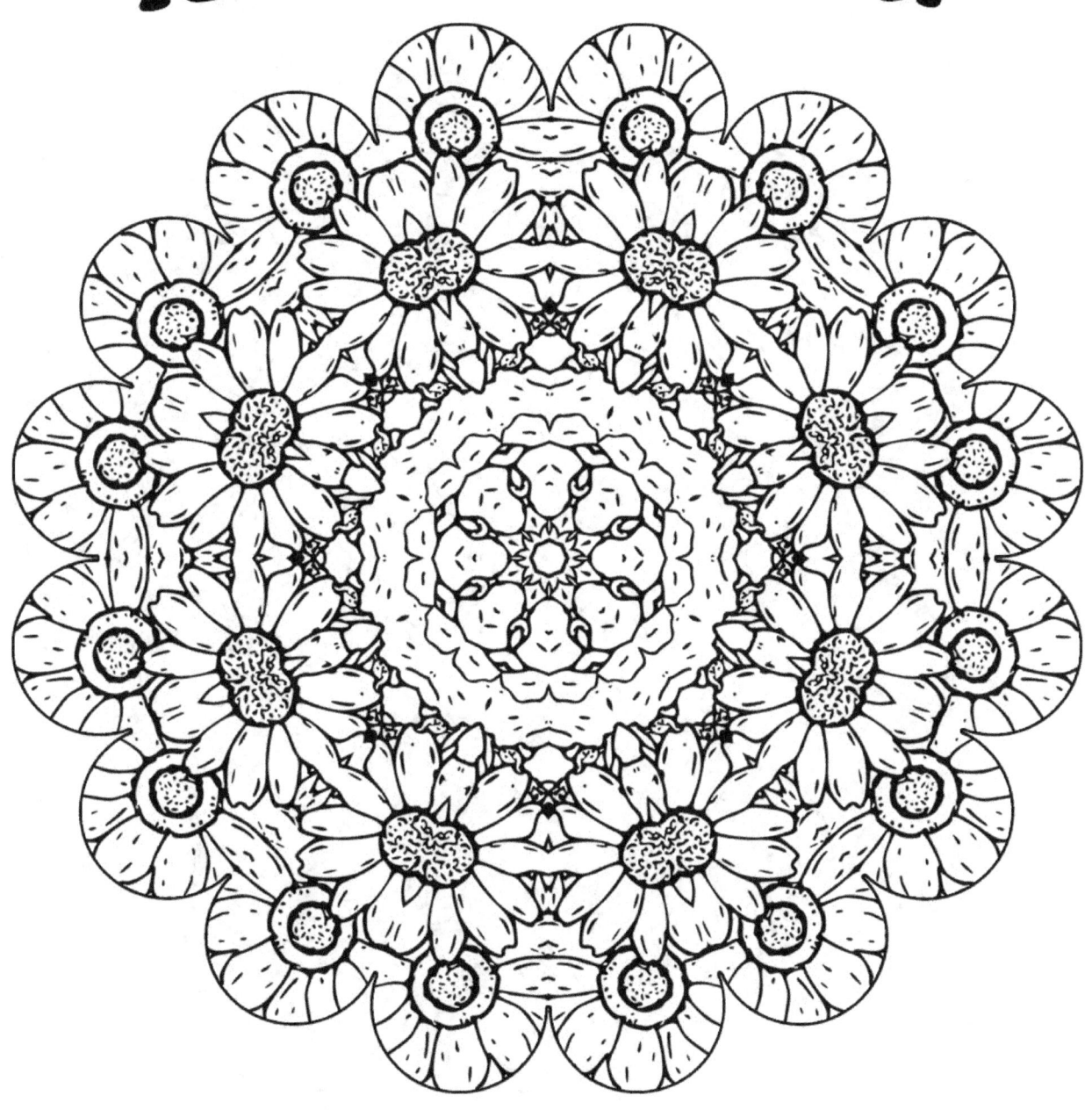

101bookclub.com

101 Flower Power

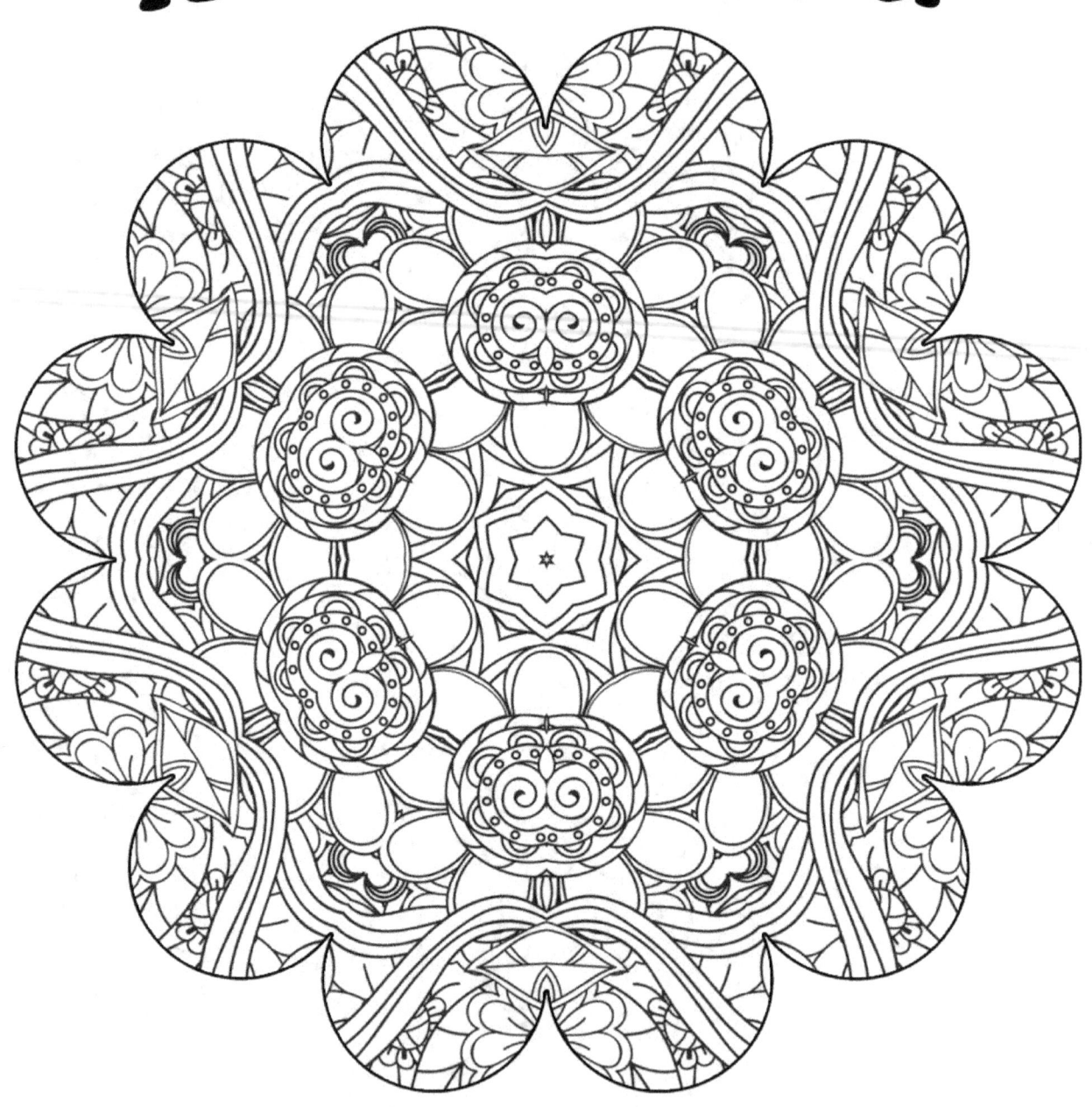

101bookclub.com

101 Flower Power

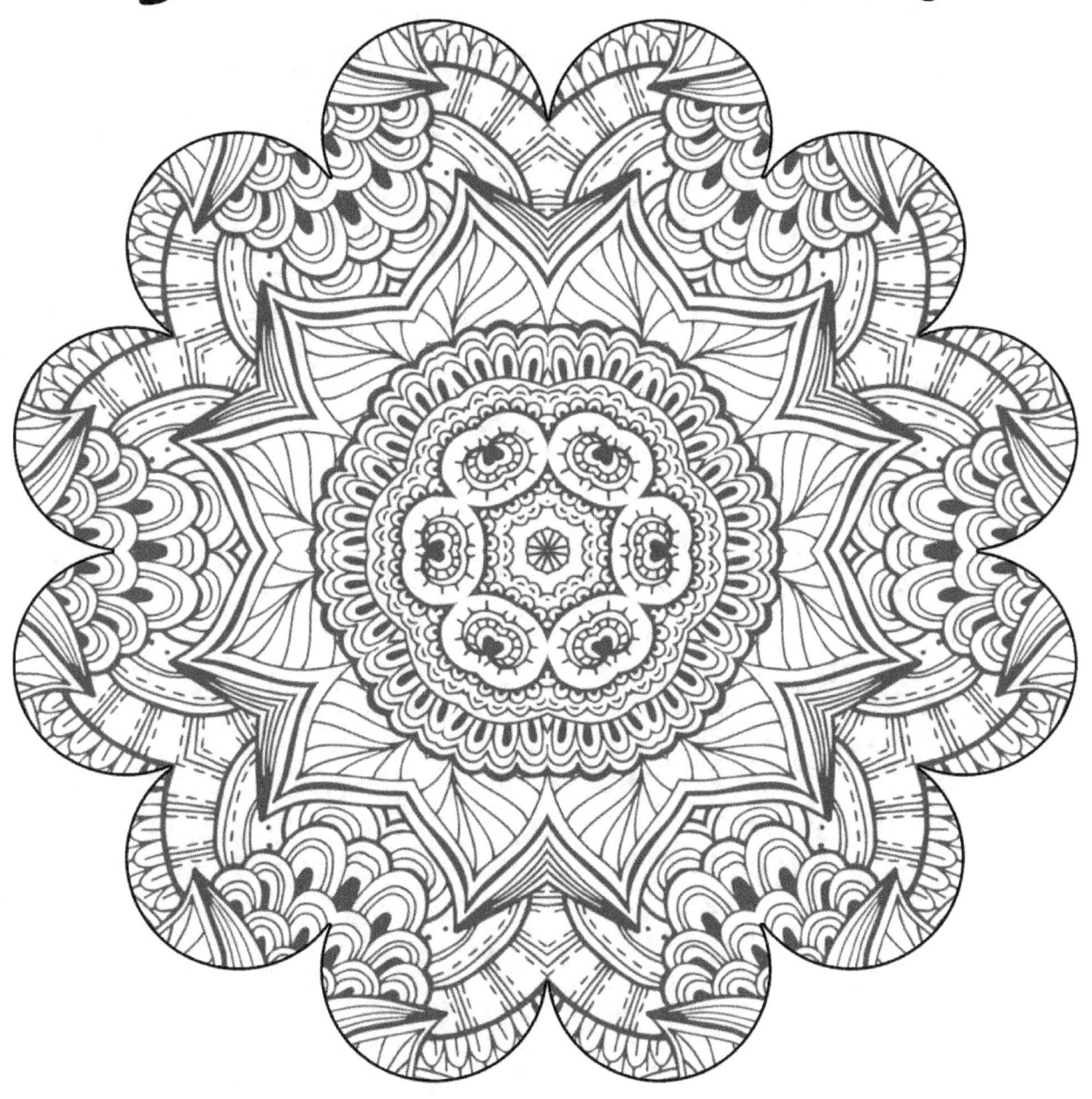

101bookclub.com

101 Flower Power

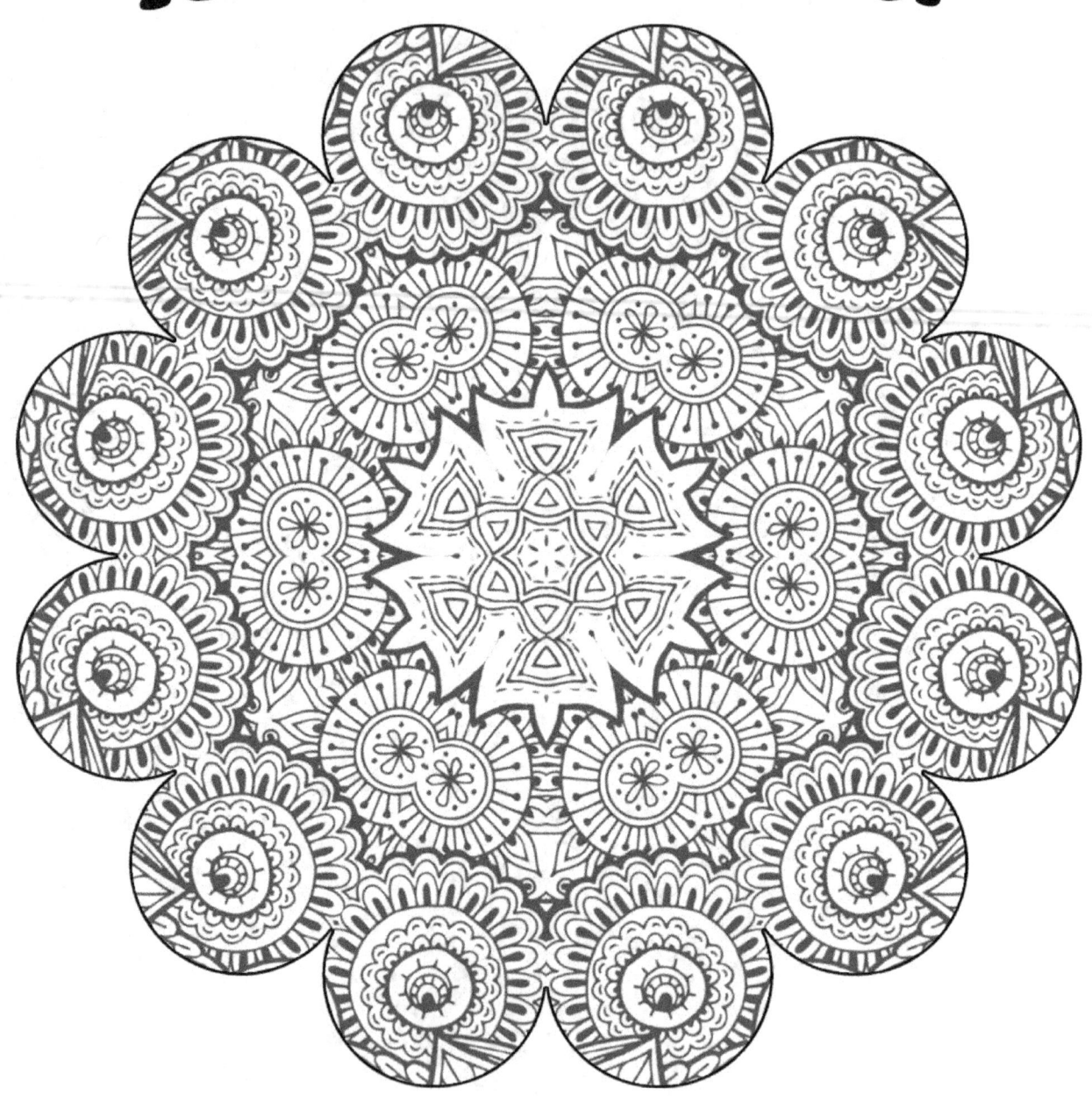

101bookclub.com

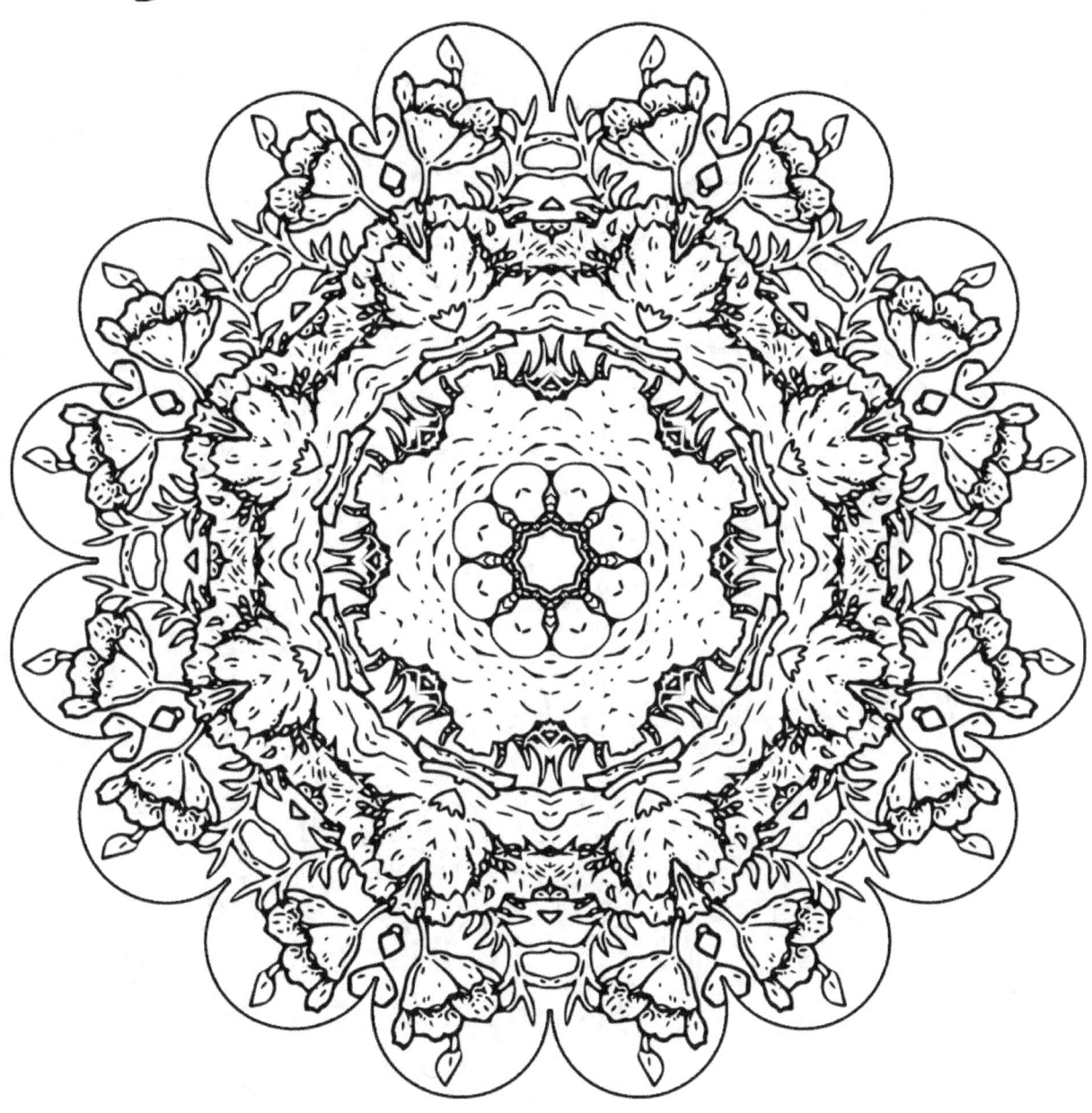

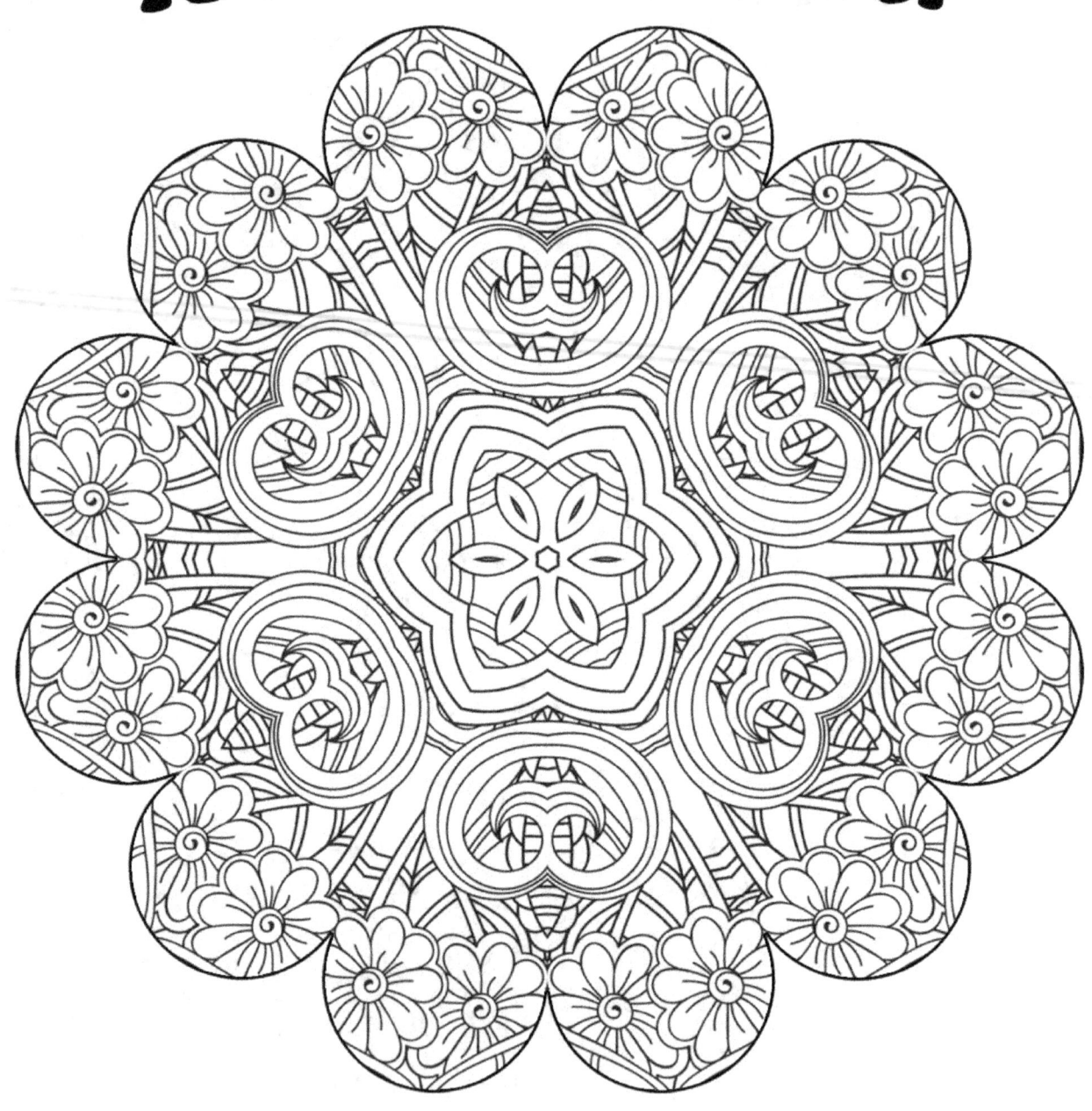

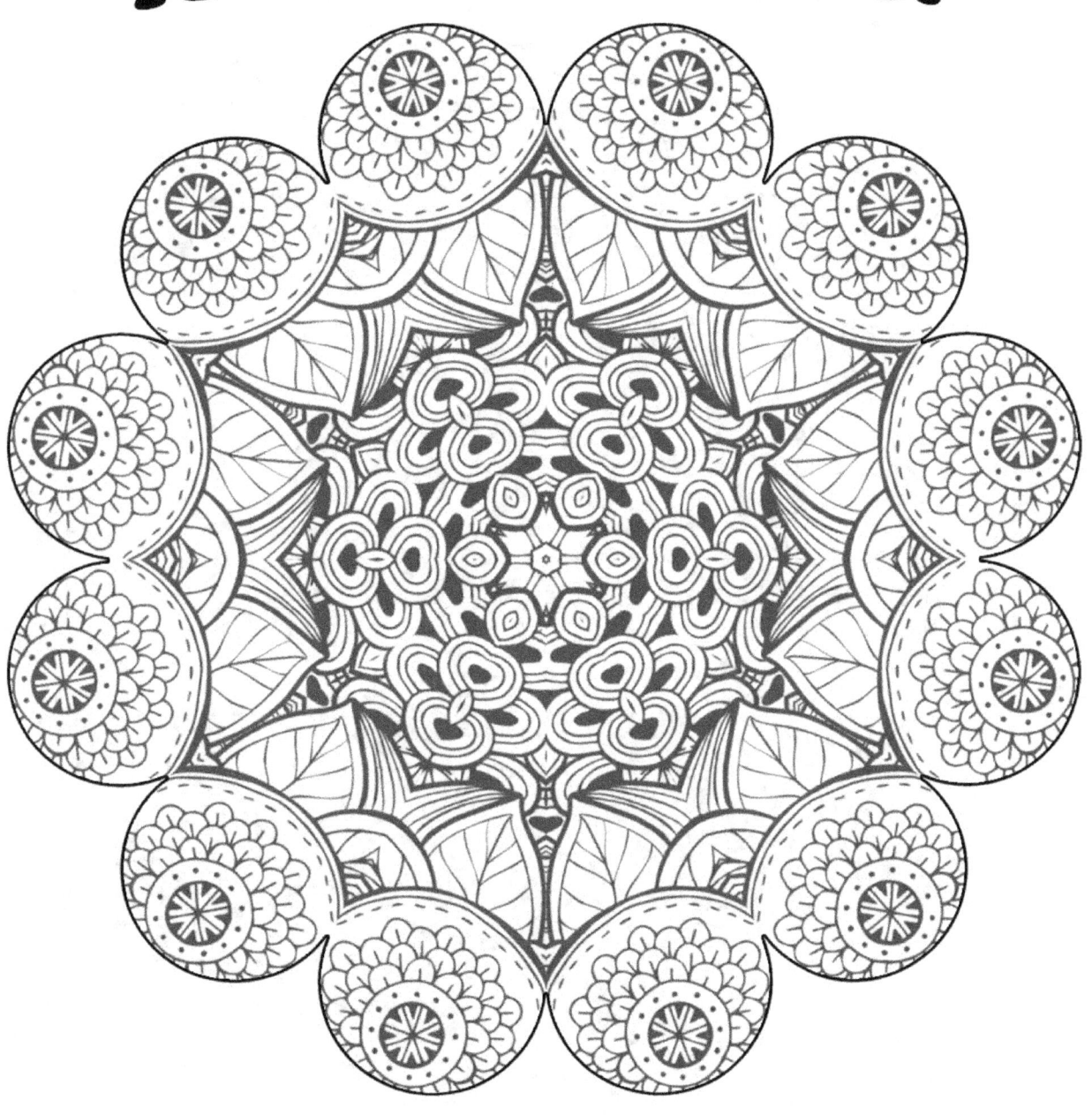

101 Flower Power

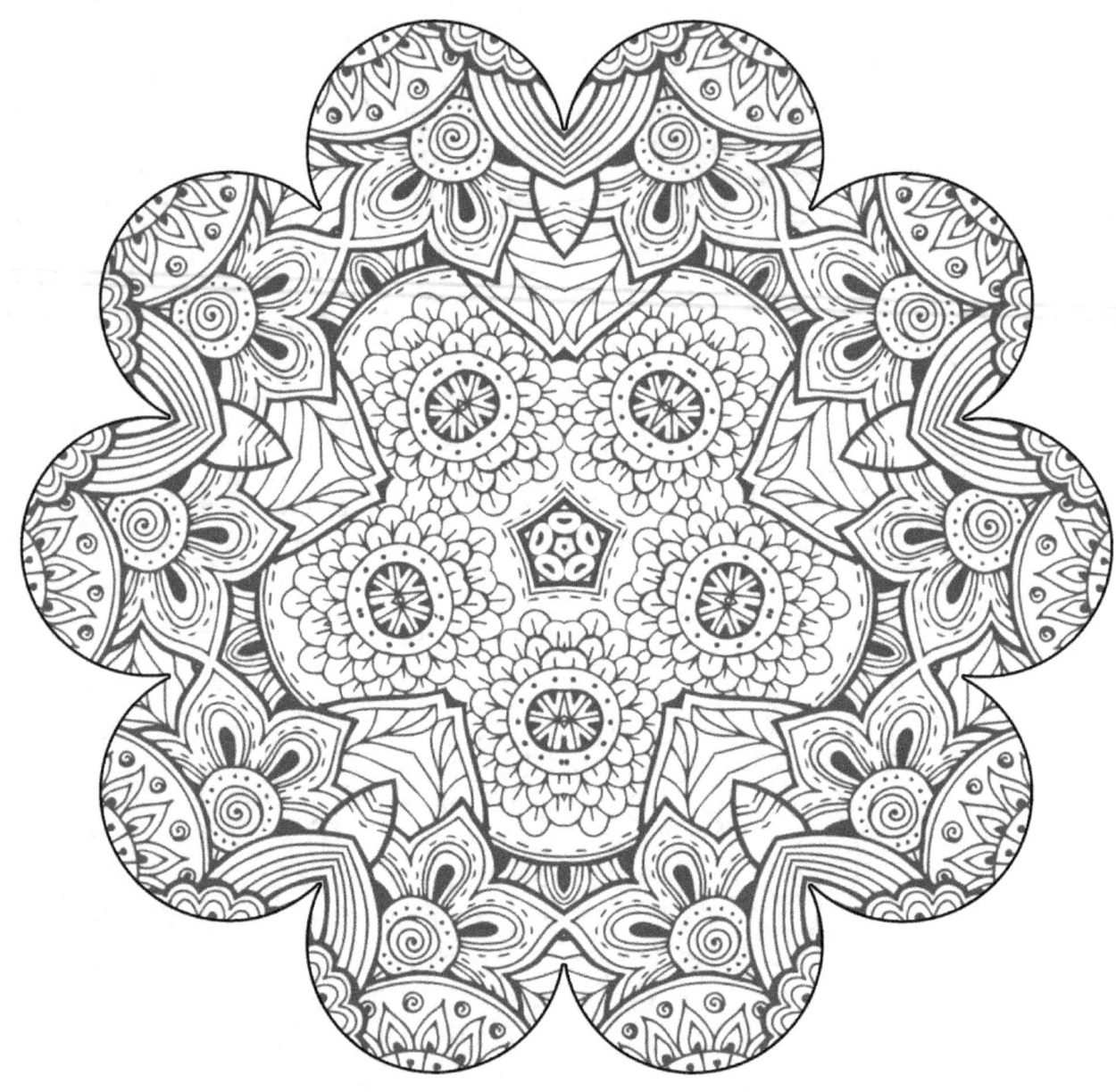

101bookclub.com

101 Flower Power

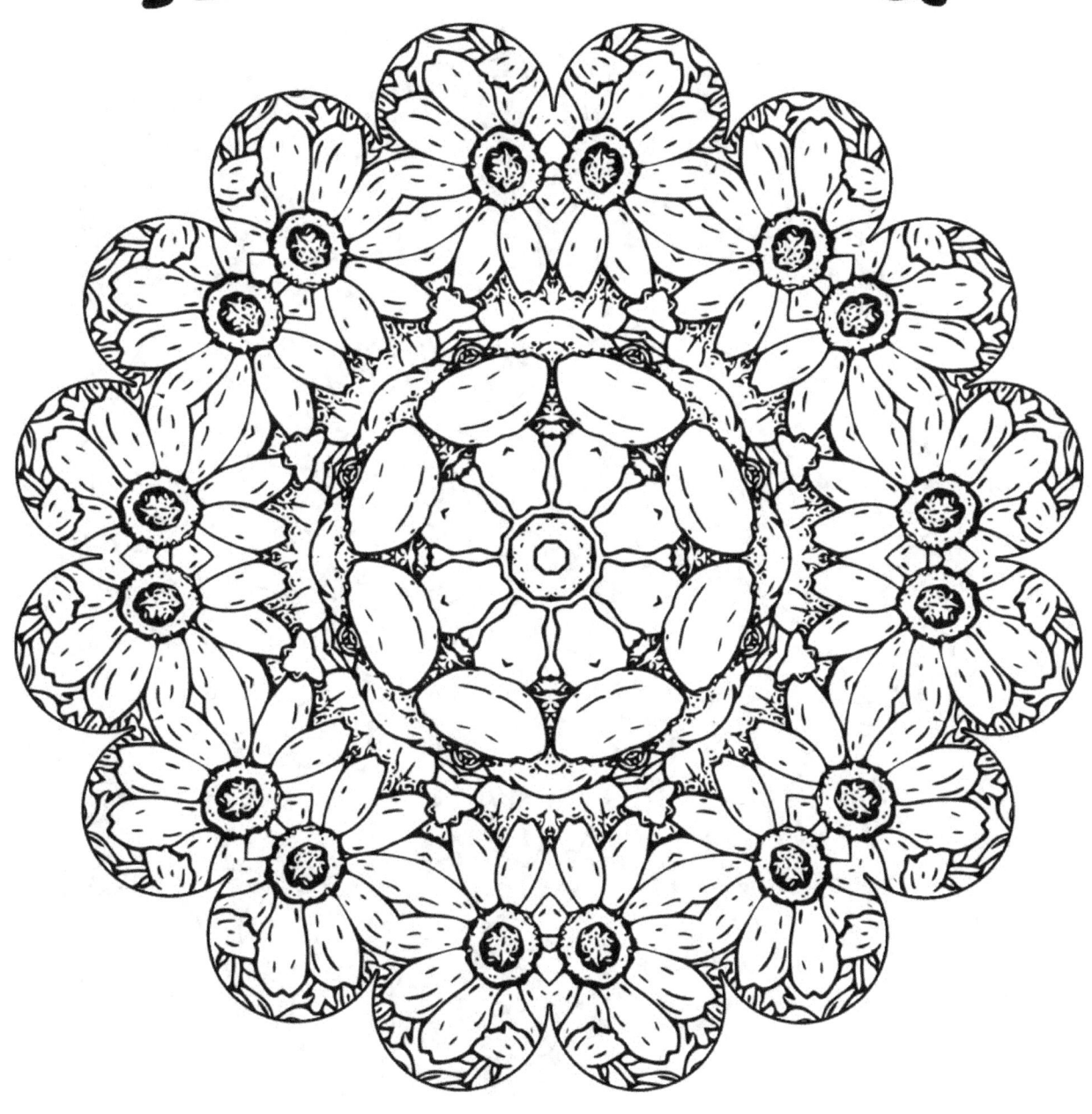

101bookclub.com

101 Flower Power

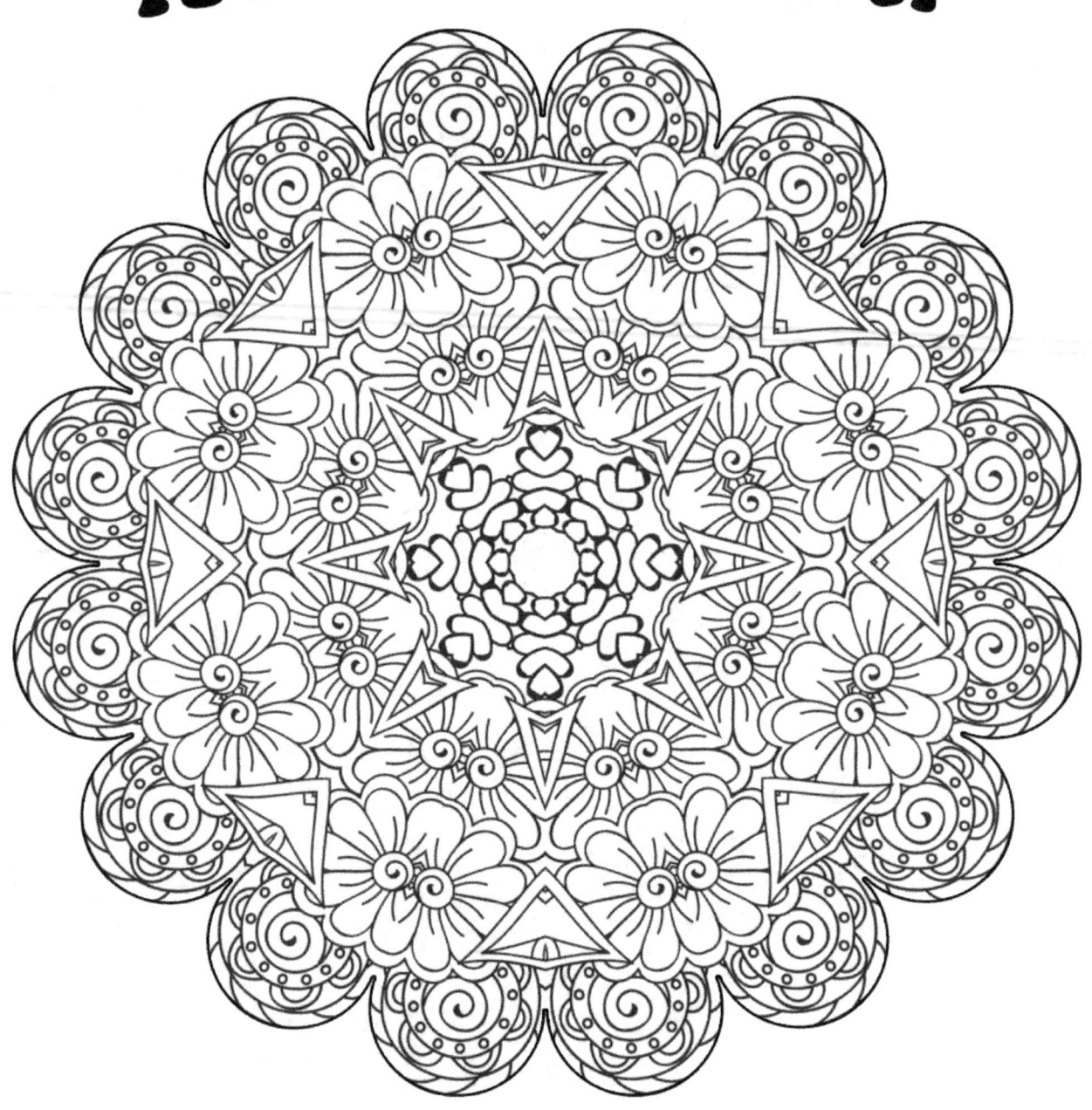

101bookclub.com

101 Flower Power

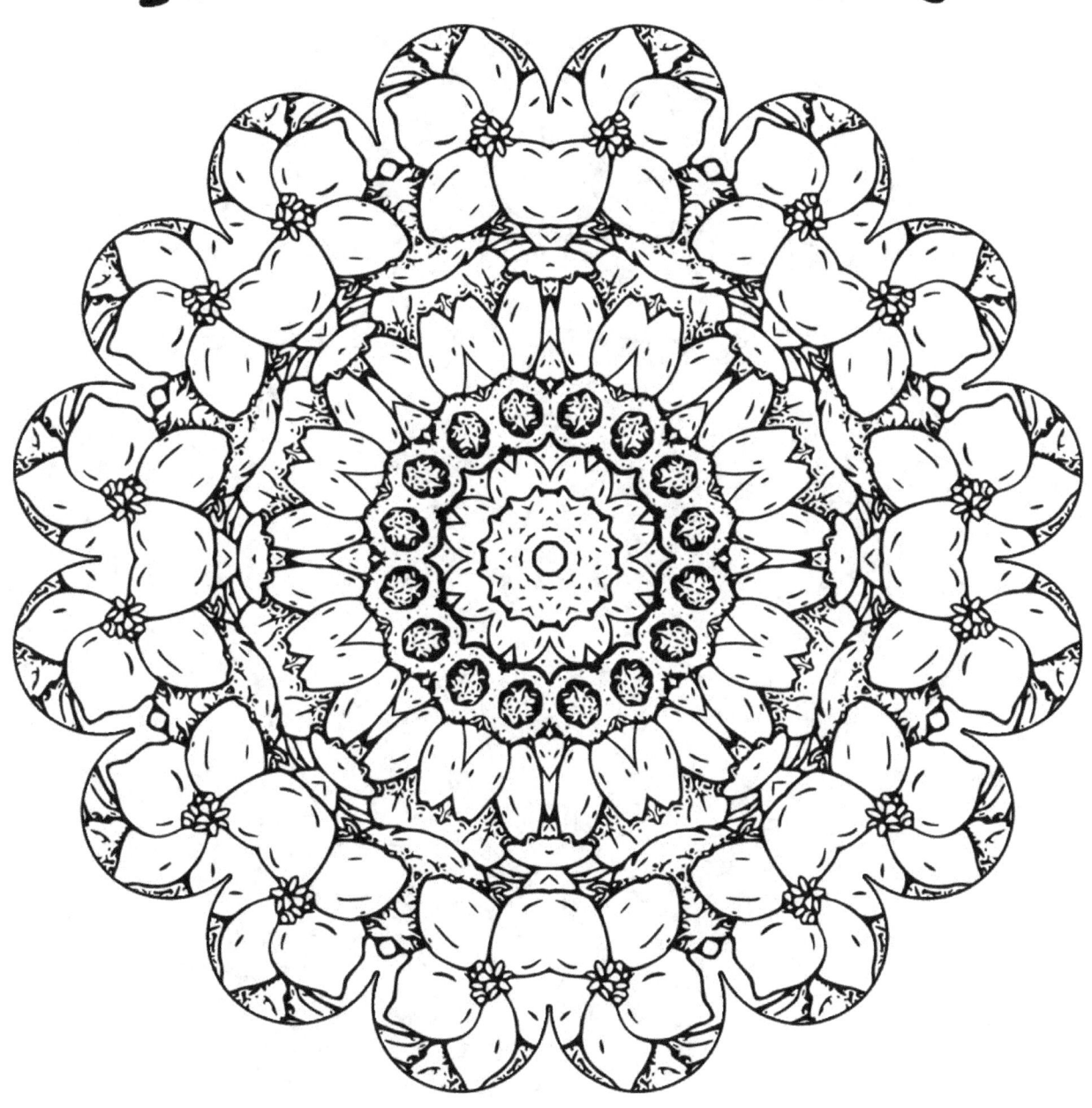

101bookclub.com

101 Flower Power

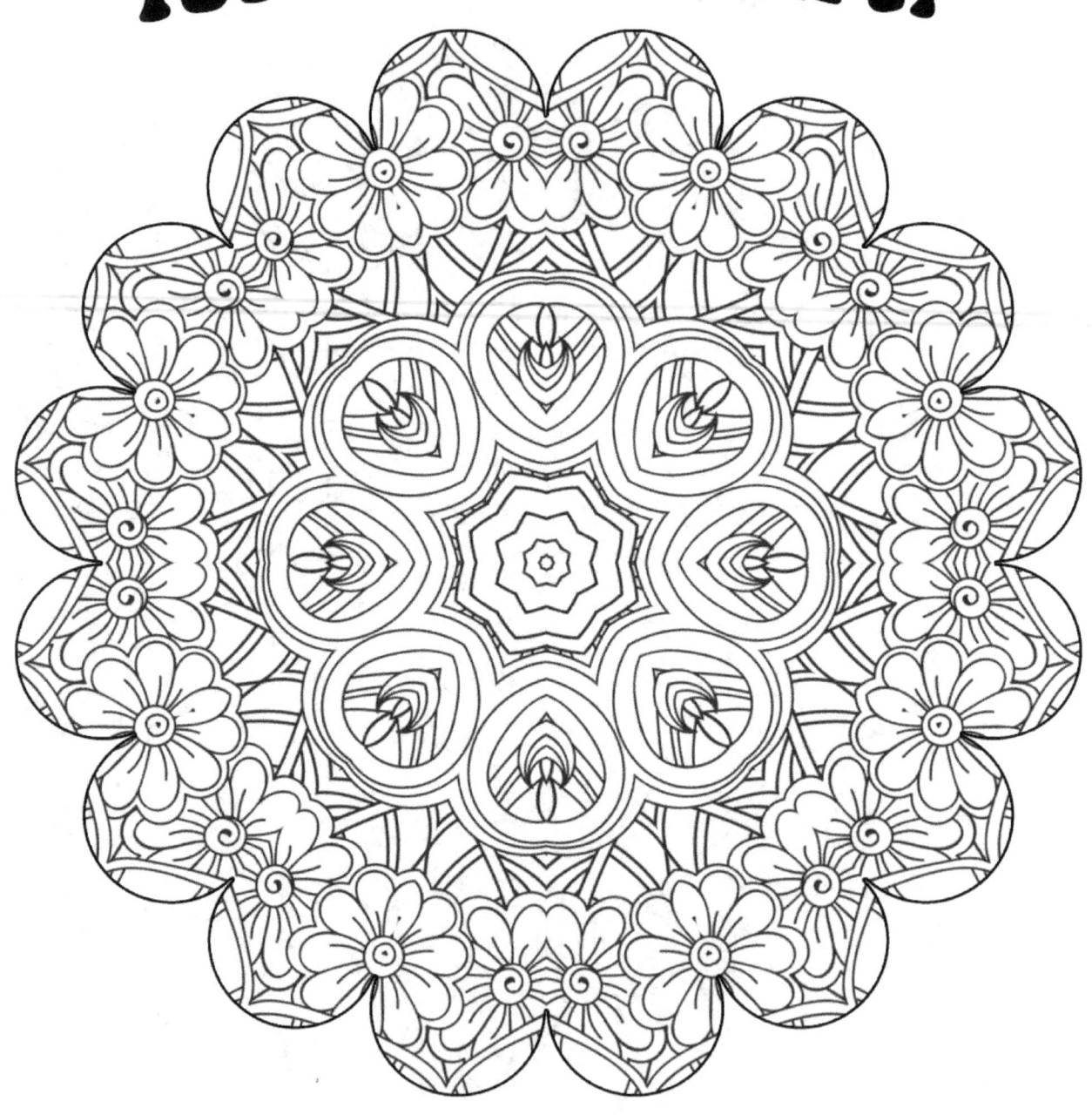

101bookclub.com

101 Flower Power

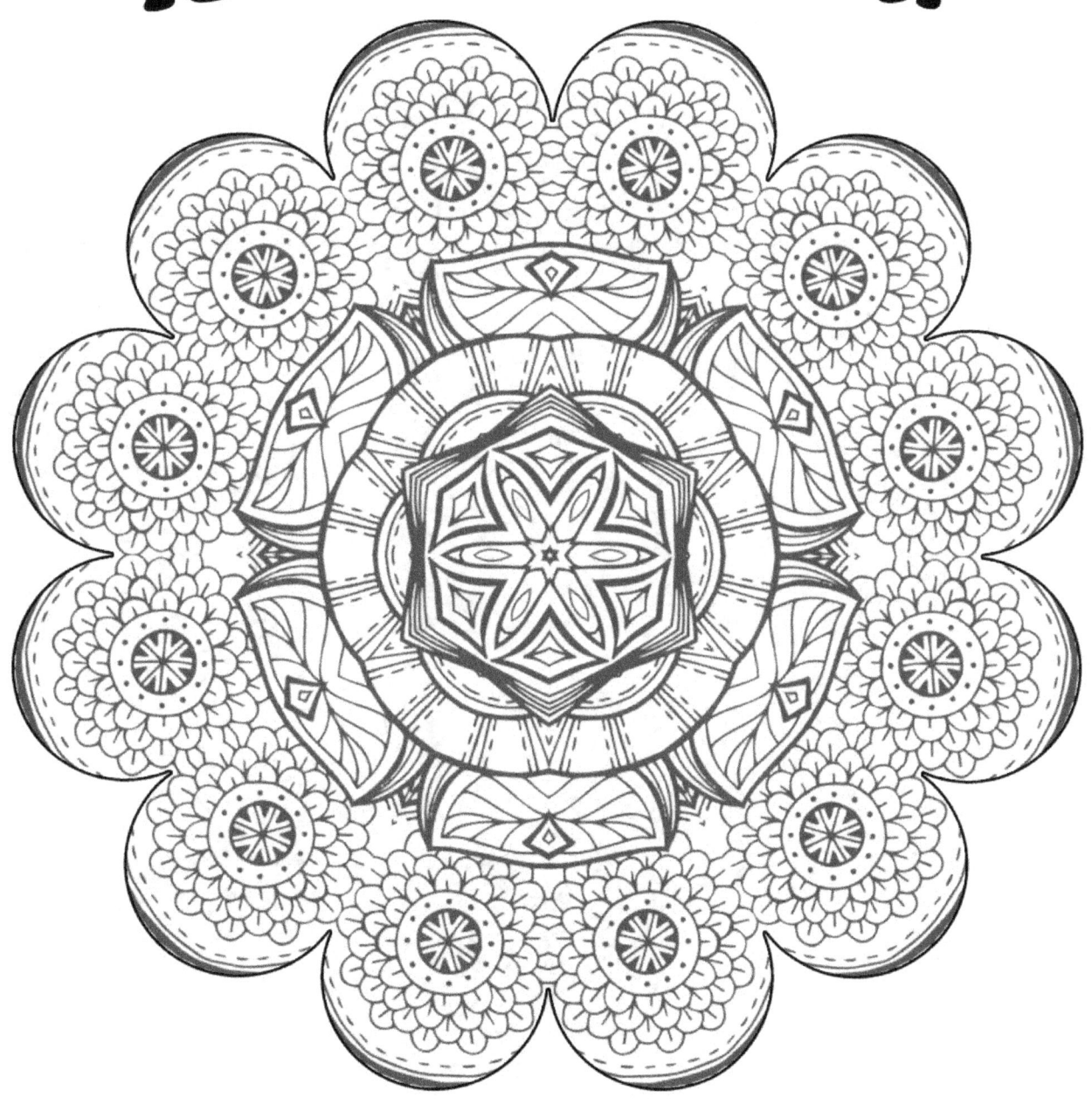

101bookclub.com

101 Flower Power

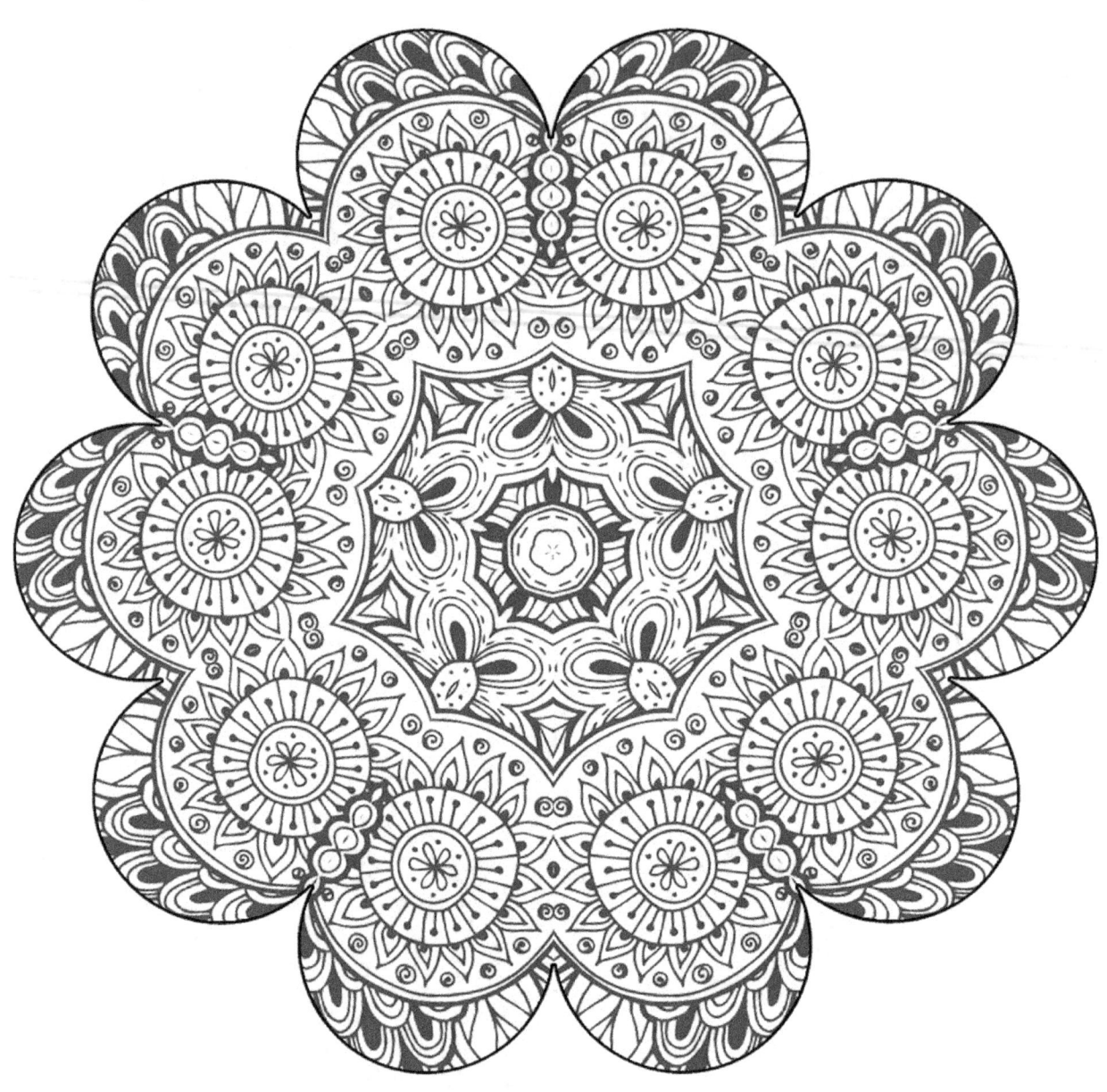

101bookclub.com

101 Flower Power

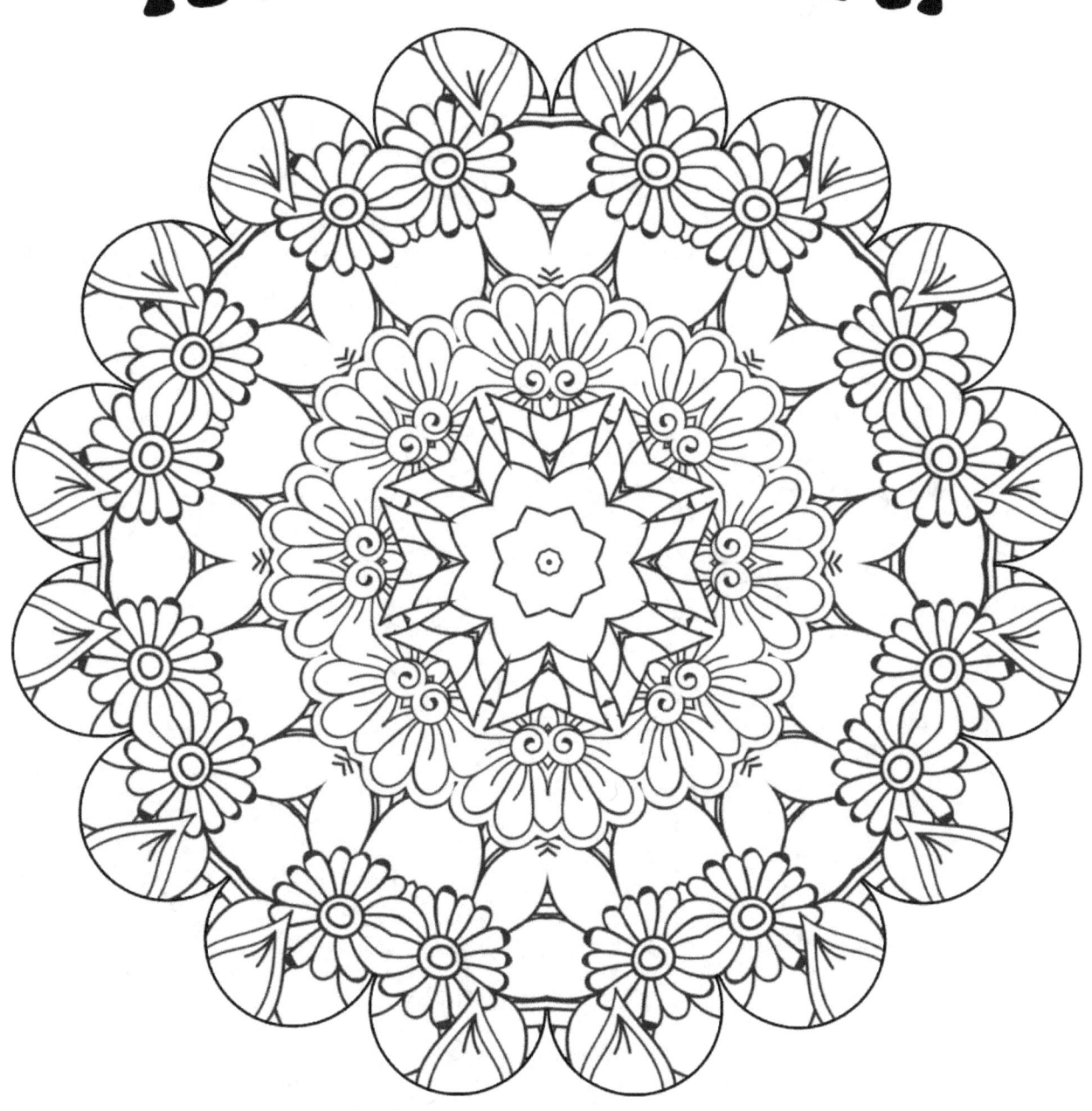

101bookclub.com

101 Flower Power

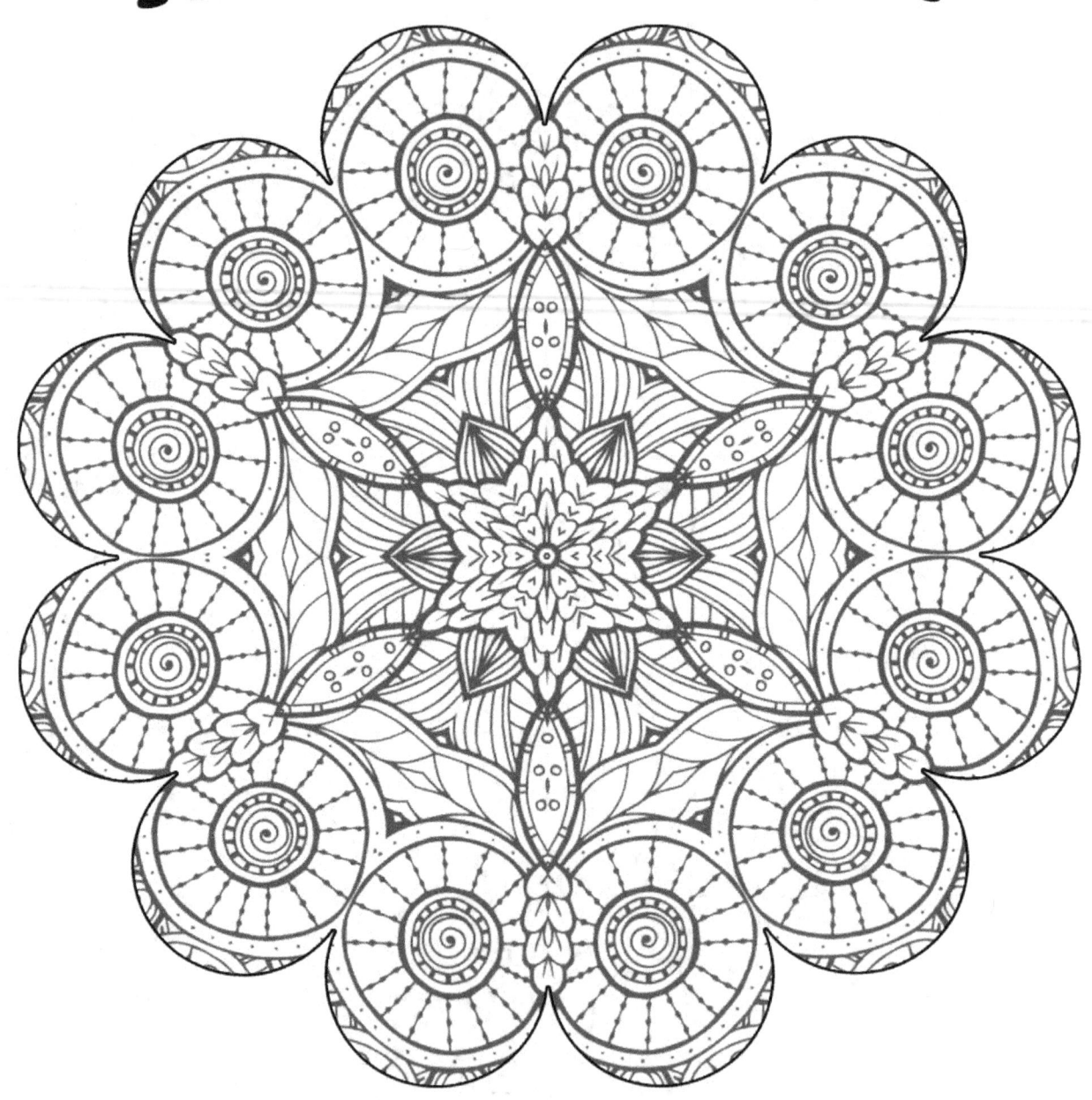

101bookclub.com

101 Flower Power

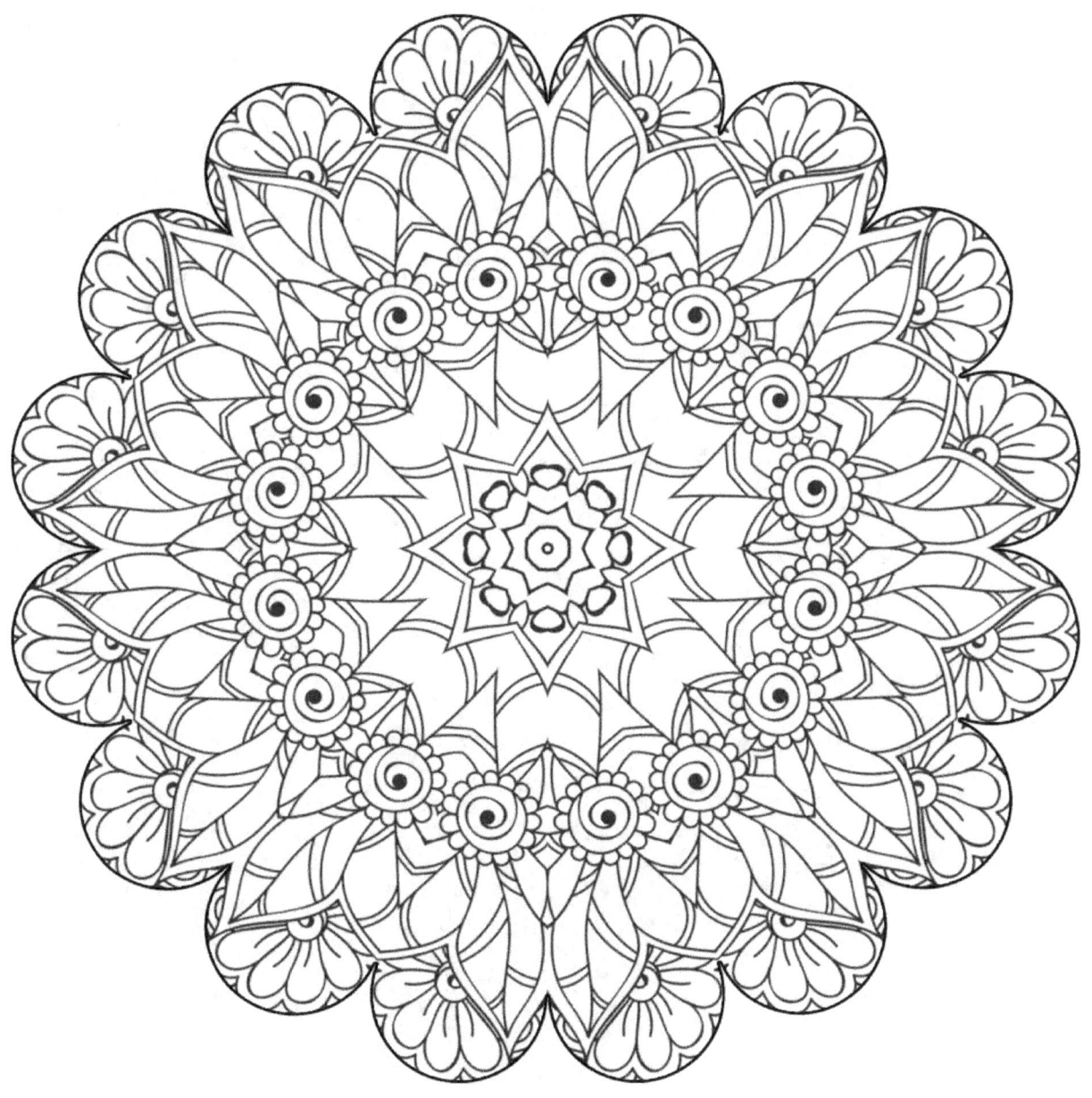

101bookclub.com

101 Flower Power

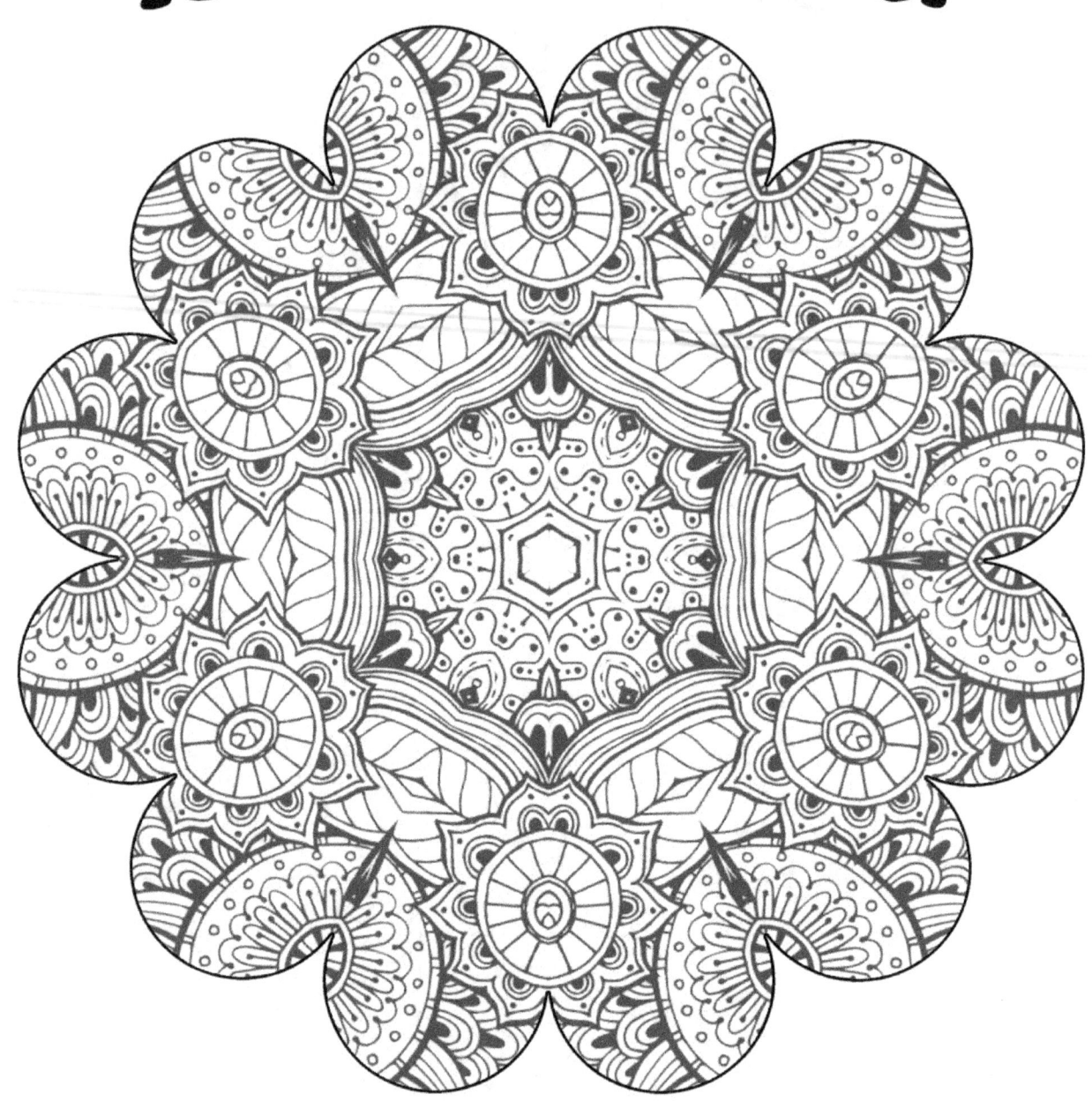

101bookclub.com

101 Flower Power

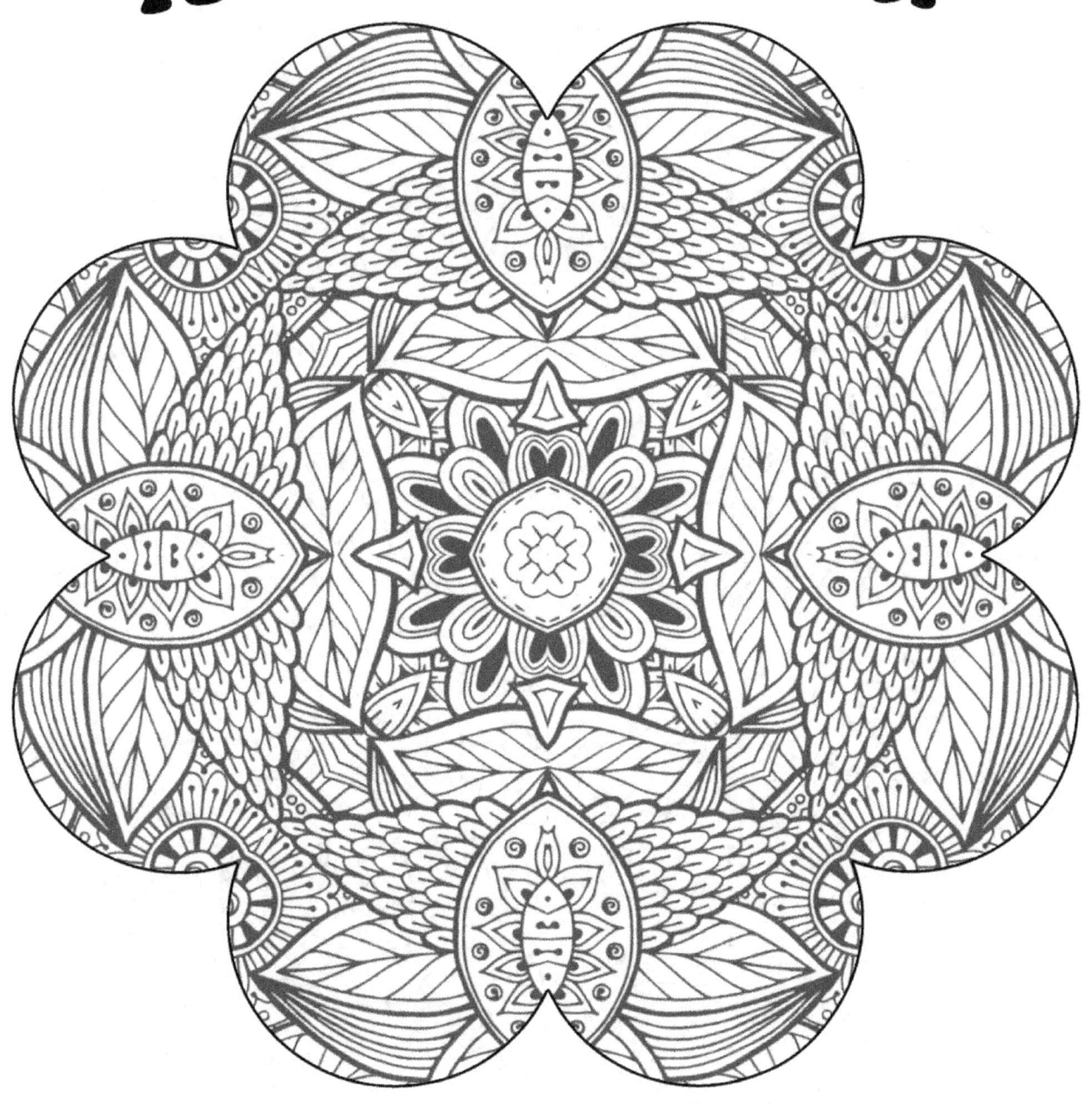

101bookclub.com

101 Flower Power

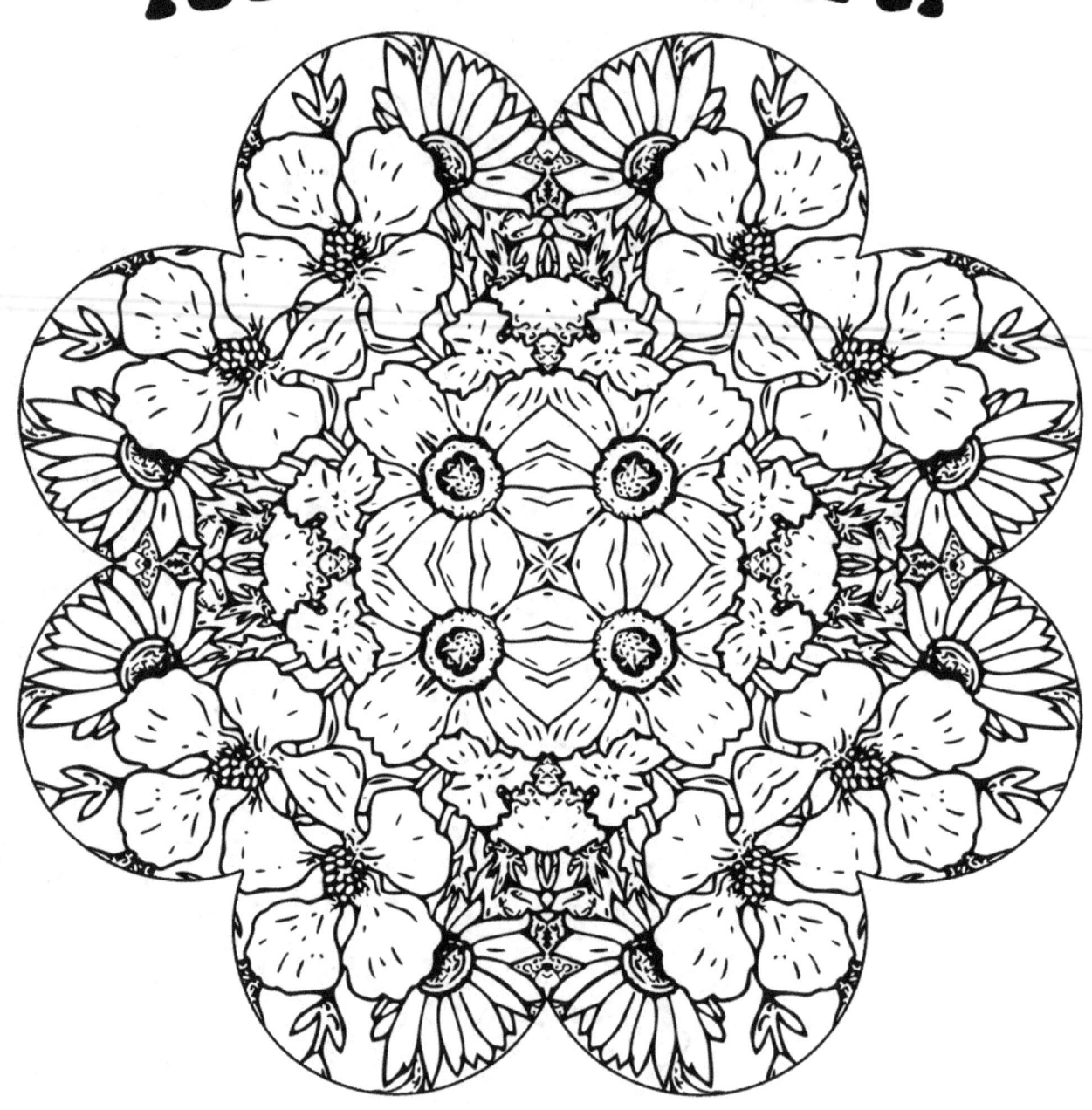

101bookclub.com

101 Flower Power

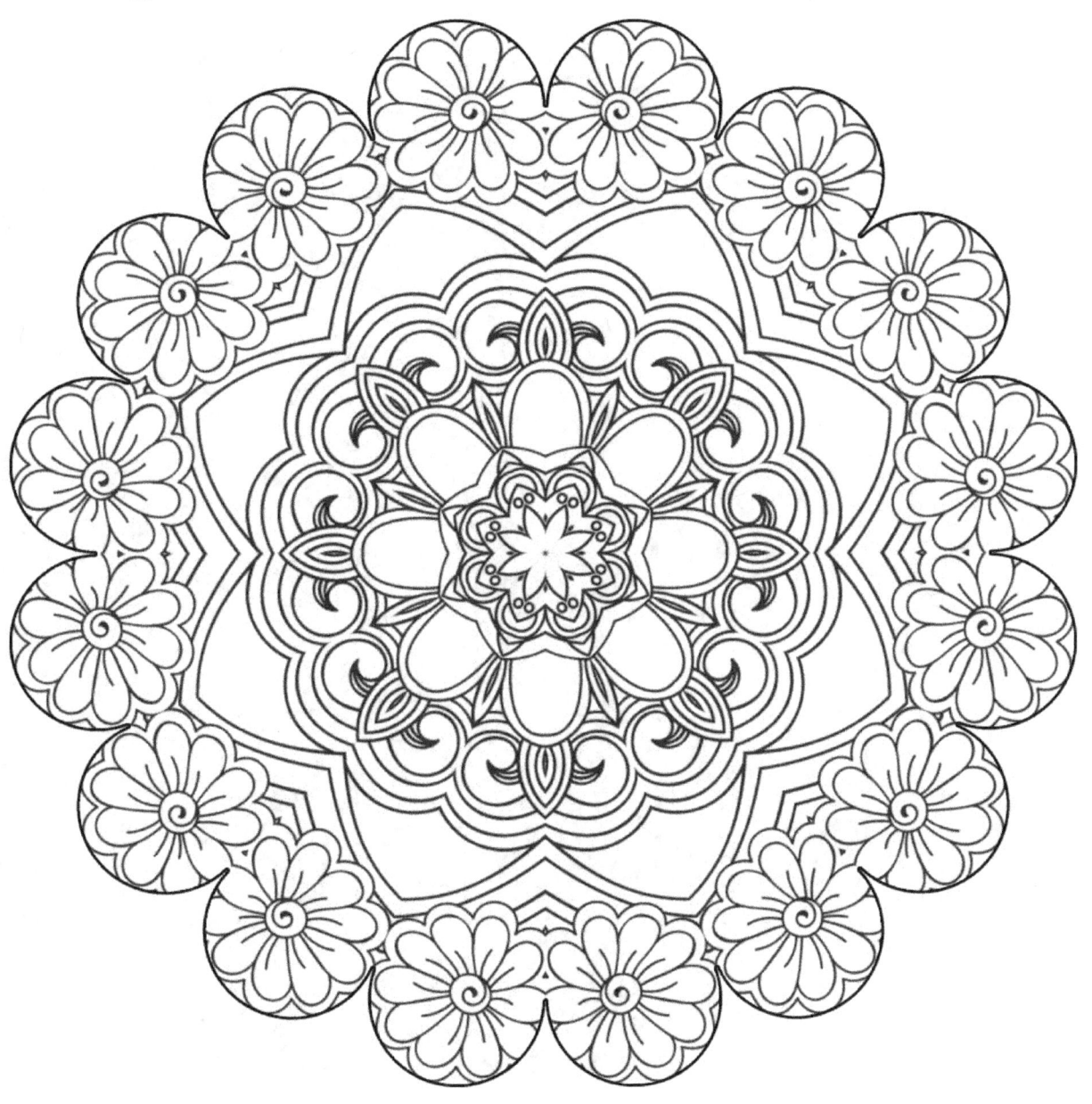

101bookclub.com

101 Flower Power

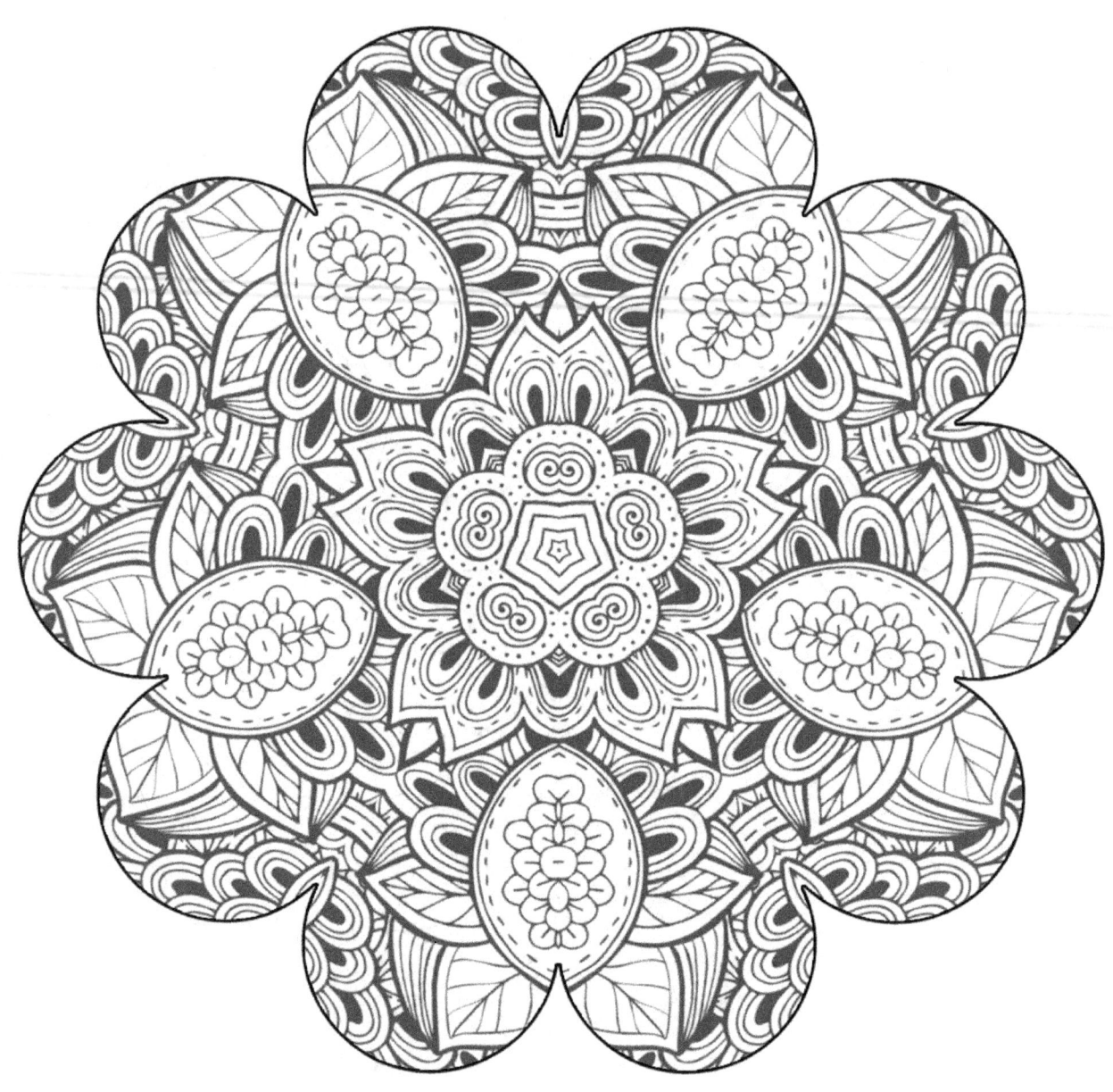

101bookclub.com

101 Flower Power

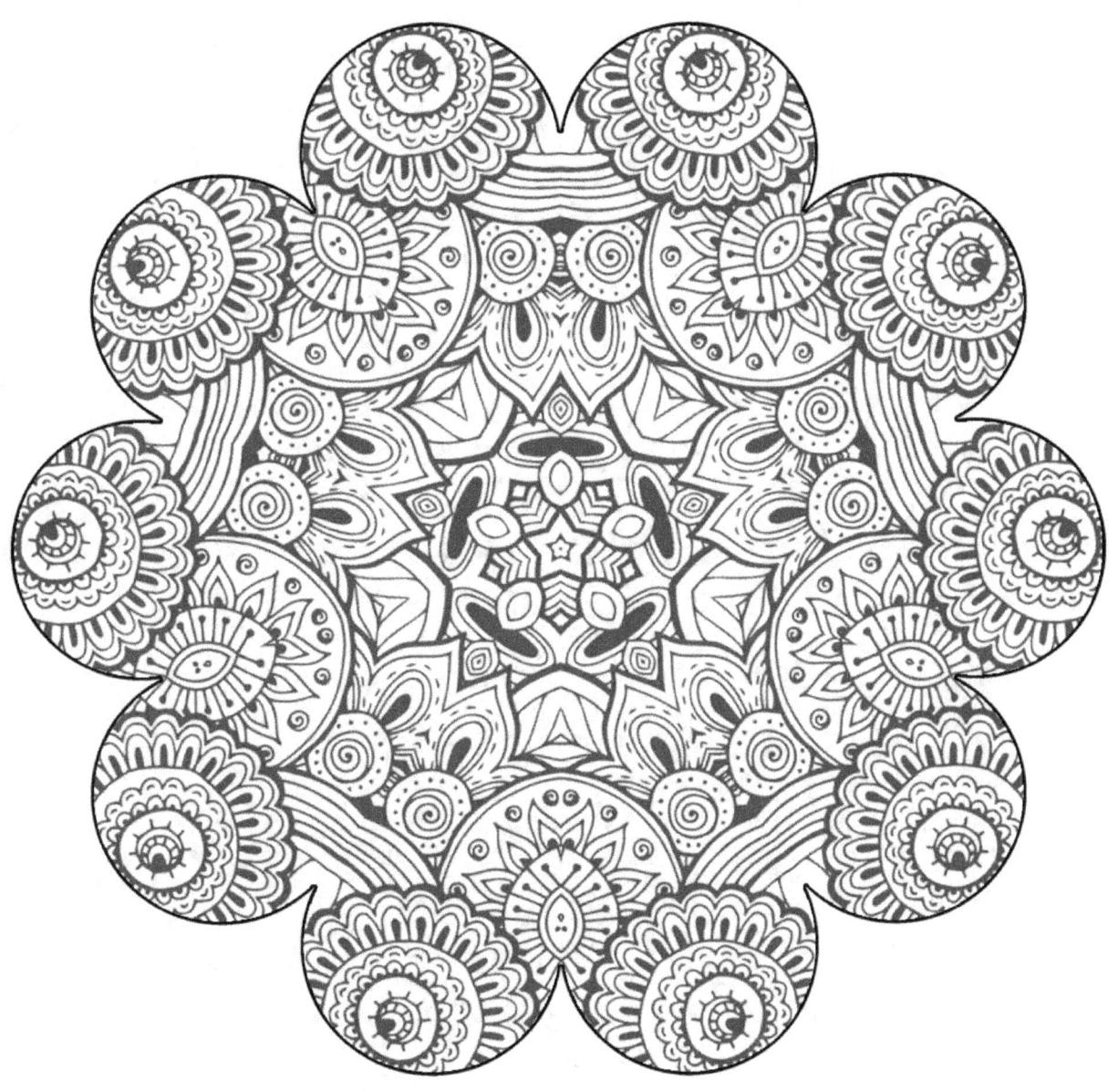

101bookclub.com

101 Flower Power

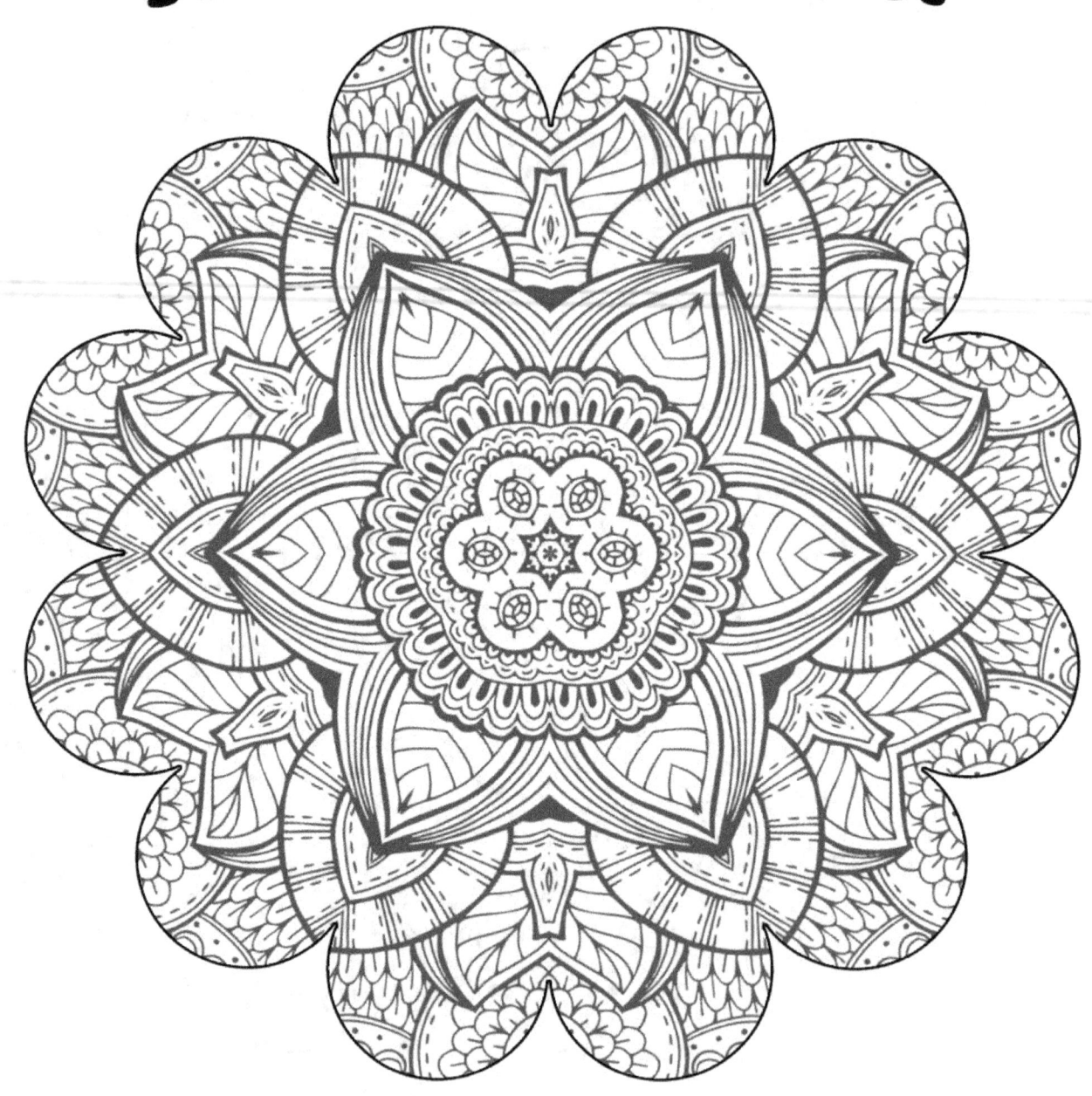

101bookclub.com

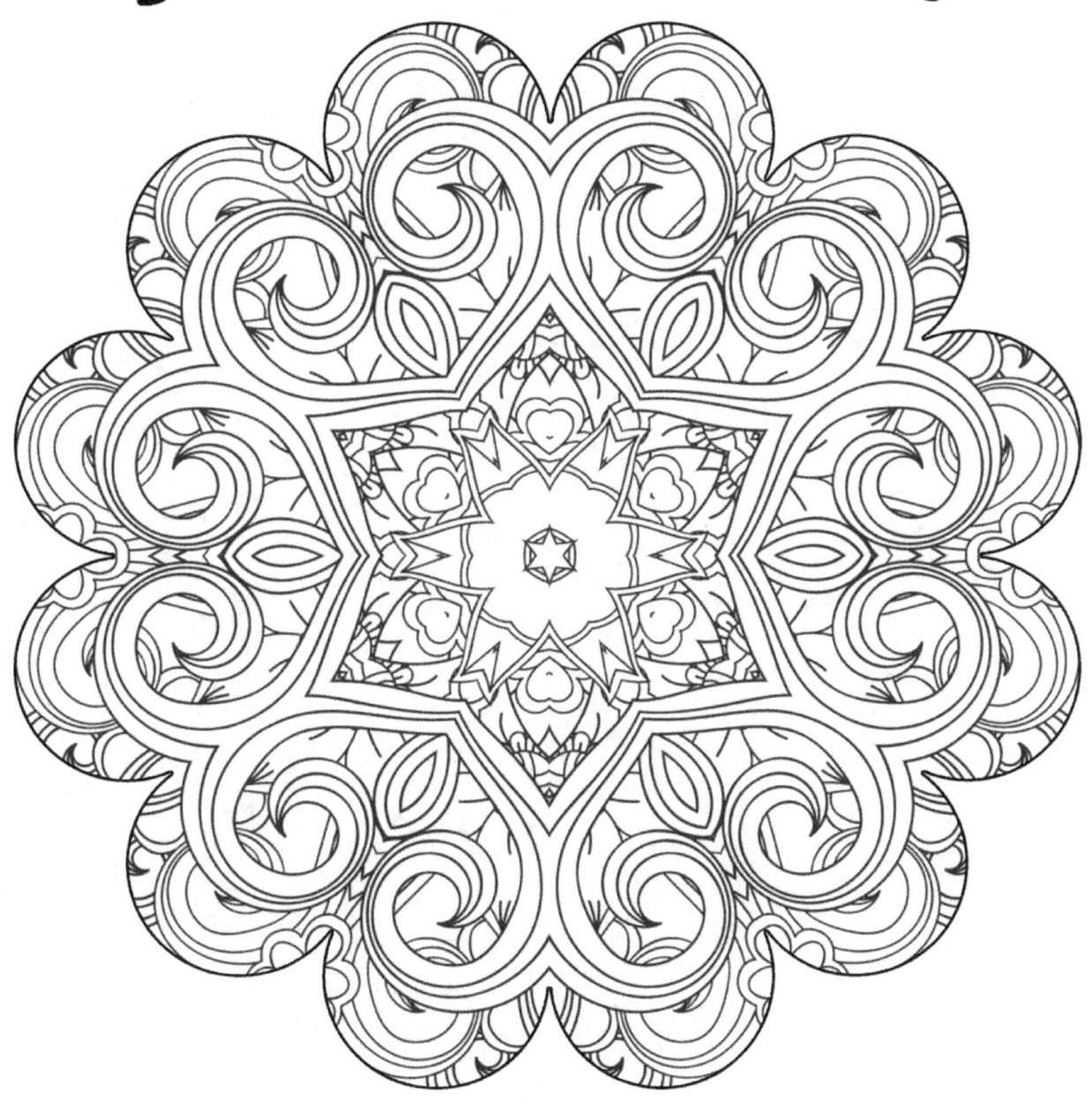

101 Flower Power

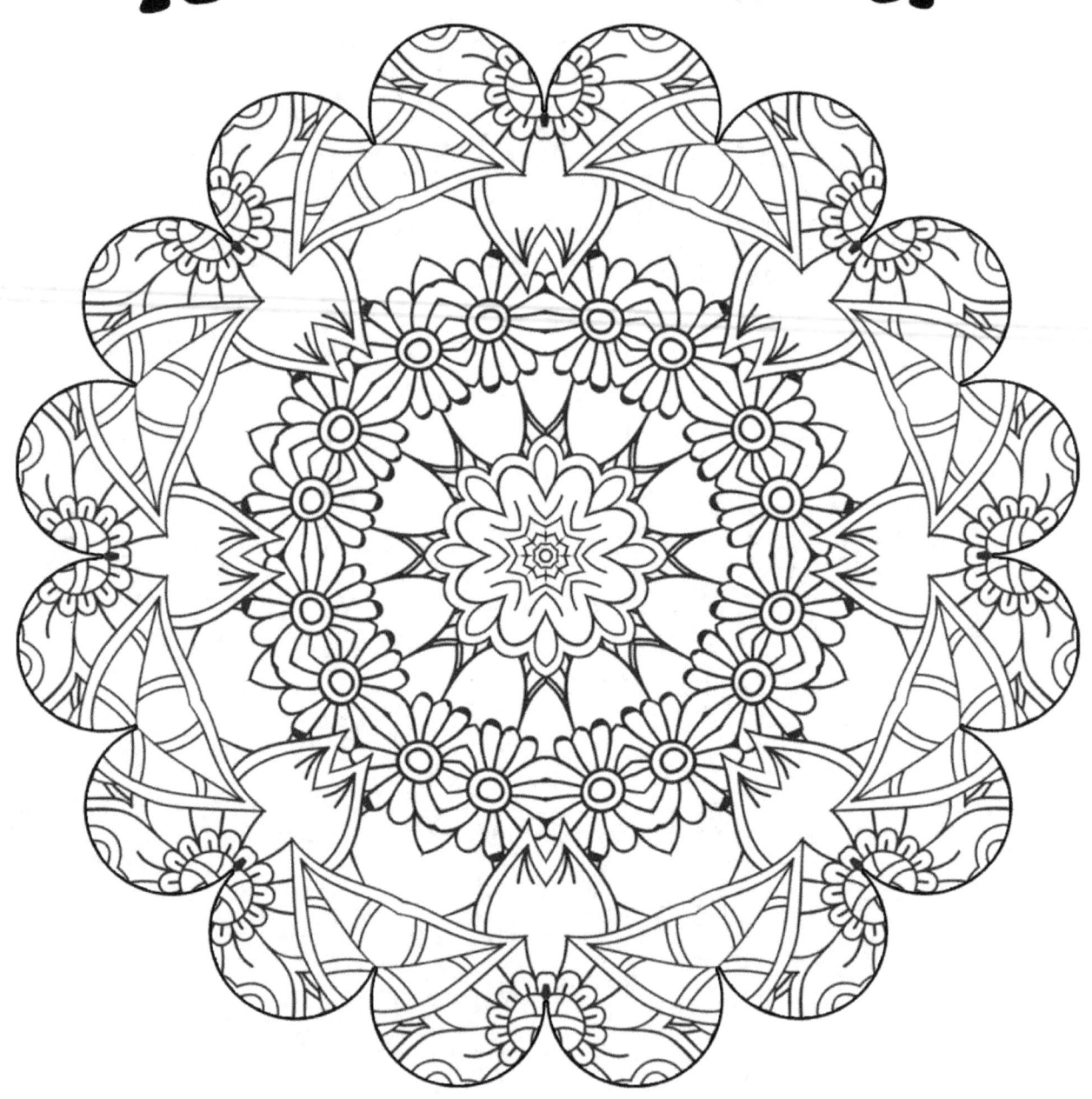

101bookclub.com

101 Flower Power

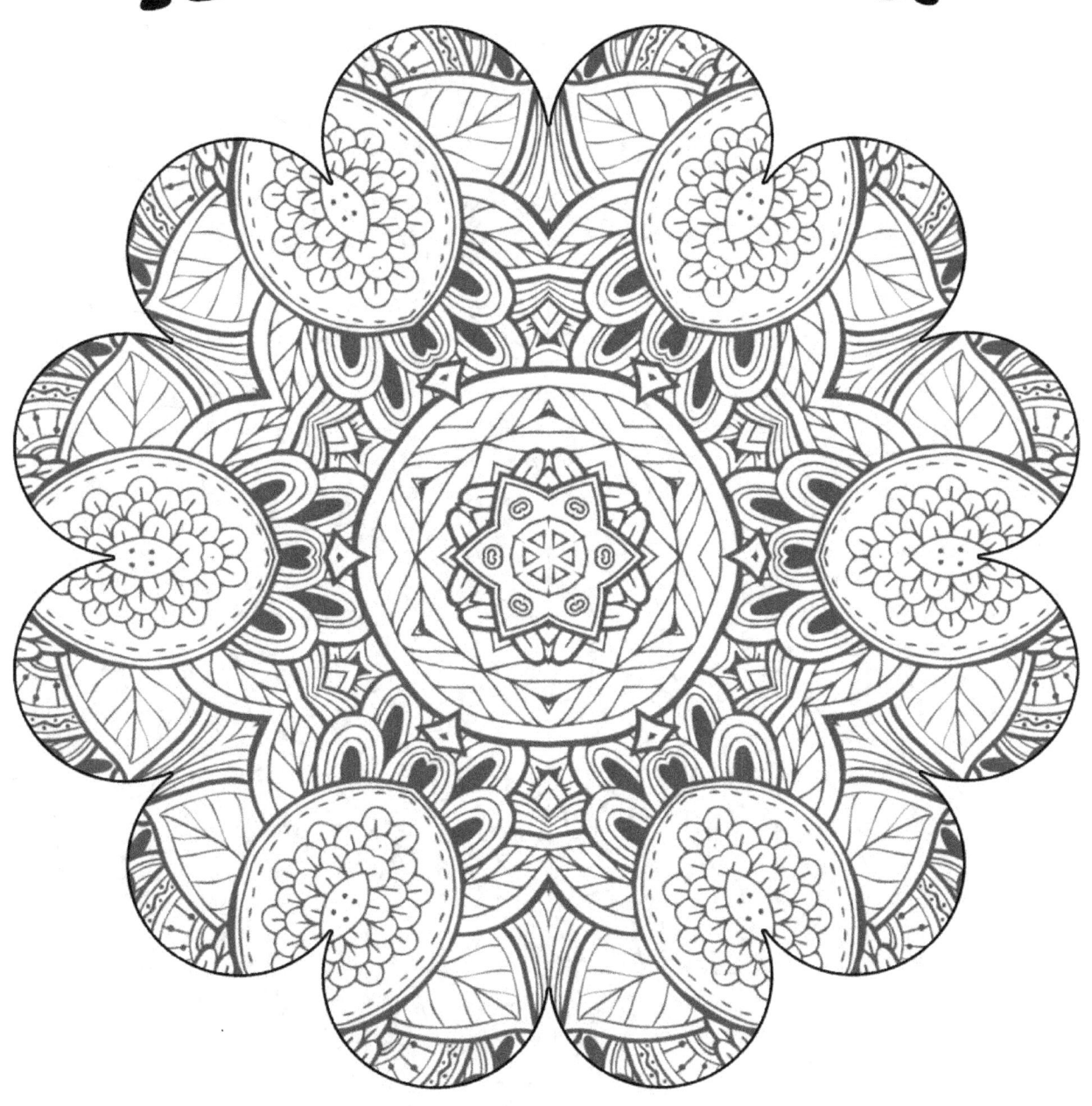

101bookclub.com

101 Flower Power

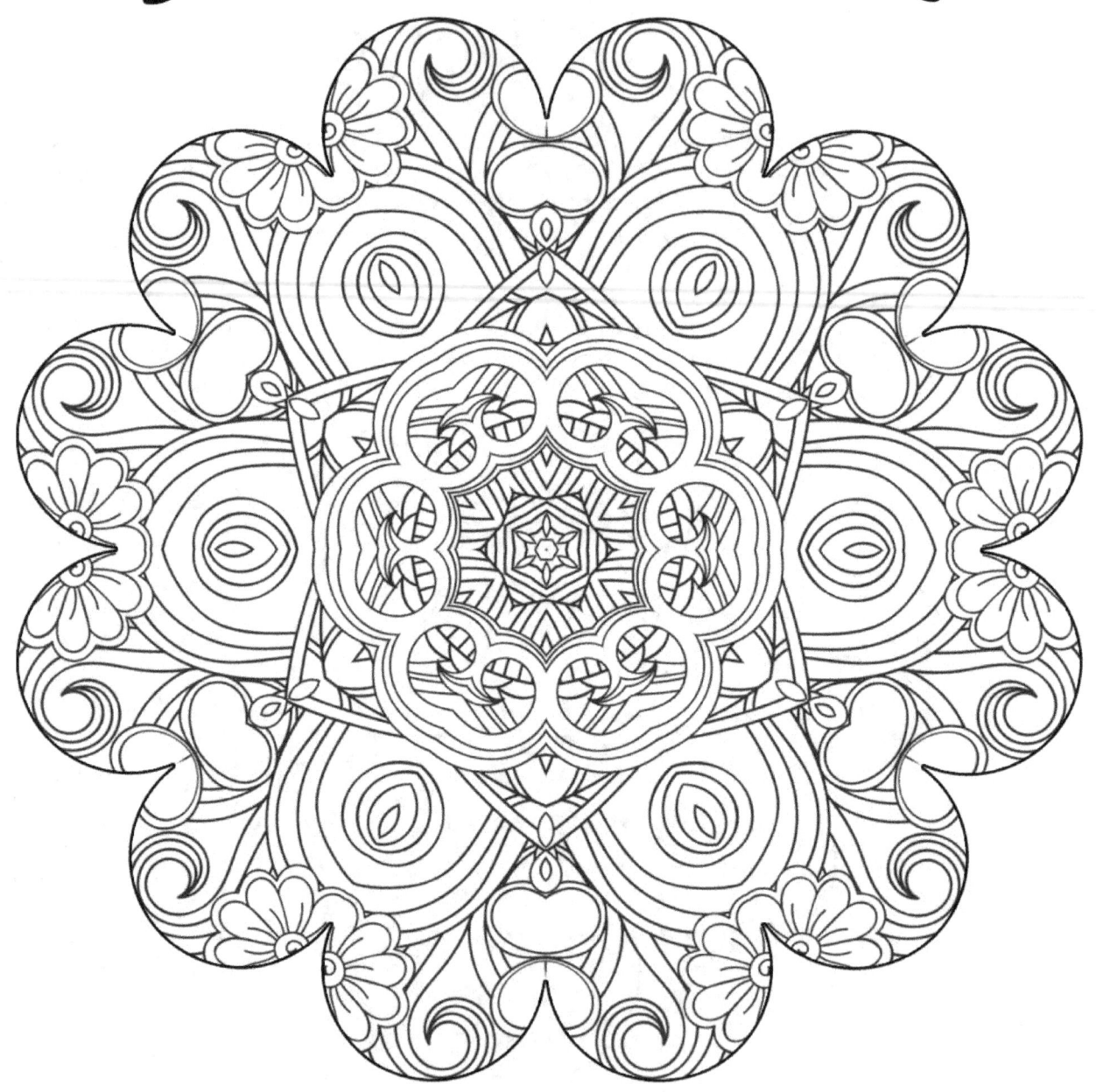

101bookclub.com

101 Flower Power

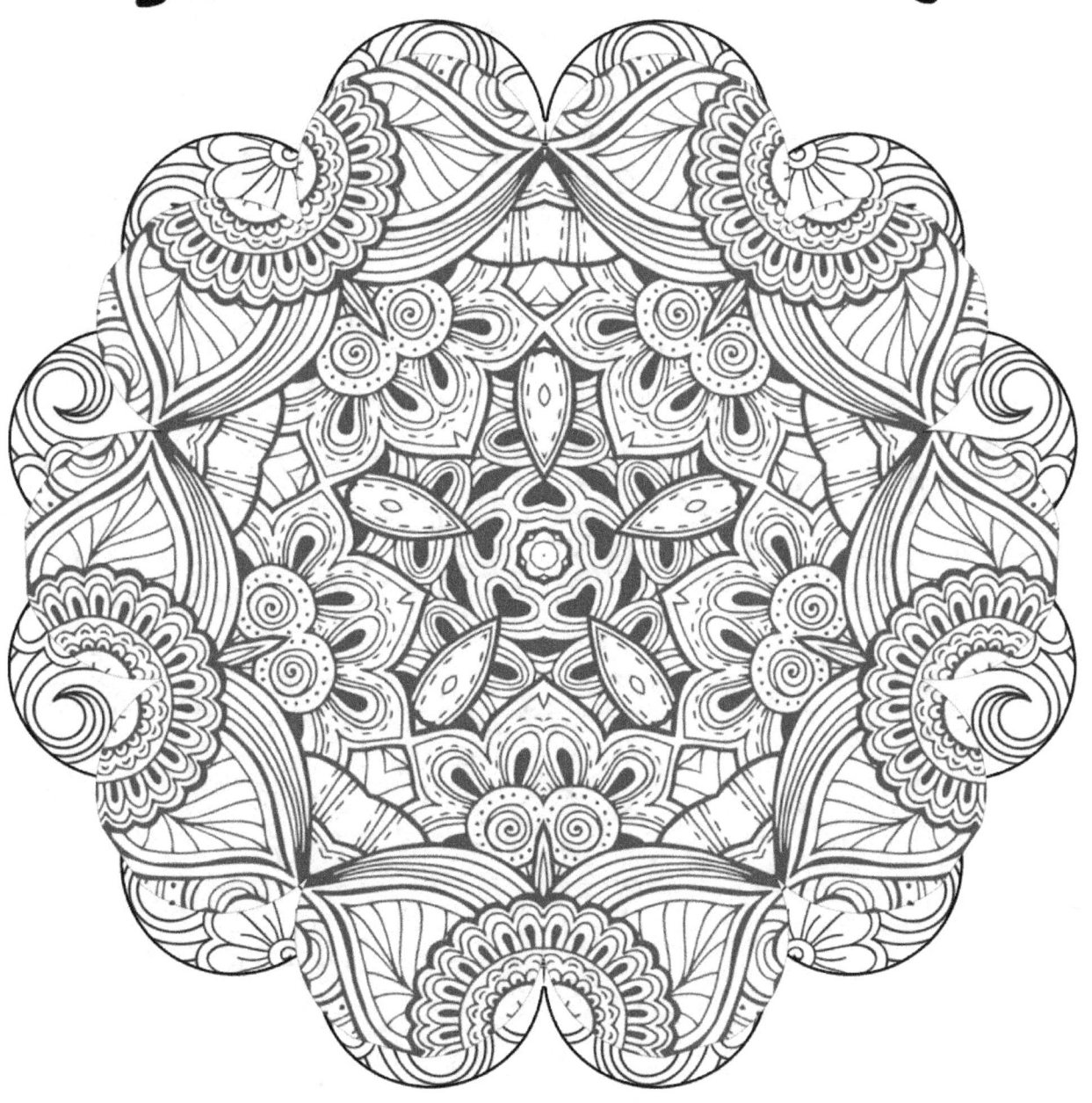

101bookclub.com

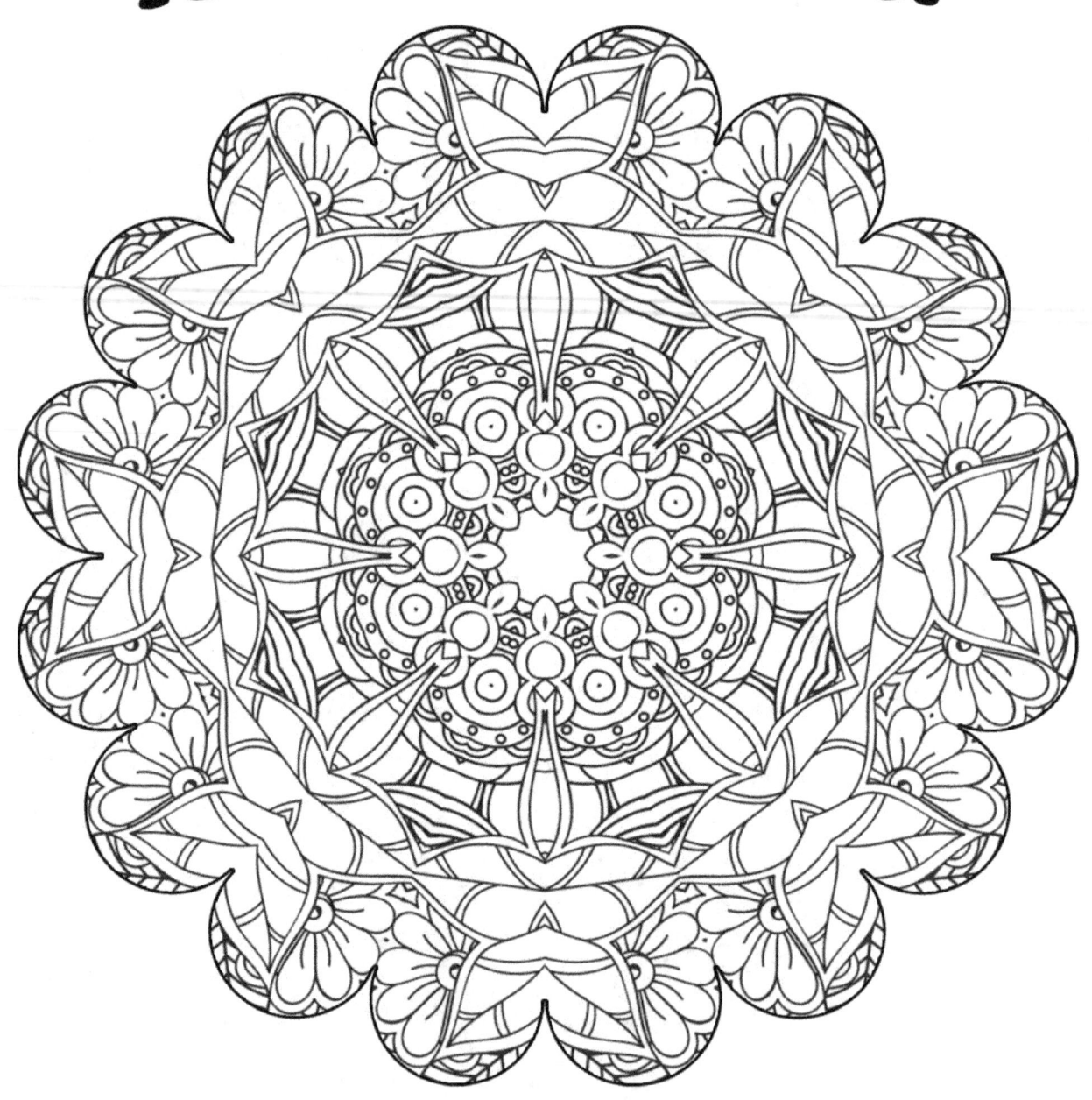

101 Flower Power

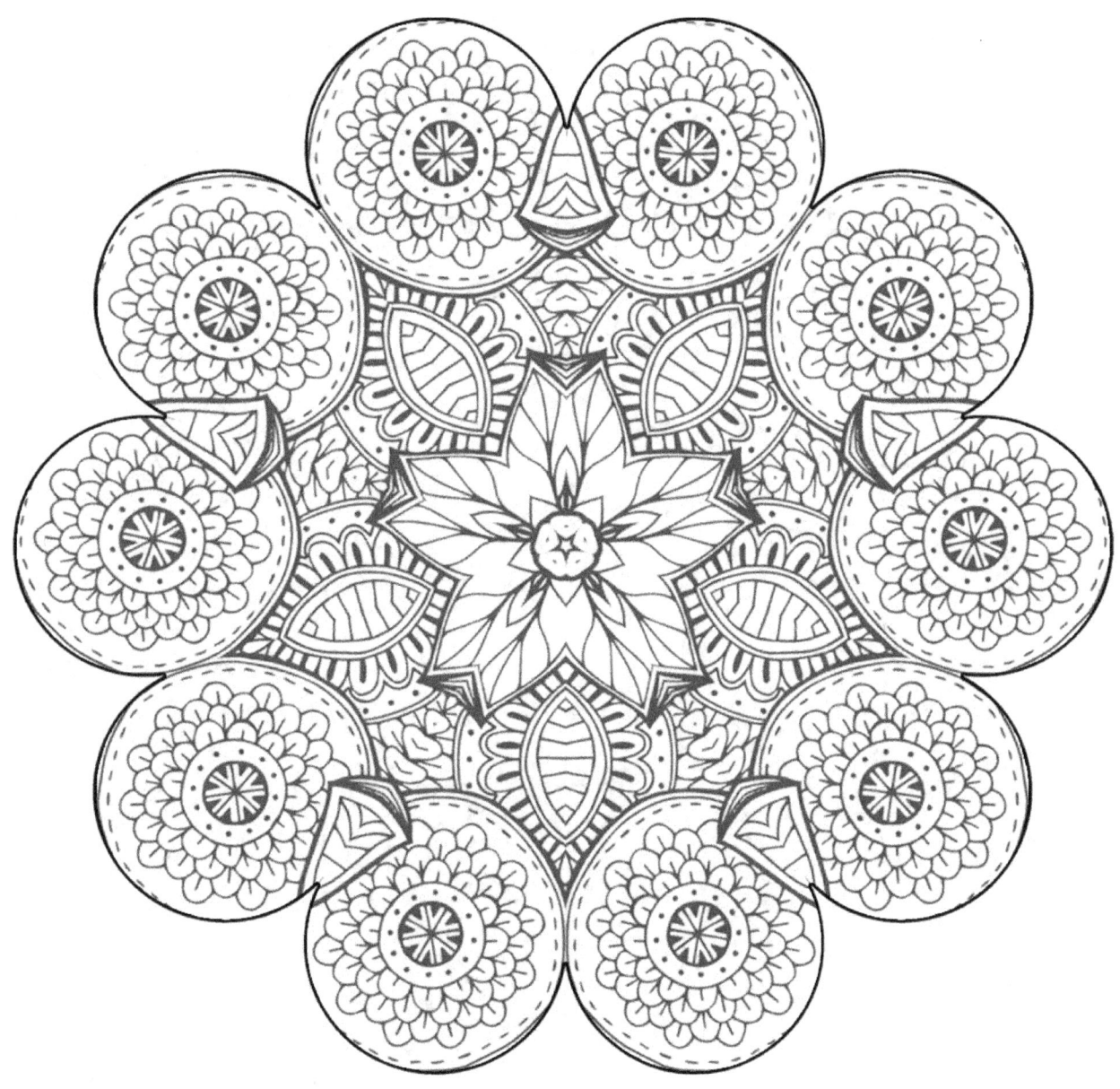

101bookclub.com

101 Flower Power

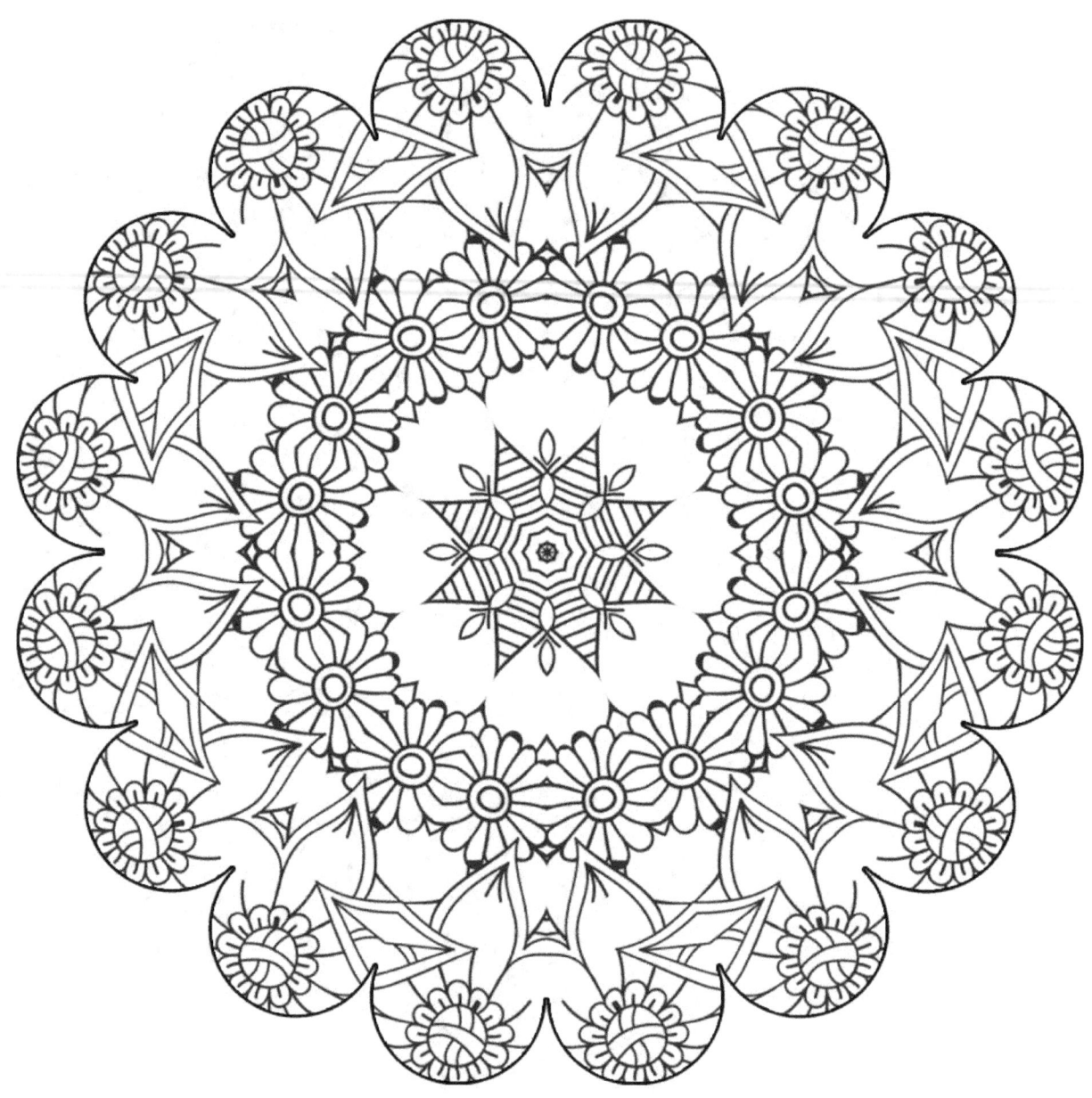

101bookclub.com

101 Flower Power

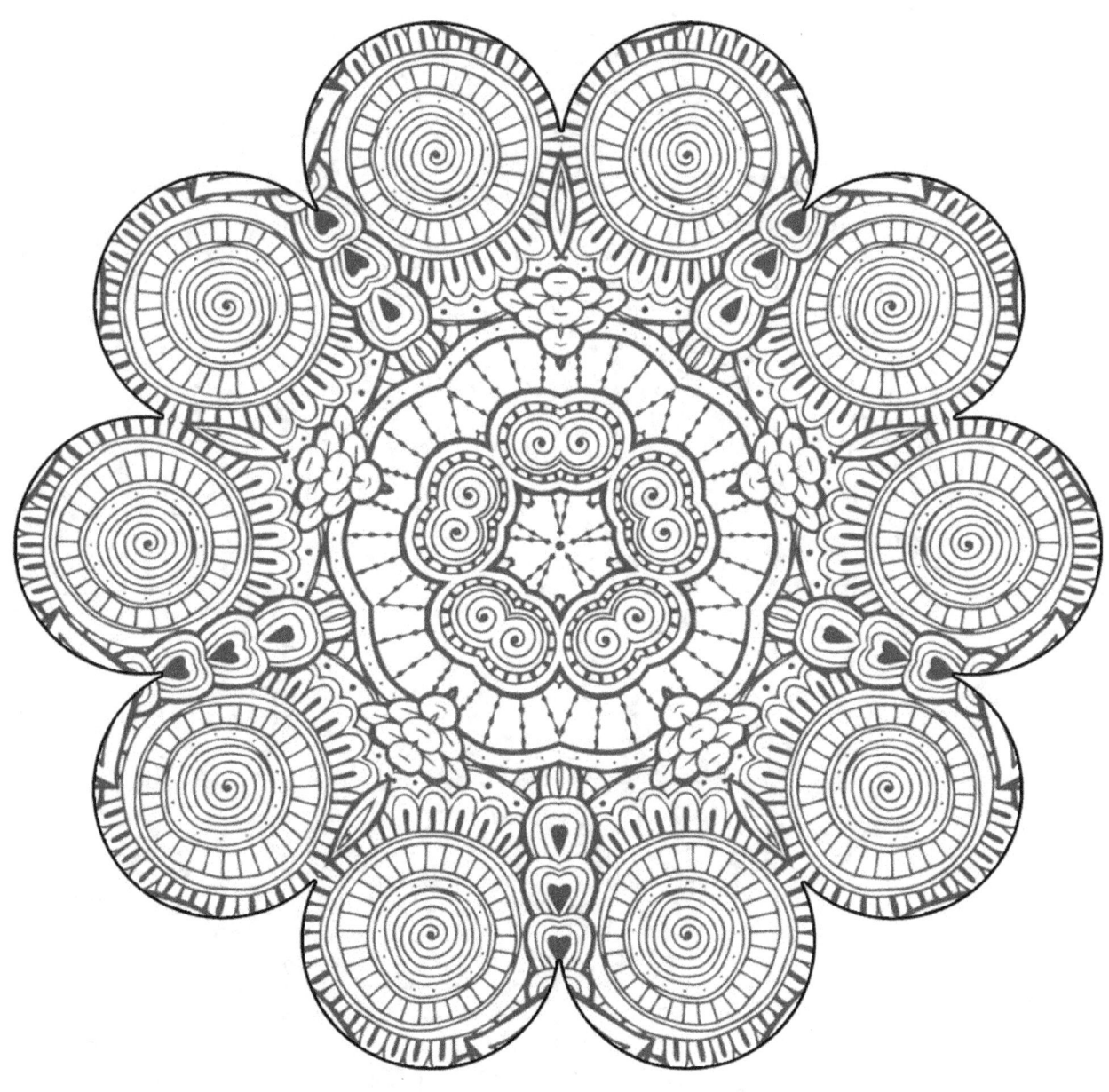

101bookclub.com

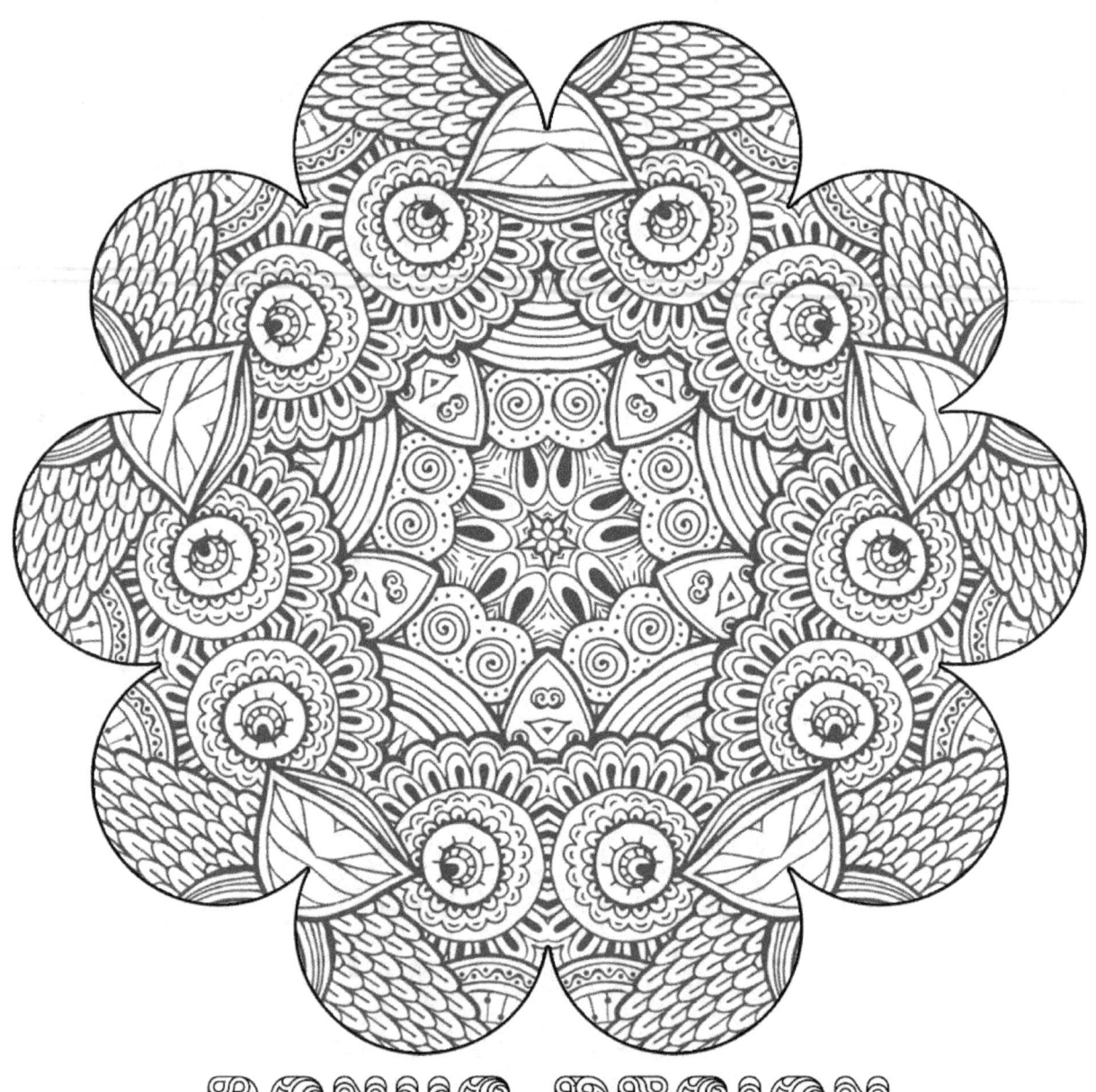

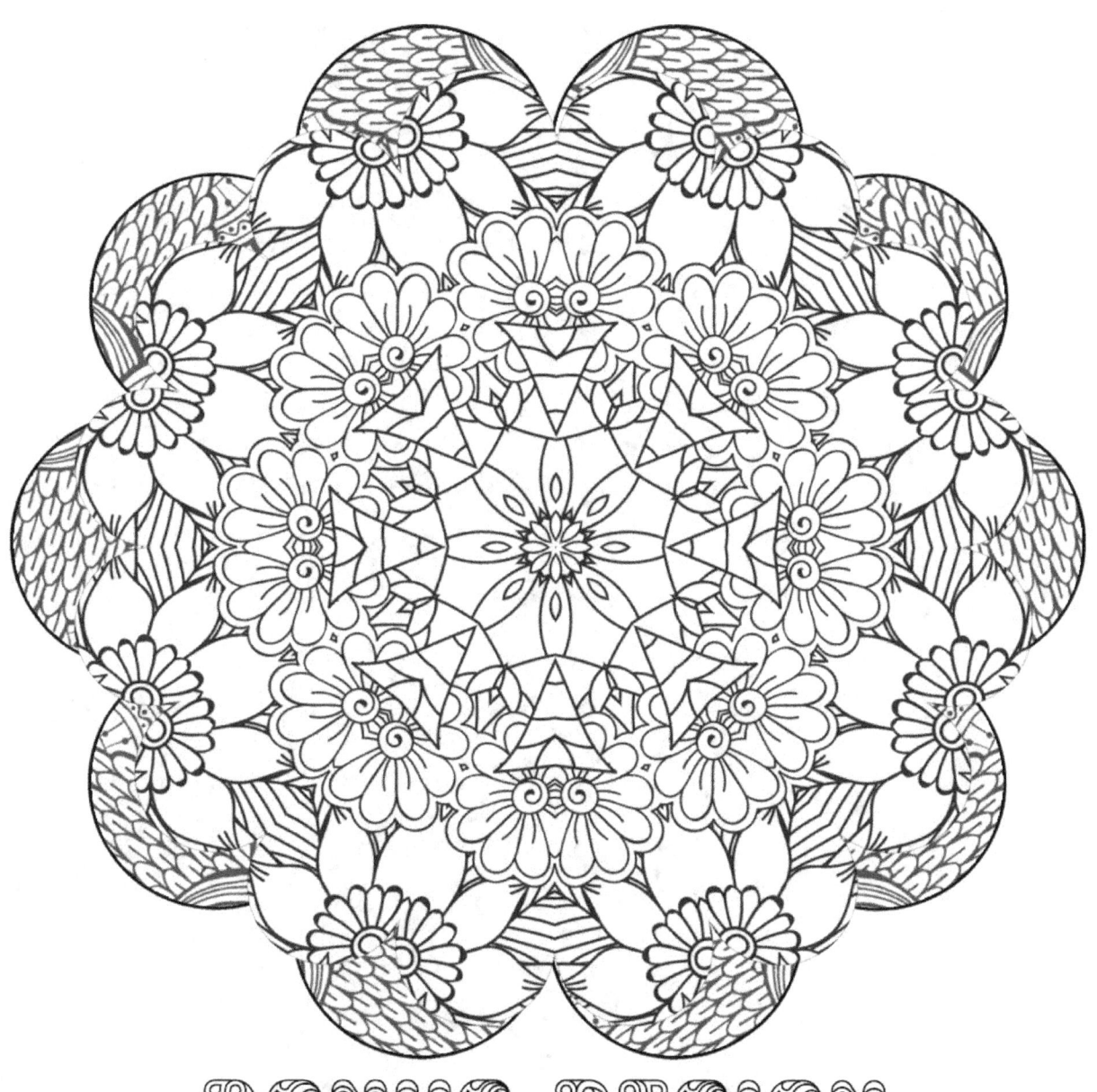

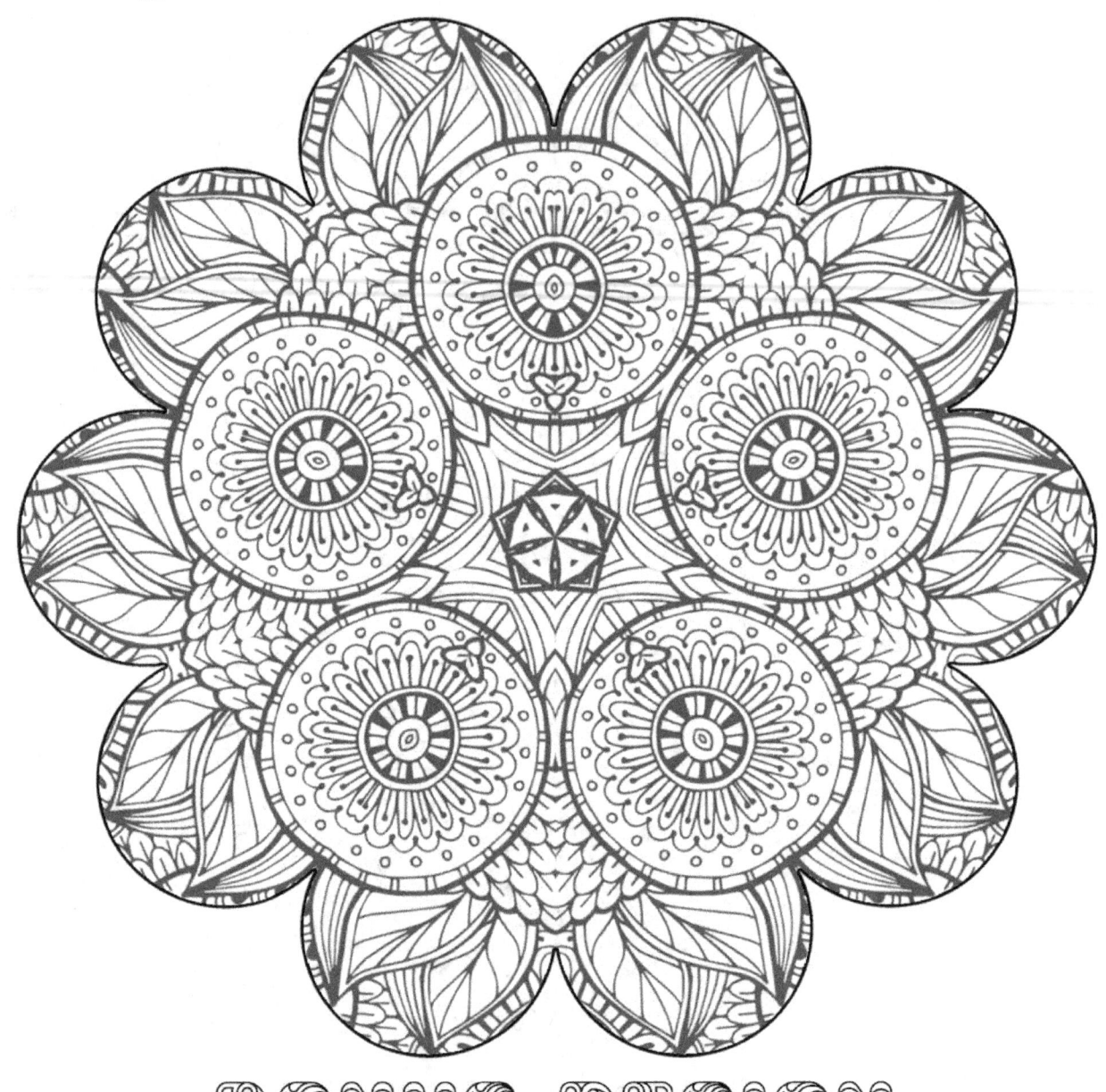

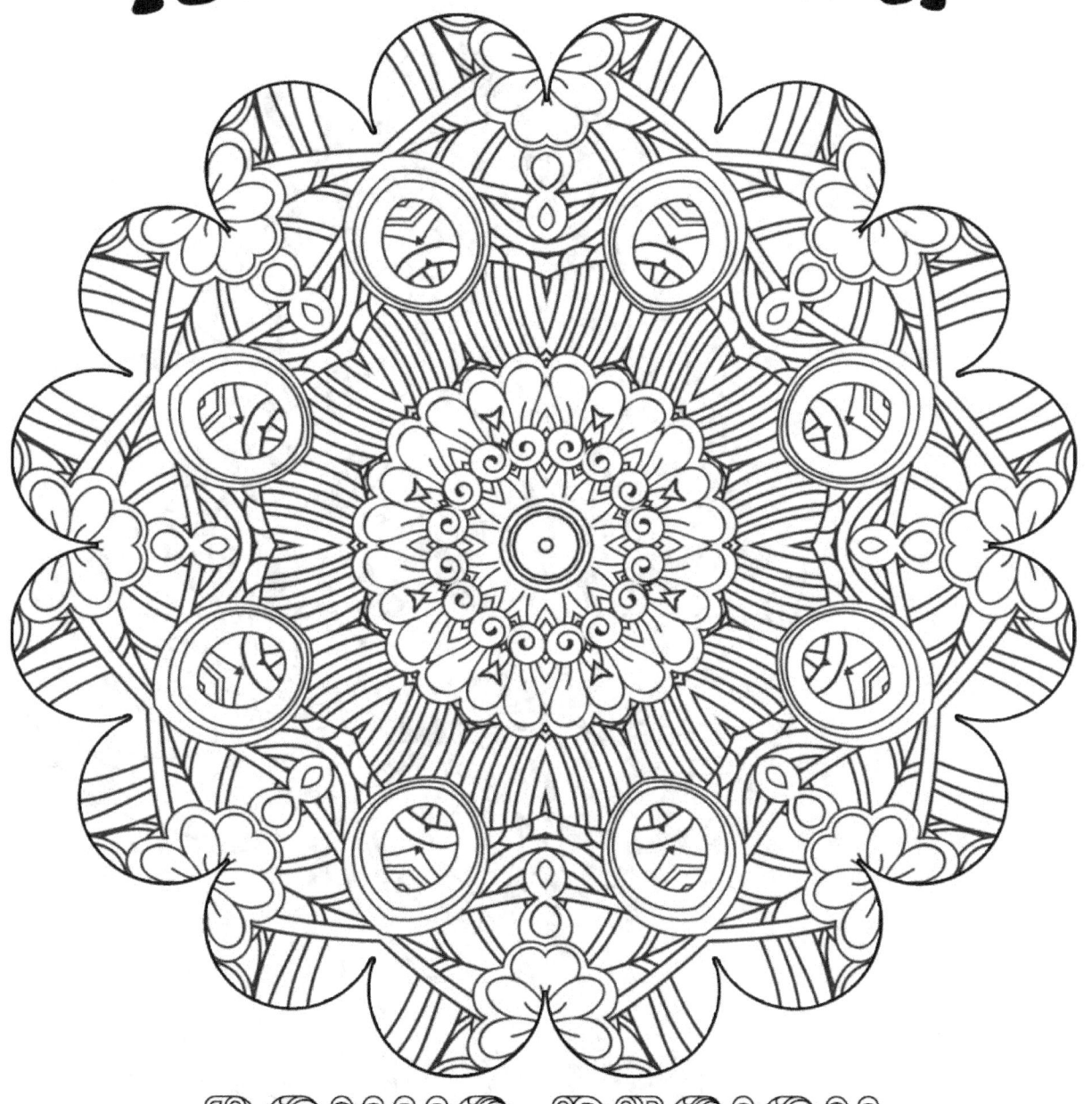

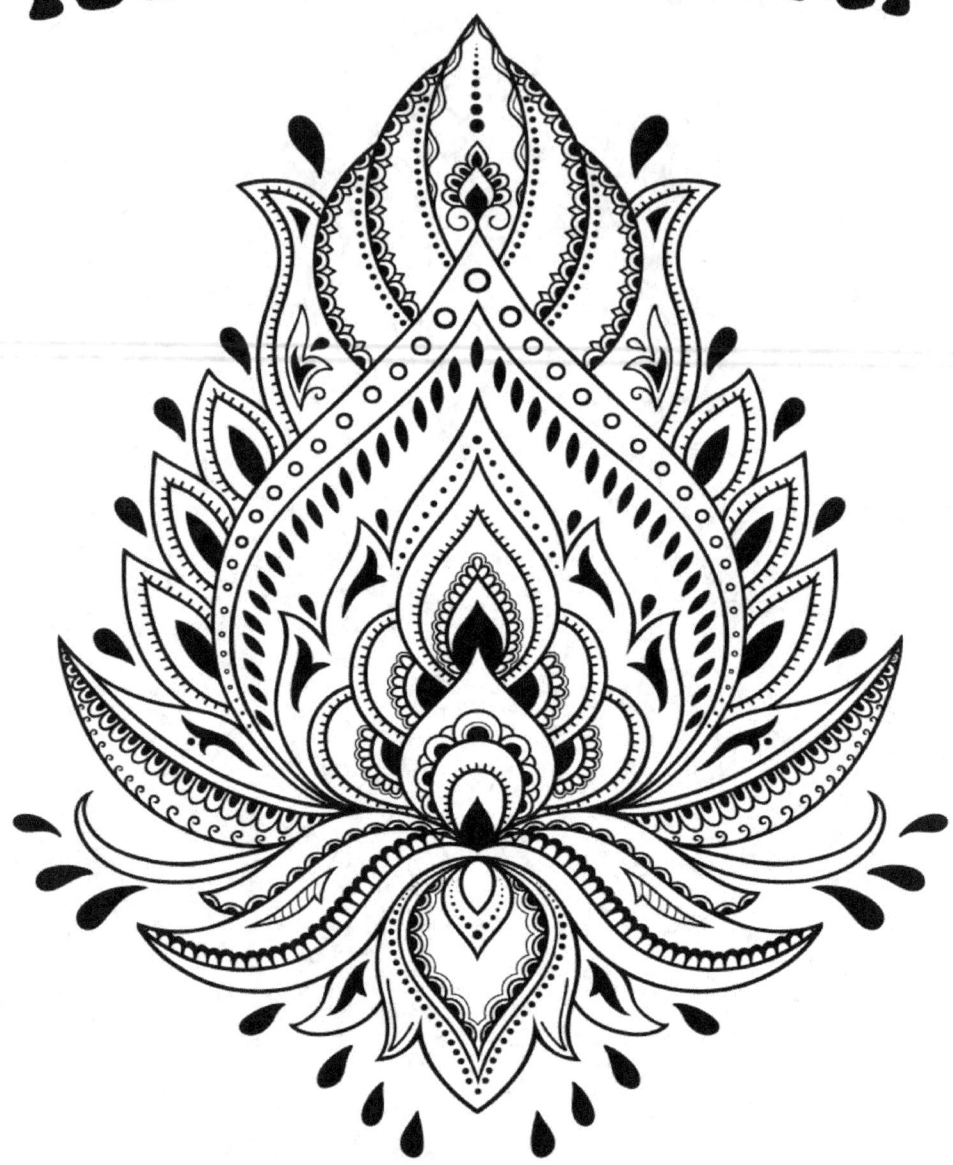

101 FLOWER POWER
Groovy Coloring Book
Curated by Todd Cotton

If you enjoyed this book, you can learn more about our ever-growing library of books and products (*or even join the club for substantial discounts!*) at:
http://www.101bookclub.com/

Please like us on Facebook at:
https://www.facebook.com/101BookClubTeam/

If you have questions or ideas for new books or products for your 101 Book Club Library, contact us via email at *info@101bookclub.com*!

Best wishes in your future endeavors!

Peace!

Todd Cotton

If you enjoyed this book, we think you will LOVE our 101 Bible Heroes Coloring Book! Check it out at *http://www.101bookclub.com/*.

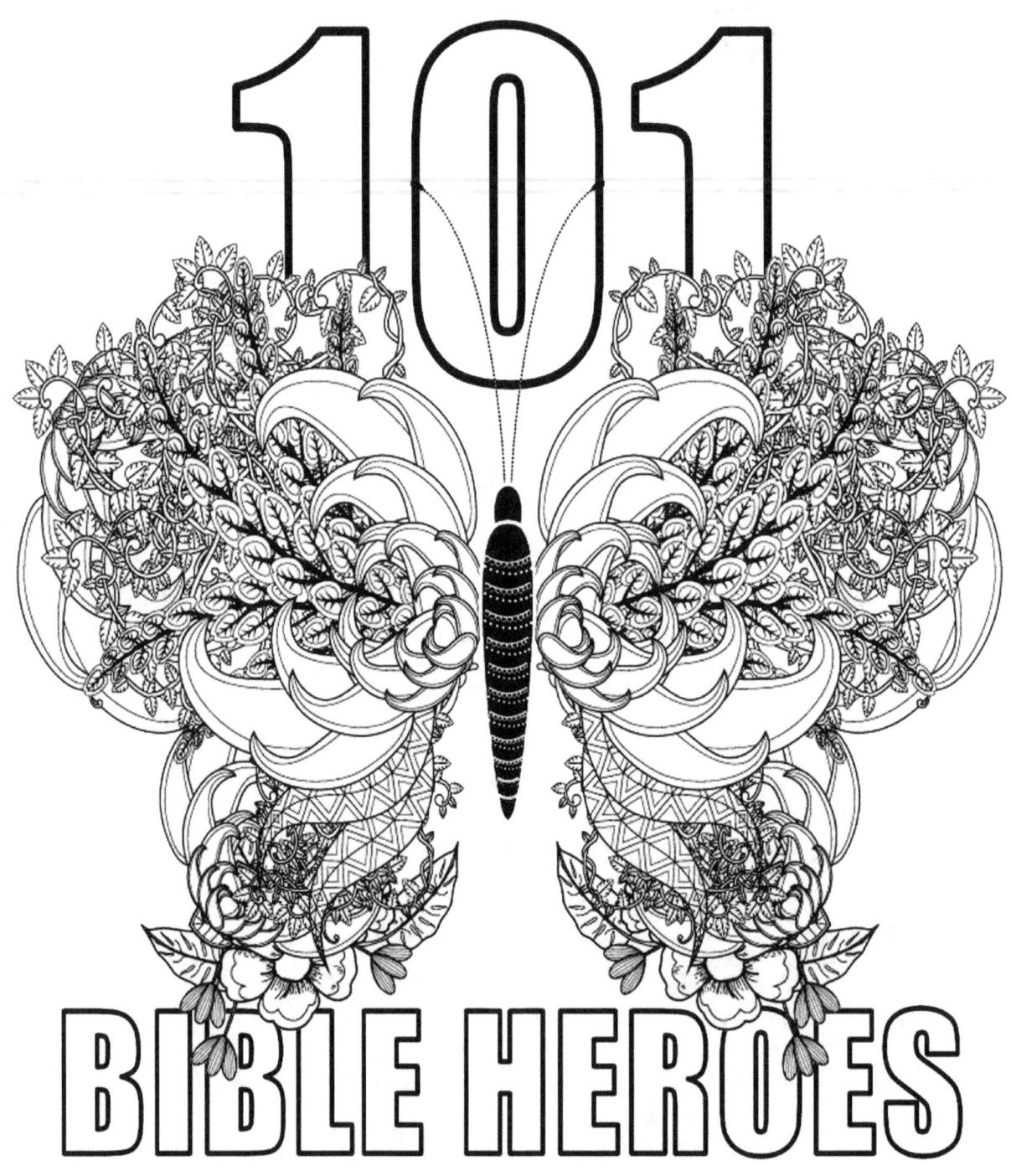

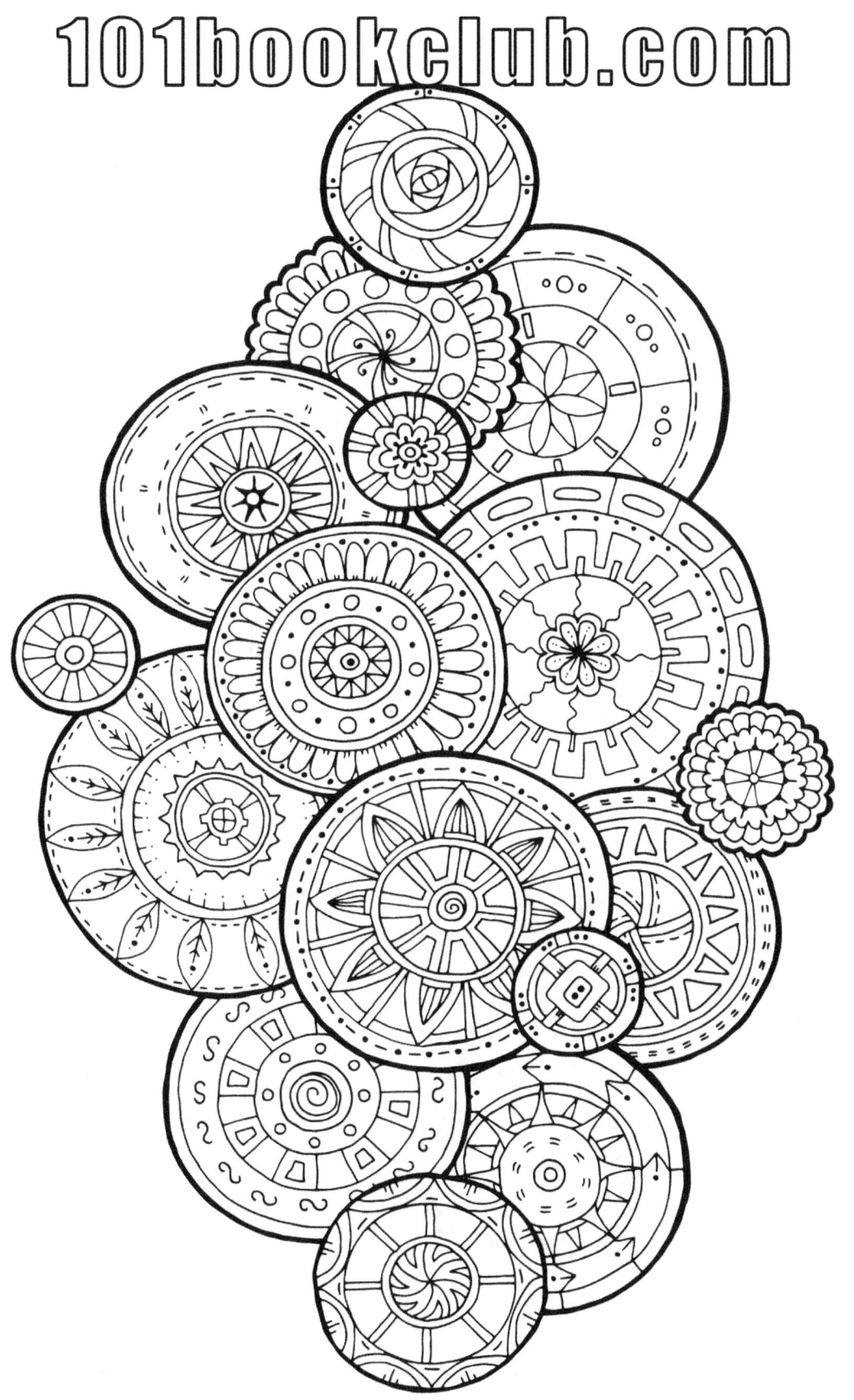

www.ingramcontent.com/pod-product-compliance
Lightning Source LLC
Chambersburg PA
CBHW062219220526
45471CB00009B/3270